ERRATUM   Women in Utopia

The above daguerreotype c. 1847 is of
Robert Dale Owen. Courtesy of the National
Portrait Gallery, Smithsonian Institution,
Washington, D. C. Gift of Andrew Oliver

The photo on page 106 of the text is incorrectly
identified as Robert Dale Owen. The photo
was misfiled at the Library of Congress; the
identity of this individual is unknown.

WOMEN
—— IN ——
UTOPIA

WOMEN

THE IDEOLOGY OF GENDER

IN

IN THE AMERICAN

UTOPIA

OWENITE COMMUNITIES

CAROL A. KOLMERTEN

INDIANA UNIVERSITY PRESS
BLOOMINGTON AND INDIANAPOLIS

The paper used in this publication meets the minimum requirements of American
National Standard for Information Sciences—Permanence of Paper for Printed
Library Materials, ANSI Z39.48-1984.

∞ ™

Manufactured in the United States of America

Library of Congress Cataloging-in-Publication Data

Kolmerten, Carol A.
Women in utopia : the ideology of gender in the American Owenite
communities / Carol A. Kolmerten.
p. cm.
Includes bibliographical references.
ISBN 0-253-33192-7 (alk. paper)
1. Owen, Robert, 1771–1858. 2. Collective settlements—United
States—History—19th century. 3. Utopian socialism—United States–
–History—19th century. 4. Women and socialism—United States–
–History—19th century. I. Title.
HX696.09K65 1990
335'.973'09034—dc20   89-45416
                                                              CIP

1 2 3 4 5   94 93 92 91 90

For Laura and Derica
and Aidan

CONTENTS

Acknowledgments

This study began in 1974 when I read my first *New Harmony Gazette* for an American Studies Seminar in graduate school at Purdue University. The paper I wrote for that seminar led to a dissertation, which led many years and many versions later to this book. Over the past fifteen years I have built up a heavy load of debts. I am pleased now to acknowledge at least a few of them.

At Purdue, Cheryl Oreovicz, Chester Eisinger, and Virgil Lokke offered me support and numerous suggestions. At Hood College, where I have taught for eleven years, Arthur Martin, the head of public services at the Apple Library, helped me track down many obscure volumes. I am also grateful for the administrative support I received at various times from Martha Church, Hood's president; Barbara Hetrick, the dean of academic affairs; Hadley Tremaine, the chair of the English department; and Ruth Watson, the secretary of the English department. My two Board of Associates Summer Grants, my Hodson Beneficial Faculty Fellowship, and the Cole Fund allowed me uninterrupted time to write. My research has also been supported generously by the resources and people of the National Endowment for the Humanities, the American Council of Learned Societies, and the Lilly Library.

I owe special thanks to several colleagues in various colleges and universities who have read all or portions of this book in various manuscript stages. Lyman Tower Sargent offered me his insights and detailed comments at a critical stage of the text. Gregory Claeys shared his expertise on Owen with me. Jerry McKnight, Kerry Strand, Glenda McNeill, Janis Judson, David Hein, and Elke Dorr all read chapters of the book and offered valuable critiques from various perspectives.

My largest personal debt I owe to Stephen M. Ross, who read every word of countless versions of this book without complaint. His astute criticism was always couched in constructive and supportive language; thus he prompted me to refine my analysis again and again. He was, above all, a kind and thoughtful reader whose suggestions helped me to create meaning out of several file cabinets full of documents, letters, and notes.

At Indiana University Press I have met with nothing but supportive help. Risë Williamson, my editor, offered extensive, substantive comments and excellent editorial assistance with a sense of humor and friendliness. Her suggestions have improved the quality of the book immeasurably.

I am indebted to various publications that published early versions of the ideas in this book: portions of chapter 3 appeared in *The Journal of General Education* and in *Utopias: The American Experience,* edited by Gairdner B. Moment and Otto F. Kraushaar (Scarecrow Press)

The best part of preparing this book has been finding its sources. This often meant visiting small historical societies for a day or two or spending a summer, as I did one year, at the Beinecke Rare Book and Manuscript Library. Everywhere I went I met with courtesy and enthusiasm for my project. I am grateful to many of the places I visited for permission to quote from their various collections. Specifically I would like to thank the Abernethy Library of American Literature at Middleburg College, the Beinecke Rare Book and Manuscript Library, the Cincinnati Historical Society, the Co-operative Union Library, the Labor Management Document Center at Cornell University, the Greene County Historical Society, the Houghton Library, the Indiana Historical Society, the Indiana State Library, the Lilly Library, the Massillion Museum, the Motherwell Library, the State Historical Society at Wisconsin, and the Workingmen's Institute at New Harmony. I extend special thanks to Katherine Haramundanis, who allowed me to quote from the Garnett-Pertz Collection housed at the Houghton Library.

Finally, I wish to thank my family—Stephen M. Ross, Laura Kolmerten McAfee, Derica L. Ross, and Aidan D. Ross—who have, with good grace, spent their summer vacations visiting small historical societies all over the United States. While other children visited Disney World, my kids camped in Madison, Wisconsin. While other couples traveled to exotic lands, Steve and I spent our free time in Xenia, Ohio, or Haverstraw, New York. My family's unstinting sense of humor and their ingrained nonsexist approaches to all work around the house freed me from the burdens of so many of the women I write about. For that and for them I am ever grateful.

WOMEN
—IN—
UTOPIA

INTRODUCTION

Utopian Visions within a Patriarchy

> To build a new fabric of social happiness comprehending equally the interests of all human beings, has never been contemplated.
>
> —William Thompson, *Appeal. . . ,* 1825

I became interested in Robert Owen and his American communal experiments almost twenty years ago when I, like so many other young women and men, was searching for an alternative to traditional family life as I had seen it while growing up in the 1950s and early 1960s. My personal search led me to an urban commune, founded, I was told, in the spirit of Robert Owen. Though I had not heard much about Robert Owen, what I hastily read of him intrigued me: here was a rich man who devoted his life's fortune to founding a utopian community based on egalitarianism.

After visiting the commune, though, I decided not to join, unable then to verbalize exactly what bothered me about it. Looking back later, I realized that the smocked, earth-mother women, baking their own bread, gently instructing the young children, and thoughtfully performing all of Woman's Time-Honored Tasks was the image that haunted me. As a guest in the house, I sat back and talked to the men, while the women quietly scurried from room to room taking care of my needs: Did I want herbal tea, they inquired? Would I like some Tassajara Whole Wheat Bread, just warm from the oven? Would my daughter, then a toddler, like to join with the other children in a game of capture-the-flag? Though the men assured me that the community was "completely egalitarian," and that I could go "out" to work just as they did, I nevertheless perceived a potential conflict in being Woman behaving like Man.

My instincts were quite right, as numerous popular and scholarly studies on countercultural communities of the 1960s have verified.[1] Almost without exception, women in the countercultural communities of the 1960s lived at best with only the promise of sexual equality, never with its reality. Rather than being liberated from "woman's work"—the endless cooking and washing and cleaning that cannot be pointed to with a proud "look what I did"—women in these communes found that they were more likely to live traditional female roles than were women working in the main-

1

stream culture. Young women who left home to join a countercultural commune often found that their most radical activity was washing everyone's dinner dishes night after night. Yet many of the commune women joined together in group living because they, like me, were trying to escape from an ideology of gender that prescribed separate and unequal women's work and men's work. Why did the women always end up in the kitchen with most of the work to do, away from the power? It was this notion of women's powerlessness linked inexorably with "women's work" that led me into a fifteen-year search through American history and literature to find the answer.

I learned over the course of the next decade that my apprehension concerning relations between the sexes in countercultural communities had been foreshadowed in over two thousand years of utopian thought. Social critics long before Robert Owen had imagined communities where human dreams could be fulfilled, where life obeyed natural or spiritual laws, and where everyone could work harmoniously in a chosen social order. Almost without exception, though, these dreamers of utopia have been flesh-and-blood men (not the generic kind), who have woven their fantasies into social fabrics that have perpetuated the power of people like themselves. It is not surprising that the great utopian thinkers of the Western world envision their good place/no place to be a world where men retain control. Utopia has always been conceived as a male construct, with women being defined by their relation to those with the power and providing a permanent class of secondary citizens created, as it were, to serve the men by guaranteeing that all the bothersome, endlessly trivial work will get done without question. The result is that utopian dreams in many ways replicate the culture from which they spring.

Utopian visions, with few exceptions, have always been grounded firmly in one of the most obscure abstractions of modern history: patriarchal power. Although the literal power a father had and has over his wife and children gave us the words "patriarchy" and "patriarch," the term "patriarchy" also refers to an ideology, a set of ideas about the way the world is organized. As an ideology, patriarchy hides within the consciousness (or subconsciousness) of women and men at the same time that it informs the social and political structuring of the society as a whole. It permeates everything, functioning through unconscious gender training that infuses all of a culture's institutions. Most individual men and women accept its traditions, customs, and inevitable divisions of labor as "natural."[2]

Because of this overwhelming and pervasive ideology, imaginative thinkers have rarely been able to create a world, even a fictional one, that considers men and women equally. "Utopian" thinkers have been able to critique most of the institutions of the culture in which they live—economic systems, religious systems, educational systems—but no one, wrote Robert Owen's friend William Thompson in 1825, could comprehend all people's "interests" when thinking imaginatively about utopia. The reason is that even the most "utopian" of thinkers have been unable to question the primary "given" in a patriarchal system: the unequal relationship between the sexes.

Our very assumptions about the way the world works, about what is "natural" and "good," are tied up in an inevitable fact of our existence: "Fathers" rule. Traditionally, fathers have presided over families (by paying the bills, sitting in the most comfortable chair, driving the family car), over nations (as presidents, chiefs of staff, chairmen), over all of society's valued institutions (economic, political, educational, religious). Thus we learn from infancy the ways of the patriarchal world in our schools, marketplaces, and churches, and we learn our lesson so well that patriarchal priorities become "natural" long before we are grown. Our history classes ("his" story) tell us about wars and presidencies, not about housework or quilting. Traditional women's work of raising children—arguably the most important task of a culture—has almost always been devalued or "ghettoized" by its separation from the paid workforce. Young children growing up in a patriarchal culture soon learn (obliquely, of course) just who has the power—male principals, not female teachers; male doctors, not female nurses; male policemen, not female metermaids—because, as Gerda Lerner has said, the family "not only mirrors the order of the state and educates its children to follow it, it also creates and constantly reinforces that order" (*Patriarchy*, 217). Most women learn their lesson on how to obtain power from the powerful: by being daddy's little girl, cajoling, talking sweetly, batting eyelashes, wearing sheer, impractical clothing, high heels, perfume—knowing all the time who has the power and who does not. Those girls and women who do not learn this important lesson are labeled "bossy" or "aggressive."

Perhaps the most pernicious manifestation of patriarchy as it infused American institutions in the 1820s—the decade Robert Owen came to America to establish his utopian community—was the attitude toward women and their "proper" place that accompanied the growth of industrialism in the Western world. The first half of the nineteenth century in the United States has been characterized by American historians as an era swept by extensive change. Rapid industrialization and the concomitant urbanization that followed in its wake changed forever how people worked and where they lived. With the flocking of men and women to the factories and the subsequent expansion of cities, America was rapidly transformed from a rural to an urban society. At the same time, the new manufacturing subjected an agrarian people to numerous dislocations and readjustments.

Until the early nineteenth century, home was a vital part of the world, a center of work, a subsistence unit. In it, women and men raised and prepared food, produced clothing. Children learned by observing and participating in the family's activities. With industrialization, however, the economic basis of family life diminished. Men left home to "go" to work; production and consumption within the home became defined as "women's work." While women continued to prepare food and other necessities to be consumed within the home, their work also included creating a private haven from the competitive "outside" world, socializing children into being adults with personalities appropriate to the demands of industrial capitalism, and becoming, increasingly as the nineteenth century elapsed, consumers. These shifts in the functions of the middle-class family led to a new definition of the relationship between "home" and "work."[3]

As numerous social historians have illustrated, industrial growth caused drastic role changes and power shifts for all members of a family. From the onset of the industrial revolution in the United States, women's employment was shaped, in Carl Degler's words, "around the family, while man's work, in a real sense, shaped the family" (395). Families lived and moved as man's work decreed. The industrial revolution thus exacerbated the distance between public and private spheres. Family life, then, with which women have always been associated because of childbearing and nursing, became increasingly separated from public life, or from the sphere of power.[4]

This demarcation of spheres of action—one for women, another for men—when combined with the rising industrialism of the early nineteenth century led to a mythologizing of "Woman" that was unprecedented in American history. According to historian David Kennedy, a country beset with territorial expansion and the birth of modern industrialism puts a high premium on the forces working for order and cohesion. The family as it came to be shaped in the nineteenth century, with its wife/mother center, seemed to be such a force.[5] As Tocqueville commented in 1835, man's appetite for change needed order and "regularity of morals," which women personified. The very idea of Woman and her stationary "place" provided a firm base from which the arrow of technological progress could be launched.

Woman reached her ultimate mythic proportions as a "regulator of morals." Her purity, one of the most deeply cherished abstractions of nineteenth-century patriarchal America, represented, in the words of William Taylor and Christopher Lasch, a "desperate effort to find in the sanctity of women, the sanctity of motherhood and the Home, the principle which would hold not only the family, but society together" (35). Because the industrial revolution created an amoral (or immoral) atmosphere, the idealized home, complete with its nurturing Mother/Woman, offered a compensatory sense of humanity, and, on a more concrete level, it put a consumer in the home to educate the children and purchase products.

During the decades that the industrial revolution was transforming early nineteenth-century America, a revolution in perception was providing the intellectual framework for the mythologizing of woman's abstract roles and sacred sphere. The emphasis of American romanticism on imagination, on intuition, on traditional "female" virtues helped to spread the Cult of the True Woman. The True Woman, a term coined by historian Barbara Welter, symbolized the romantic desire of a romantic age to replace the deductive by the impulsive, the rational by the religious ("Anti-Intellectualism," 71). In Welter's words, woman's nature transcended the marketplace, where man was mired by his passions and his greed. When man spoke of something more mysterious than himself, he spoke of "her," the True Woman, a being so pure, pious, submissive, and domestic that she could live only in myth. In an age when the building of a nation did not require purity and morality for its builders, the image of a True Woman, the idealized pure being who occupied the central position in America's mythology in the nineteenth century, provided a repository for these values. As Welter says, "if women had not existed, the age would have had to invent them."[6]

The "morality" demanded of women by the Cult of True Womanhood was representative of the moral focus of American romanticism. Certainly all the ideal characteristics ascribed to American women in the early nineteenth century were romantic ones; at the same time, male perceivers invested in woman a "divine" authority that nicely masked her lack of concrete power. Eager to get on with his making and doing, spurred on by his own romantic vision of aggressive individualism, nineteenth-century man, according to Welter, balanced his acquisitive self with feminine-romantic virtues conveniently stored at home.[7] Translated into its most popular American form—evangelical religion—romanticism maintained female "delicacy" and "purity," while "allowing" woman to be idolized.[8] This feminization of religion during the early nineteenth century cleverly put to use woman's ideal characteristics, while freeing man for work in his separate world, a world where morality and purity interfered with "progress." Woman's separate sphere and ideal virtues, so useful for industrialism and so conveniently glorified by the romantic movement, were translated into culture-wide values by the development of a national publishing industry capable of transmitting common ideas throughout the United States.

The Cult of True Womanhood swept the country with the force of an evangelical revival, converting everyone in its path. By the 1830s, "home" was woman's only proper sphere and there woman was supposed to create a haven for her husband. The only woman fit to occupy this noble sphere was a True Woman. Such a woman's life's objective was to nurture and serve the men and children in her life; her highest responsibility was to exert a moral influence upon her husband, her children, and through them, upon society. She was everywhere considered separate from and unequal to man.

This glorification of woman's place in her home and of her ideal feminine characteristics was forcefully and constantly reiterated by the voices of authority in nineteenth-century public life: woman's "place" was dictated for individual women through the voices of the "experts." Different groups of professionals—all authorized by their status in a recognized institution to prescribe characteristics of Woman to women—justified women's and men's totally different spheres through their advice giving.

The clearest and most obvious rationale for the separation of the sexual spheres can be found in the views of woman's physiology held by nineteenth-century physicians. Through the popular writings of these doctors, the relegation of woman to the sphere of domestic functions was given a "scientific" basis.[9] Everyone could see that woman's physical appearance was drastically different from man's: she was smaller, rounder, and not as strong as a man. Her body was constructed for bearing and nursing children. Not only was woman's body completely different from man's, but her observable physical differences reflected internal, intellectual, psychological, and temperamental distinctions as well. Unlike man, whose impulses were subject to his control, woman's hidden sexual organs controlled her; she was both the product and the prisoner of her reproductive organs. Her uterus, believed physicians, was connected to her central nervous system; therefore, women were under the influence of emotion, while men were under the influence of reason. Motherhood, then, was woman's biological destiny; women who thwarted biological imperatives suffered increased nervousness, illness, and early death. Woman's proper sphere was the home, where she could engage in domestic tasks suitable to her "pure" nature. Those women who ventured out of their homes and into association with men were going against nature's dicta and were jeopardizing the ideal characteristics given to them by their unique nervous system.

The dicta of biology were, conveniently, believed to be God's laws as well. Countless clergymen in the nineteenth century wrote didactic tracts and preached sermons that reinforced the precepts of science about woman's true place in society. But instead of using scientific "evidence," ministers uncovered countless biblical examples to "prove" that woman's place was in the home. Clergymen picked and chose carefully from the Bible in order to demonstrate the qualities of the ideal woman who was to occupy the home: she was to be gentle, affectionate, and retiring, and her chief role in life was to further the "formation of character" of others.[10]

Educators, as well, voiced the same sentiments as the physicians and ministers. Female intellects, the educators agreed, were not capable of bold, masculine attainments but, rather, were designed to "please and console. . . . whatever is sentimental and touching is peculiarly worthy of [their] regard."[11] Because woman was weak and dependent, she should be educated not for herself, but so that she could better "influence" others. "If ladies were disciplined in logical reasoning, in literary taste, and capable of communicating their own thoughts with ease," wrote Catherine McKeen in Henry Barnard's *American Journal of Education* in 1856, how "immeasurably would their means of radiating light be increased" (578). Girls' education was not calculated to lead them away from their divinely appointed sphere; instead, the young women who attended the first girls' schools in America learned that their most appropriate duties lay in motherhood.

The principles of woman's fixed place and immutable characteristics were not only reiterated by voices of authority but also repeated by women themselves. Gaining prominence in the 1820s was a group of increasingly popular women writers, the "domestic" authors, whose advice to women filled the pages of handbooks, gift books, and dozens of "Lady's" magazines. Instructing women to cultivate their "feminine" capacities to better nurture and influence those around them, the domestic writers spread the Cult of Domesticity throughout the United States.[12] Women such as Lydia Sigourney, Catharine Sedgwick, Lydia Maria Child, and Sarah Hale, though not widely known in the twentieth century, were among the most popular writers in the 1820s and thirties. Despite the aesthetic weakness of much of their literature, these women reflected the cultural expectations of the True Woman in their didactic advice handbooks and columns as well as in their fiction and poetry. Primary in the minds and pens of these women was their oft-repeated categorical imperative: they were wives and mothers first and writers second. This imperative is especially revealing because not one of the four women mentioned had a "happy" marriage at the time she was writing about the "glories" of the marital state. Lydia Sigourney had a miserable home life and repeatedly asked her husband for a separation. Lydia Maria Child and her husband, David, were separated for over ten years. Sarah Hale became a writer and editor only after she was widowed, and Catharine Sedgwick never married.

Nevertheless, the domestic writers strove to convey the importance of marriage and the family. Marriage was "unquestioningly the most blessed of all human relations," said Lydia Maria Child in her immensely popular *Mother's Book* (165–66). Domestic life was, Child continued, "the home of woman's affections, and her pleasantest sphere of duty." This "blessed" human relation was meant for every woman because "God appointed you for marriage. He has designed you for it," admonished the spinster Catharine Sedgwick in her popular advice book for girls, *Means and Ends* (116). God also designed woman "as the preserver of infancy, the teacher of childhood, and the inspirer . . . of man's moral nature," wrote Sarah Hale in her ambitious *Women's Record* (viii). Lydia Sigourney agreed with her contemporaries and said of motherhood:

> My friend, if in becoming a mother, you have reached the climax of your happiness, you have also taken a higher place in the scale of being. . . . How this new affection seems to spread a soft, fresh green over the soul. Does not the whole heart blossom thick with plants of hope, sparkling with perpetual dewdrops? What a loss, had we passed through the world, without tasting this purest, most exquisite fount of love. (*Letters to Mothers*, 9)

The domestic writers did not hesitate to describe the woman who was best fitted to reign over the sacred sphere of the home: that woman was a True Woman, the pure, pious, self-sacrificing epitome of idealized womanhood. A True Woman, according to the images the domestic writers constructed, learned how to please others by creating an idyllic domestic situation from her "pure and lofty feeling," her "charm of manners and conversation," and her "cheerful temper." A True Woman was advised that home "naturally" occupied the first place in woman's thoughts and was inevitably the only source of happiness. A True Woman's role in the rearing of her offspring and care of her household was perceived as "angelic and divine. . . . inspiration springs up in her very paths . . . it follows in her footsteps." By performing all of her domestic functions, the ideal woman became the "luminary which enlightens, . . . it was she who made 'home, sweet, home.' "[13]

A True Woman was not a primary player on her nineteenth-century stage; she merely influenced the actors by her self-sacrificing denial of any active role for herself other than "pleasing others." Mothers in magazines like *Godey's* were advised to "blunt" the sensibilities of their intelligent young daughters and to "sedulously direct" them to a "cheering view of female influence." As women, then, their minds would be constituted and adapted to play upon and influence the "finer parts" of men's natures. As one domestic writer summed up, the True Woman's sphere is "not to govern, but to direct; and her moral influence, in the humblest grade, is as powerful as the influence of one of her sex who rules a nation or occupies a throne."[14]

While this image of the True Woman crouched in every nook of the popular psyche in the early nineteenth century, Robert Owen announced his plans to change the world through egalitarian communal living. When Owen proposed in 1825 to create a Community of Equality at New Harmony, Indiana, his ideas were revolutionary. He wanted nothing less than to overthrow an outdated "social system" and replace it with a new moral world where private property and religion would end. Only in a community where all lived without money and religion could women and men live as equals, Owen wrote. Only in a community of equality could men and women be freed from what Owen called the bonds of "ignorance, superstition, and hypocrisy."[15]

At New Harmony, Owen promised that without the necessity of perpetuating private property, without the "need" to condemn women to a life "enslaved" as a piece of property, women and men could live together "in virtuous and happy connection . . . solely with a view to their happiness."[16] At New Harmony, woman's "false and vicious" place within the traditional family would be abolished and the place hitherto occupied by "domestic drudges" kept in a state of mental childhood would no longer exist. "False notions" about differences between the sexes, which existed in

individual minds or were reinforced through institutions founded to perpetuate these differences, would no longer keep men and women the
"artificial beings" these institutions made them. At New Harmony women
would no longer depend on their husbands economically; they would,
Owen proposed, receive equal education with men, would be relieved of
individual cooking and housework, and would have, along with men,
sufficient leisure for mental improvement and rational enjoyment.

Few utopian thinkers before Owen considered women in their plans to
create a perfect place. Utopian thinkers until the late eighteenth century
had primarily been of two molds: either visionary writers of philosophy or
fiction such as Plato or Sir Thomas More, or religious patriots/patriarchs
who sought a concrete heaven on earth, and who correctly perceived that a
sect had a better chance of survival by separating itself from a hostile
world. At best, as in Plato's *Republic,* women's needs were expected to be
the same as men's, their liberation presumed to occur in relation to men's.
At worst, as in Sir Thomas More's *Utopia,* or in most religious communities,
women were expected to exist in a pervasively regulated state serving
men's needs.

The few utopian thinkers before Robert Owen who did imagine communities based on sexual egalitarianism did not carry out their plans. In the
autumn of 1794, Robert Southey, Samuel Taylor Coleridge, and Robert
Lovell planned their egalitarian "pantisocracy" community based on
William Godwin's principles, where property would be held in common,
and all people, men and women, would be equal. The publisher of the
Pantisocrats wrote that their community was to be "a social colony in which
there was to be a community of property and where all that was selfish was
to be proscribed." It would "regenerate the whole complexion of society,
and that not by establishing formal laws, but by excluding all the little
deteriorating passions, injustice, wrath, anger, clamor, and evil speaking,
and thereby setting an example of human perfectibility."[17] Southey and
Coleridge, rejecting the advice of one of Godwin's friends to found the
community in England, traveled to Bristol to charter a boat to take them to
America and the banks of the Susquehanna, but while waiting for a ship,
they married Bristol sisters and their idealistic plan dissipated.

Robert Owen, on the other hand, did come to America and did found
America's first community where men and women were guaranteed equality. Unlike most rich entrepreneurs, Owen devoted his fortune to establishing a utopia. Other less well-known Owenites also dedicated their energies
to establishing other communities in America. On paper their plans look
potentially more liberating for women than any previous endeavors.

We need to reassess the Owenite communities established in nineteenth-
century America for a number of reasons. First, Robert Owen's experiment
at New Harmony and the other Owenite communities that sprang up in the
East and Midwest provide us with a unique opportunity to look at the

world in a microcosm. Owen intended to create a world that would be, like all utopian communities, a "city on a hill" for others to emulate, separate from the biases and prejudices of the mainstream culture. The Owenite communities did become little worlds unto themselves, with carefully written constitutions that guaranteed equality for all people. Reformers who journeyed to an Owenite community believed themselves to be a new version of a chosen people, self-selected to begin life afresh in a new state of society. Given their insular nature, intentional communities offer particularly rich environments for studying the evolution of an idea such as egalitarianism. In the mainstream culture, any notion of equality is instantly compromised by the reality of tradition, of habit, or of economic necessity. But in a separate intentional community, all could and should be possible.

A second reason for looking again at the Owenite experiments is to uncover untold stories of the many Owenite communities and to rescue from obscurity the reformers who established them. Few people have heard of Samuel Underhill, Robert Jennings, Daniel Roe, or Frances Wright. Their attempts to weave women's emancipation into communal living have heretofore remained buried in the archives of local historical societies.[18] The stories of these reformers tell of dedication, often for a lifetime, to Owenite ideals. The legacy these men and women left us created a tradition that has lasted over 150 years, infusing American political and social life with such reforms as free thought, workingmen's rights, the abolition of slavery, the advocacy of birth control, and the liberation of women from ignorance and powerlessness.

Until recently, few scholars have noted the Owenites' place in the history of women's liberation, or even Robert Owen's place in the history of socialism.[19] The term "socialism" comes, in fact, not from followers of Marx or Engels but from an Owenite publication of the mid-1820s, *The London Co-operative Magazine,* as a way of describing matters dealing with Robert Owen, Great Britain's "Father of Socialism." By the mid-1840s the word "socialist" was used in the United States and England to refer to followers of Robert Owen. Although most Marxist/feminist critics today consider Friedrich Engels responsible for creating "a new way of looking at the family and at women," Engels borrowed his ideas linking the rise of private property with women's subordination rather shamelessly from Owen.[20] For Owen, a socialist critique meant emancipating all of humanity through communal living. For Engels, Marx, and the long line of socialists who would come after them, class alone determined a person's ideological perspective. As Barbara Taylor has pointed out in her study of British Owenism, Owenite schemes to emancipate all of humanity were displaced in the mid to late nineteenth century by Marxist socialism, which increasingly focused on the economic struggles of a single class, leaving women out of the socialists' search for liberation. Concomitantly, issues like marriage and family life were transformed from political questions into private ones (xvi, 287).

Besides giving Robert Owen and the many other Owenite reformers their due for creating and trying to implement a socialist theory that they believed would liberate the world, we also need to reassess in what ways the American Owenite communities did "succeed" and in what ways they "failed." For most of Robert Owen's contemporaries, and for most scholars today, the records of the Owenite communities signal a colossal defeat; the "success" of a communal experiment has almost always been measured by how long a community has lasted, not by what it attempted to do. Similarly, most communities are also judged by how different they are from the mainstream culture—by what sacred beasts they slay and what taboos they challenge. Certainly, in this respect as well, Owenite communalism in America looks, at first glance, to have been a failure, perhaps because it tried to slay so many beasts and thus strayed too far from the mainstream culture. In fact, I will argue that neither assessment is accurate. The Owenite communities were not failures simply because they did not withstand some measure of time. Any attempt to create a more perfect world cannot be labeled a "failure" because it did not last over two or three years. The Owenite tradition in America, as we shall see in chapters 4 and 5, lasted throughout a century and continues to inspire people today. At the same time, I will argue that the real "failure" of the communities was not that they were short-lived, but that they did not do enough—specifically that they never implemented the equality they sought.

All the official documents of the Owenite communities promised egalitarian happiness (see chapter 2). As we submerge ourselves in the discourse of the women who populated the communities, though, and compare the women's own words in private texts such as letters and journals to the official public discourse of the communities' constitutions, newspapers, and lectures, we find a glaring discrepancy between the public promises and the private realities of the communities (see chapters 3, 4, and 5). Such a discrepancy is also evident in the mixed messages of the Owenite reformers, who appeared to be advocating egalitarianism in public pronouncements but who refuted it in their private behavior. The tension generated by the clash of promised equality and actual practices never resolved itself in any of the communities; rather this struggle played itself out again and again in all the Owenite experiments that populated the American landscape in nineteenth-century America. We will be occupied throughout this study with the reasons particular Owenite communities never achieved any genuine equality between men and women.

From a feminist/historicist perspective, we will also confront the broad cultural dilemma of why, when rational women and men set out on a journey toward equalitarian communalism, they could not reach their prized destination. The answer, we will see, is disarmingly simple to state yet maddeningly complex to unravel: Owenite reformers could not, finally, disentangle themselves from the mainstream culture they sought to reform. They lugged with them to communal life some heavy ideological baggage. Their instincts were for and their habits were of a patriarchal system. Though they all advocated a socialist state, their socialism in no way altered the priorities of a patriarchy, with power resting firmly in the hands of men. Despite their professions of equality, almost all the reformers accepted an ideology of gender that labeled women a separate species that did not need or want equality. The one Owenite reformer who did understand the evils of the patriarchy—because she was a woman—discovered at the end of her life that women who try to alter the way the world is organized end up bitterly hated, with no more to show for a lifetime of Owenite reform than utter ostracism from both family and society (see chapter 4).

It remains for those of us in the twentieth century to continue the Owenites' search for egalitarianism, but first we must understand their history so that we are not doomed to repeat it. My final goal in this text is to identify the confluence of ideology and event that blended inevitably into the cultural practices that relegated women to powerlessness and domesticity, practices that affect us today as clearly as they did in the Owenites' day.

CHAPTER
1

THE BRITISH BACKGROUND AND
THE AMERICAN LANDSCAPE

To begin to understand the American Owenite movement, we must place this phenomenon and its founder in an ideological and cultural perspective. Robert Owen's ideas on equality evolved slowly over a period of twenty-five years. Leaving his birthplace, Wales, in 1789 at the age of ten, reputedly with only forty shillings in his pocket, Owen, in a tradition soon to be popularized in nineteenth-century novels glorifying capitalists on the rise, journeyed to London to make his fortune.[1] Success in each of his ensuing apprenticeships led to his eventual management of the New Lanark mills in southwestern Scotland and marriage to the daughter of the mill's owner. After becoming manager and part owner of the New Lanark Mills in 1800, he set about transforming New Lanark from a dirty mill town to a showplace of cleanliness and enlightened education. If Owen had died on his thirty-fifth birthday in 1814, he would surely be known today (if at all) only as a benevolent patriarch, a man who insisted upon numerous reforms to make working and living in new Lanark healthier and happier for its residents. But slowly Owen's "plan" for improving the lot of all poor people, trapped landless and uneducated in a burgeoning industrial revolution, evolved into a vision that he believed would transform the world.

Robert Owen's plan was rooted in the same ideology as the French and American revolutions: a new way of looking at the world that had its roots in Enlightenment thought. This new perception was based on the idea that every man had the natural right to determine his own political and social destiny, because, since all human knowledge was acquired through the senses, all men were potentially equal; they had the potential for equality if their environments were equal.[2] Robert Owen absorbed the great Enlightenment thinkers' ideas, as well as their innate biases about the way the world worked and about women's place in that world.

Perhaps Owen's greatest gift was his ability to amalgamate others' ideas and turn them into his own.[3] Owen unashamedly latched onto ideas from the Enlightenment thinkers he was familiar with, synthesizing them into his own expanding "theory." From Locke he took the idea that the character of man is a tabula rasa at birth; from Rousseau, that children collectively may be taught any sentiments and habits because humans are basically good and it is institutions that pervert this natural goodness; from the Utilitarians, the importance of happiness, which can be attained only by conduct that must promote the happiness of the community; from William Godwin, the notion that private property has to be eliminated in order for equality to exist; and from Adam Smith, the premise that wealth results from labor. Taken together, these statements appear unrelated, a hodgepodge of the best in late eighteenth-century male-dominated philosophy, but together they formed the nexus from which Owen's later communal plans would spring.

THE BRITISH BACKGROUNDS

Owen's first fifteen years at New Lanark were marked not by revolutionary theory but by his ever-present patriarchal insistence on reform and efficiency. Upon taking over the mills in 1800, Owen cleaned up the town where the workers lived. He enlarged and rebuilt the workers' houses, created "bug patrols" to inspect the kitchens, removed dunghills piled high on the public streets, and fashioned paths and walkways for the workers on his private land. The invasion of privacy by the weekly house inspections outraged the women of New Lanark, according to a former teacher at the New Lanark school, but Owen's leadership prevailed, nevertheless. Because of his own lifelong aversion to alcohol, Owen set up groups of people to report on public drunkenness and, at the same time, developed a set of rules for good behavior. As Owen says in his autobiography, "My first task [at New Lanark] was to make arrangements to supersede the evil conditions with which the population was surrounded, by good conditions" (*Life*, 84).

Although Owen did not pay the highest wages in the area, he did provide a fairly priced mill store, a novelty in a mill town where the workers were by definition captive consumers.[4] At the same time, Owen reduced working hours for children as well as for adults in his mills, paid all doctors' fees, and continued to pay weekly wages to disabled workers. As an innovative leader and forerunner of the behaviorist B. F. Skinner, Owen encouraged good workmanship in his mills by devising and using a set of colored blocks to signify the productivity of the worker. The color of the "telegraph"—from black (bad) to white (excellent)—revealed to Owen at a glance a given worker's efficiency; thus Owen claimed he never had to say a word of blame to a negligent worker. Owen sums up the results of his experimentation in his mills in his autobiography:

This experiment at New Lanark was the first commencement of practical measures with a view to change the fundamental principle on which society has heretofore been based from the beginning; and no experiment could be more successful in proving the truth of the principle that the character is formed *for* and not *by* the individual, and that society now possesses the most ample means and power to well-form the character of every one, by reconstructing society on its true principle. . . . (*Life*, 85)

As early as 1813 Owen had published his first significant essays, collected together under the title *A New View of Society*, on this very point. It was here that Owen laid out the foundation of his philosophy. These essays criticized the errors in "our forefathers' systems," whereby children's characters were formed without any guidance. Owen proposed that because children could be taught any sentiments and habits, countries should establish rational plans for educating children and thus form the character of their people. His first several essays in character formation and the necessity of national plans for educating all children led him to his most famous axiom: that the character of man, without a single exception, is always formed for him.[5] Such emphasis on the importance of environment and of early education would lead Owen by the end of the decade toward his communal theory.

Although Owen had trained his workers in industrious habits and had begun to clear the foundation for his infant school as early as 1809, it was not until January 1, 1816, that Owen opened, with great fanfare and spectacle, his Institution for the Formation of Character at New Lanark. Using the opening of the New Lanark Institution as an excuse to do one of the things he loved best—lecture—Owen spoke to his workers on the educational benefits and comforts (such as shorter working hours) available to the inhabitants of New Lanark; his aim, he reiterated, was the Benthamite's "happiness to all."[6] His theory was based on his belief that character was formed for people, not by people. Pleased with his successes to date, Owen also directed comments to other manufacturers about how they could benefit by improving their workers' conditions. Owen, easily assuming his role as an industrial reformer, believed that his example at New Lanark illustrated that when conditions for workers and their children improved, profits for manufacturers increased. His glowing descriptions of what he had done and would do at New Lanark brought endless streams of educators, factory owners, and other reform-minded dignitaries to New Lanark.

Owen's greatest success at his mills, the one he cared about the most, was the New Lanark school, the most important element of the New Lanark Institution for the Formation of Character. From the age of one on, children of the mill workers were given lessons taught by "sensible signs"— the common elements around them such as maps, conversation, animals, plants—and were entertained by General Noun and Corporal Adverb, rather than "annoyed with books." The children in the infant classes, from just over one year old to five years old, remained in school only half of the day; during the rest of the day, they amused themselves "at perfect freedom." The older children, from five to ten, studied academic subjects such as reading, writing, natural history, geography, history, and religion (just the "facts," not the "abstruse doctrinal points") as well as singing, dancing, playing musical instruments, and military marching. All of the children learned their lessons without fear of punishment or "artificial" rewards, because Owen firmly believed that punishment or reward was useless, given his dictum that the characters of children were formed for them, not by them. A former student at the New Lanark schools remembers being one of the boys Owen caught in the woods cutting hockey sticks, or "shenteys," but instead of punishing the boys, Owen gave them his famous "the blame is not justly yours" speech. Owen himself believed that the children at the New Lanark schools were "by far the happiest human beings I have ever seen." Owen charged parents nothing for the infant school or for evening classes for students over ten who spent their days working in the mills; for the full-day students parents paid only three pence a month, a bargain for the finest school available in Scotland at the time.[7]

Convinced of the rightness of his reform-minded benevolent patriarchy, Owen expanded his concerns from his New Lanark mills to issues concerning children and poor laborers everywhere in Great Britain. He became involved in establishing factory relief laws for children and helping Great Britain's unemployed, who were caught up in the current industrial catch-22, with the supply of workers far exceeding demand. In 1815, in his first public campaign, Owen convened a meeting of Glasgow manufacturers to discuss child labor laws, but he was not satisfied with the response. Though the Factory Act passed in 1819 did limit child labor, Owen never believed that the act would accomplish enough. Trying a different tactic, in March 1817 Owen wrote a report for the Parliamentary Committee on Poor Laws, hoping to solve the country's escalating economic problems within the framework of governmental aid. The plan he presented to this group was a first version of his soon-to-be-famous communal plan and his first step away from traditional reform channels.

Hoping to find occupations for the poor, Owen proposed that agricultural communities be formed so that the poor could support themselves. Both Owen's model village at New Lanark and his recent reading of John Bellers's 1696 essay on the creating of "colledges," in which 1,300 people in useful trades worked for one another, led him to believe that the benefits of communal living could solve his country's unemployment problems.[8] Specifically, Owen suggested that from five hundred to fifteen hundred people could live in newly built squares of buildings, including public kitchens and schools, private apartments for married couples, and dormitories for all children over three years of age—all to be surrounded by at least one thousand acres of land. In this community, designed as a parallelogram, people who were ignorant and useless in industrial society would soon be able to support themselves; meanwhile, their children would be provided with useful training and exorcised of their "bad habits."[9]

In this first communal vision, though, little predicts Owen's later attitudes toward utopian egalitarianism, except the intentional design of the community. As in all his following plans, Owen imagined people living in a carefully constructed parallelogram (depicted in an engraving in the illustration section) with connected buildings including a school at one end, a public kitchen and dining room, and individual rooms for all adults at the other end. Outside the parallelogram would be gardens, crops, and livestock. Owen's parallelogram conjures up images of a modern medieval castle. Rather than serfs working for a king, the poor would work for themselves and for a wealthy landowner who would furnish the land and buildings.

In the community itself, Owen proposed strict sex-segregated work roles for men and women, with children living in a dormitory with other children so that mothers could no longer teach their children bad habits and narrow ways of thinking. He wrote that women should be employed

> First,—In the care of their infants, and in keeping their dwellings in the best order.
> Second,—In cultivating the gardens to raise vegetables for the supply of the public kitchen.
> Third,—In attending to such of the branches of the various manufactures as women can well undertake; but not to be employed in them more than four or five hours in the day.
> Fourth,—In making up clothing for the inmates of the establishment.
> Fifth,—In attending occasionally, and in rotation, in the public kitchen, mess rooms, and dormitories; and, when properly instructed, in superintending some parts of the education of children in the schools. ("Report," 163)

Men, continued Owen, were to work primarily in agriculture and also, to a lesser degree, in the "manufactures" as well.

In August 1817 Robert Owen put his plan in front of the public for the first time, only to have it jokingly referred to as "Owen's Parallelogram" (Beer, 171). Spurned by other manufacturing owners and by government officials who did not take his plan seriously, Owen in a public meeting denounced religion as the barrier that prevented men from understanding how his plan would bring happiness to all concerned. Many of Owen's potential supporters reacted in horror against the "infidel" in their midst. A committee of David Ricardo and other influential economists tried to raise subscriptions for an experimental community, but few came in. Owen himself cites this particular speech as marking a turning point in his up to this point eminently successful life. Fifty years later Friedrich Engels would praise Owen's insight for criticizing the opiate of the people, but in Owen's day, his castigation of "the priesthood" precipitated his fall from grace and set into motion his thinking about a restructuring of society rather than its gradual reform.

Beginning to believe himself separate from the cadre of wealthy land-owners for the first time, Owen continued to refine his "plan" by incorporating the ideas of his friends and acquaintances. David Ricardo's ideas, for example, helped him to refute Malthus's prophecies. Casting a pall over all economic writing in the early nineteenth century, Thomas Malthus had written in "An Essay on the Principle of Population" in 1798 that population increased geometrically while the food that sustained life increased arithmetically; thus the condition of the poor would become more and more hopeless, and, unless famine or war intervened to diminish the population, starvation was inevitable. Ricardo disagreed with Malthus, citing that manual labor, properly directed, was the source of all wealth, and that properly directed manual labor could support a huge increase in population. Ricardo had, as had Owen, been influenced by Adam Smith, who believed that labor was the source of all wealth, but Ricardo added his notion of the importance of manual labor to Smith's classic theory. Owen, using Ricardo's modification of Smith's ideas, rewrote his plan, and his May 1820 version has in it the main tenet of Ricardian economic theory—the importance of manual labor. Specifically, Owen introduced into his communal plan the notion of "spade cultivation," his formulation for cultivating the soil with individual workers using a spade, rather than a plow, to break the soil. Owen believed, for a time at least in the early 1820s, that spade cultivation would prepare the soil in such a way as to produce more crops and thus feed more people. Expanding his plan to include spade cultivation was particularly pleasing to Owen because it allowed him to illustrate how his communities, besides solving the "poor problem," could also refute Malthus.

Even more important than Ricardo to the evolution of Owen's plan, though, was William Godwin. Called by Owen's biographer, Frank Podmore, "his master,"[10] William Godwin was probably the most important influence in Owen's life during the time he was developing his plan in the second decade of the nineteenth century. Much of the phrasing and many of the ideas in Owen's works come straight from Godwin, who, in his book *An Enquiry Concerning Political Justice*, had written how circumstances form people's character, how important a rational education is, how happiness, in effect, is knowledge. During the men's twenty-three-year acquaintance they met intermittently, but they saw each other regularly about eight times a year during the period 1813–18, when Owen was formulating his social and economic theories. On one of Godwin's earliest visits in 1813 he claimed he had converted Owen from the system of "self-love" to benevolence.[11]

For William Godwin, the root of inequality was private property, and for many years he tried to convince the landowning Owen of the rightness of his views. Both men believed in the Utilitarians' premise that happiness for the greatest number was the greatest good, but for Godwin, without equality there could be no happiness. Owen, coming from his perspective as a landowning "giver" of rights to his New Lanark workers, had at first thought of his communities only as a place where poor workers could earn enough to support themselves, where their children could be given an excellent education, and where wealthy men would become even wealthier as they profited from the poor working their lands. But with Godwin's persistent urging, Owen began to rethink his plan, finally agreeing with Godwin by the end of the decade that equality was the most important element to the foundation of a new moral world.

The equality that Owen accepted as a premise for a good society was an abstract one, tempered as it always was with his biases toward patriarchal power and women's "innate" inequality—both unquestioned "givens" in early nineteenth-century thought for most people. Taking his cue from Godwin, Owen did not concern himself with women's inequality in society per se; instead he focused on the idea of marriage and its relationship to private property. In 1793, four years before he was to marry Mary Wollstonecraft, Godwin wrote that marriage was based on the absurd expectation that the inclinations of two people should remain the same for a long period of time.[12] Furthermore, Godwin wrote, "marriage is an affair of property, and the worst of all properties" (*Enquiry*, 272), with women being monopolized by men, and men watching each other in perpetual jealousy. Godwin had himself derived his own abstract views on marriage from Jean-Jacques Rousseau, who wrote in *Discourse on the Origin of Inequality* how the cultivation of the earth necessarily brought about its parceling and the rise of private property, which in turn created a state of inequality among people and new roles for women. A contemporary of Godwin's and one of his friends, Thomas Holcroft, carried these ideas further, writing that all private property was evil; marriage made women private property; therefore, marriage was evil (Marshall, 88). Godwin's solution to the evils of marriage, at least before he met and married Wollstonecraft, was to theorize that it should be abolished. Owen, not married to a Wollstonecraft, latched onto Godwin's ideas on marriage, particularly the notion of the absurdity that husband and wife should remain the same over a period of time.

By the early 1820s Owen's gradual shift from a reforming industrial owner to a communitarian socialist was well under way, thanks to Godwin's influence. His plan, only a few years earlier simply a device to help poor people obtain food and necessities, was, by 1821, based upon the importance of equality for all. As Owen wrote in his 1821 essay "The Social System," incorporating both Godwin's and Ricardo's ideas: "there is but one mode by which man can possess in perpetuity all the happiness which his nature is capable of enjoying and that is by the cooperation of all for each."[13] This new plan, now intended as a means of achieving happiness for everyone rather than simply giving permanent productive employment to the poor, kept the important features of his previous plans: the same parallelogram, allowing for a private apartment for each adult and for communal eating, educational, and recreational space; the same spade cultivation on agricultural lands. But in this new plan Owen for the first time stressed the importance of "equality": "there can be no permanent happiness in any society in which equality is . . . excluded," declared Owen, paraphrasing Godwin (*NHG,* January 24, 1827). Each individual, in his rethought system, would possess equal advantages—equality of housing, food, clothing, instruction, employment, and treatment. And because Owen was now interested in the happiness/equality (inseparable terms to Owen, as they had been for Godwin) of all people, he addressed for the first time the particular inequities in "the present system" of marriage and family life.

Speaking specifically of women's position in society, Owen promised to alleviate women's "drudgery" while allowing them sufficient leisure to improve their minds and enjoy life. Though he promised that community life would relieve women's drudgery, Owen in no way altered his thinking about the efficacy of traditional "women's employments"; these employments remained the same as in previous plans. Owen, like Godwin, was more interested in marriage and, specifically, in the unhappiness surrounding a marriage where neither party loved each other, rather than in different roles for women. Believing strongly that marriage should promote happiness, not misery as was often the case, Owen predicted that marriage in his new communities would present "a striking contrast to that which is exhibited in common society." Misery in the latter, wrote Owen, reflecting Godwin's and Wollstonecraft's views, came from a defective education, an inequality of condition, and a lack of acquaintance due to "artificial and insincere character created by the present systems"—conditions that would be ameliorated in his Social System. Should these precautionary measures not be sufficient to ensure the happiness of both the husband and the wife, and should the union prove the cause of misery to them, Owen recommended that a notice and ceremony similar to a wedding be allowed to separate them again in order to prevent the "increasing evils which must arise to those who are compelled to live together when they can no longer retain the affection for each other which is necessary to their happiness" (*NHG,* February 28, 1827).

Inspired by Owen's plan to create a new social system that could affect all people, numerous reform-minded men took up his cause locally and thus became known as the first "Owenites." Men such as A. J. Hamilton, Abram Combe, Donald Macdonald, George Mudie, and William Thompson embraced Owen's communal ideas and helped to begin Owenite societies and then implement the first Owenite experiments in Great Britain. At the same time these men, friends and disciples of Owen, to one extent or another helped change the focus of Owenism as it developed in the early 1820s, just as Ricardo's and Godwin's influence had helped Owen to modify his plan from 1816 to 1820. Because these men were attempting their own versions of Owen's "plan," they were inevitably changing it, and Robert Owen, despite his pleasure at having disciples, was not always pleased with the directions they took.

The first of the men to become converted to Owenism was A. J. Hamilton.[14] Born in October of 1793, the son of General John Hamilton, himself known for his own reform tracts, Hamilton discovered long before he met Robert Owen that traditional schooling was useless. Unhappy with life in the army, displeased with all the "artificial rank" in Great Britain, Hamilton returned to his family's land in 1816 near Motherwell, Scotland, to marry and become "a farmer." Meeting Owen at a dinner shortly after his return to Scotland, Hamilton found Owen's plans to be "in unison with nature, reason, and truth: ("Soldier and Citizen," 148). As early as 1820 Hamilton, taken with Owen's notions of poor relief, proposed that he would let from five hundred to seven hundred acres of his land at Motherwell to form "an establishment on Mr. Owen's plan." Robert Owen did not sanction the scheme because he feared the Motherwell Community would become a poor farm, despite the fact that the "Rules and Regulations" of the future Motherwell Community that Hamilton had drawn up paralleled Owen's own ideas in his 1821 essay "The Social System."[15] Though subsequent meetings followed, efforts to get the Houses of Parliament to finance the community were defeated. In 1822 the British and Foreign Philanthropic Society took up the Motherwell plan and tried to raise subscription funds; the Society did obtain over fifty thousand pounds (ten thousand from Owen, five thousand from Hamilton), but it did not reach the one hundred thousand pounds Owen believed necessary to begin a community.[16]

Inspired by his mentor Owen, Hamilon decided to take courses at Edinburgh University and there, according to his autobiography, he met Abram Combe, an Edinburgh tanner. Like Hamilton, Combe was predisposed to finding Owen's ideas appealing. Born in 1785 and raised by strict Calvinist parents, Combe admired utility from the time he was flogged as a schoolboy for not completing his "impractical" Latin lessons. His father, an Edinburgh brewer, worked next to a tanning works, and this "accidental circumstance" is how he chose a trade, according to his brief autobiography (*Life*, 5). In 1820 Combe visited New Lanark. After seeing the New Lanark schools, he wrote that he was "a complete convert to [Owen's] views" (*Life*, 8). With Hamilton he quickly set up a cooperative society, which they called the Edinburgh Practical Society, a first step toward community living based "as nearly on Mr. Owen's principles as was compatible with external circumstances" (*Life*, 8). They opened a cooperative store and school and met evenings for mutual instruction, dancing, conversation, or music. Like Owen, Combe insisted that all members of the Practical Society, more than five hundred families, abstain from strong drink and swearing.

Combe's initial attempts exhilarated him and he bet a friend that within five years the Royal Circus, then the most splendid residence in Edinburgh, would be pulled down voluntarily by its proprietors, to be converted into communities "on the new principles" (*Life*, 9). However, in reality, the storekeeper Combe had hired to oversee the Practical Society's store, reputed (by the nonreligious Hamilton) to be a "religious man," embezzled all the funds. Undaunted, Combe established a cooperative in his tannery, erecting dormitories and a kitchen for his workmen, and agreed to share the profits with them, although this venture, too, was unsuccessful because, according to Combe, the men were "unprepared in their mental habits" (*Life*, 10).

Drawn to the Practical Society, Donald Macdonald, a thirty-year-old Royal Engineer who happened to be stationed in Edinburgh, became one of its first members because of his particular interest in education for children. Knowing that the Practical Society had few funds, Macdonald suggested beginning a day school for the children of the society's members, as a "temporary and partially progressive step toward our object."[17] In only one week, Macdonald relates, the society's school had 128 children. The conditions for the school were not ideal—an inconvenient house in a busy city, teachers with questionable qualifications, principles little understood by parents and unknown to children while being denied by the public. Yet within a few months, the students had improved drastically. Macdonald was, in his words, "always there," assisting the teachers. Only travel to Ireland with Robert Owen in 1822 took him away from the school. Although the school was discontinued after Macdonald's departure, the nucleus of "believers" associated with it, including Combe, Hamilton, and some dedicated parents, formed the nucleus of Orbiston, the first large-scale Owenite community in Great Britain, established in 1825.

Meanwhile, George Mudie, a Scottish journalist and printer who had lived in Edinburgh and Glasgow until coming to London in 1820, organized London printers into London's first Owenite society, the "Cooperative and Economical Society," in January 1821 and began printing the first Owenite journal, *The Economist*. In typical Owenite style, the first issue of *The Economist* proclaims that it is a "Periodical Paper Explanatory of the New System of Society Projected by Robert Owen, Esq." and of a plan of association for improving the condition of the working classes at their present employments (January 27, 1821). Mudie created his Cooperative Society as a halfway measure, much like the Edinburgh Practical Society, until money could be gathered for communal living. The Cooperative Society, according to their "Report" dated January 23, 1821, would consist of 250 working-class families who would come together to spend money jointly to purchase necessities. As the society was located in London, most members remained at their present employments, with each male member paying one guinea weekly, for which he received lodging, food, clothing, and education for himself and his family. The members of the society believed that they would save money by buying in large quantities and would economize by cooking cooperatively. They would also benefit, they believed, from the time saved by the women of the community, who, because of cooperation, would "doubtless . . . be beneficially employed in performing services for which we are now obliged to pay."[18]

Throughout the pages of *The Economist*, Mudie consistently praised Mr. Owen's system; as he said in the issue of March 17, 1821, "I cannot hesitate to pronounce the whole scheme to be the greatest effort of wisdom the world has yet witnessed." Mudie was particularly impressed with the technological benefits possible in communal living, such as using steam to clean linens, thus saving women hours of time, or heating and cooling "centrally," through tubes to each of the rooms in the parallelogram. But Mudie was not impressed with rumors that Owen's system would aim at "equality." "In the new societies," said Mudie, "there will not be a REAL community of goods. We know of no motive strong enough to induce families to enter into a state of common property." Instead, according to Mudie, the new community would "carefully preserve the right of private property, and of individual accumulation and possession" (*Econ*, August 11, 1821).

At the end of October 1821, Mudie, competing with other Owenites, prophesied that the Cooperative Society would "have demonstrated the efficacy of the new arrangements, in the heart of the metropolis, before the establishment at Motherwell" was opened (*Econ*, October 20, 1821). By November 17, Mudie informed his readers that the society had "taken" several houses in Spa Fields. By March 1822, the constitution of the new community was printed, along with a discussion of the pleasurable life the families living there discovered. According to Mudie, the families ate breakfast and dinner together at general tables, and in the evenings they talked, read, or listened to lectures and music in the public room—though members of each family were at perfect liberty to spend their leisure hours and take their meals in their private apartments. The domestic duties of the women were the same ones prescribed by Owen: the cooking done with one fire, thus sparing a number of women from "their usual avocations" such as cooking, cleaning, or washing. Because of this freedom, the Owenites believed that some women would be able to add to their work load by "tak[ing] under their constant superintendence, without a moment's intermission, in and out of doors, the whole of the children—securing for them the best possible attention to their health, comfort, and morals" (*Econ*, March 2, 1822). The elder children were to be "carefully instructed in the principles of Christianity." In trying to keep everyone, adult and child alike, behaving acceptably in communal living, the community decided that each member should appoint "his own friendly

Monitor," whose duty was to note errors in character (*Econ,* January 19, 1822).

Despite these plans and the enthusiasm generated by the Spa Fields Owenites, Robert Owen himself had no involvement in the experiment, perhaps because of his disagreement with Mudie over religion, or perhaps because he had little interest in a community that had no intention of ever seeking communal property. Nevertheless, Mudie let Owen know of his progress. He wrote to Robert Owen on January 3, 1823, that "we are making great progress in London, as far as the conversion of numerous persons to the principles is concerned. I lecture every Monday evening, using sensible signs. . . ." He signed himself "your Faithful Follower" (RO Papers, #25).

Meanwhile, Robert Owen believed himself to have no "faithful followers." All his disciples were intelligent men who modified his plan according to their own wishes. Perhaps because of this dissension, Owen antagonized those who meant to follow him. For reasons that remain obscure, Owen did not appoint his "faithful follower" George Mudie to the Committee of the Philanthopic Society in 1823, an honor Mudie coveted. Still nursing this slight in 1848, Mudie wrote to Owen that he was "convinced that, had you cooperated with me or had encouraged me to persevere in cooperating with you, the cause of cooperation would many years ago have been successfully established" (RO Papers, #1665).

Other young men, such as John Gray, who appeared at first to be just the kind of "faithful follower" Owen wanted, also tended to modify Owen's plans. Gray, taking the "liberty" of writing to Owen in 1823, told him that he had heard his views for the first time a week ago and now wanted to "lay before [him]" his own ideas. If they were the same as Owen's, he wrote, then he would be content let Owen do the speaking on the subject. Two years later, though, Gray published an essay, "A Lecture on Human Happiness," that concluded with his promise that he would offer his own plans "altogether different from those proposed by Mr. Owen."[19]

Both Owen's considerable traveling and his growing lack of commitment to Motherwell, which he believed needed much more money to be established successfully, made many of the Owenites besides George Mudie impatient for a community to be established. Hamilton and Combe, specifically, and members of the Edinburgh Practical Society decided to begin Scotland's first Owenite community without Owen. The site they chose, Orbiston, was only about a mile from the original Motherwell lands and was still a part of the Hamilton estate. On March 18, 1825, Combe and Hamilton drew up the Articles of Agreement, which specified that the Orbiston Community would be a community of manual labor organized to eliminate the world's poverty.[20] In the same month, a large building was begun, and members moved in a year later, even though the building was not ready for occupation. Numerous hardships, beginning with members moving into an unfinished building and ending with the unexpected death of planner/manager Combe in 1827, doomed this first Owenite experiment to a short life. As Hamilton wrote, after Combe got ill and left for Edinburgh, nothing went well. Yet both men remained staunch Owenites. Combe, on his deathbed, dictated to his thirteen-year-old son the following message for posterity: "I have compared the effects of the old system with those of the new, and . . . I am quite satisfied that the new system is much superior to the old. Under the old, we really see through a glass darkly, and know even as we are known; but under the new, a very short time makes us see face to face" (*Life,* 21). Hamilton, despite losing much of his fortune in the venture, remained a believer in the efficacy of the Owenite system as well. He wrote in his autobiography in the late 1820s that "the system of Pantisocracy or Co-Operation . . . must be, sooner or later, adopted, to produce the most beneficial, most extensive results in the social happiness of mankind" (339–40).

As Robert Owen traveled around Great Britain in the early 1820s, he met many people who influenced him, but perhaps the most important to the development of Owenite thought in the 1820s was William Thompson, whom he met on a trip he took to Ireland in 1822 with Edinburgh Practical Society members A. J. Hamilton and Donald Macdonald. Thompson, rightly called by his biographer the "most important theoretician among the early Owenites," was greatly influenced by Owen's socialistic plans (Pankhurst, 1). Like Owen, Thompson accepted many of the premises of the Utilitarians—Thompson, in fact, lived with Jeremy Bentham in 1822 and 1823—while rejecting their conclusions about the benefits of a laissez-faire government. To the Utilitarians, the sole measure of the value of any social arrangement was the quantity of happiness it produced, and this happiness was obtained by the pursuit of self-interest and laissez-faire government (a convenient and timely philosophical justification for capitalism). But to Thompson, a laissez-faire government could not produce happiness. As Owen visited him, Thompson was writing a book, *Distribution of Wealth,* a tract on the importance of equality. To Thompson, as to Godwin before him, only the equality of all people would lay the groundwork for happiness. Thompson solved his problem of how to achieve a truly equal distribution of wealth when he heard of Owen's ideas of communities, where everyone could enjoy equally the fruits of one another's labor. After Thompson talked with Owen, he incorporated Owen's idea of egalitarian communities into his theory.

At the same time, Thompson gave Owen a clearer understanding of the discrimination against women in the "old world." Thompson's friendship with the forceful, brilliant feminist Anna Wheeler and their reading of Wollstonecraft had helped him understand the real problems women faced in a capitalistic society. Wheeler, after being married for twelve years to a drunkard, left her husband in 1812 and fled with her children to France, where she became involved with the Saint-Simonians and Charles Fourier. She understood, as Robert Owen never would, exactly what women's position was in the old, immoral world. The mother of six children (two of whom survived), she nevertheless read avidly of the French Revolution and of Wollstonecraft, becoming obsessed with the wrongs done to women.[21] As an upper-class wife and mother, she had been a "True Woman," had lived a life she hated, married to a man she despised. Once escaped from that life, she never forgot it, and her experiences influenced Thompson's and, through him, Owen's thinking. Wheeler convinced Thompson that almost everywhere women were condemned to eternal childhood and a lack of human rights. Thompson, reflecting Wheeler's ideas, wrote in his *Distribution of Wealth* that women everywhere were "domestic slaves" with no access to mental pursuits; they were "tools of male selfishness" who were, Thompson proposed in his vivid metaphorical language,

> supposed to have no feelings, no choice of their own: like houses or sheep, they are supposed to be quite passive as to the occupant. . . . [now when] women are brought up and treated like rational beings, and enjoy in all respects equal advantages with men, they will not, like ripe fruit or bales of cloth, be fought for; their opinion will be of some trifling weight in the disposal of their persons and happiness for life; and no greater indignity could the imagination frame for such women, than the supposition that they were to become the willing prey of the stronger or more fortunate of two contending savages. . . . (556)

After meeting Owen, Thompson developed and expanded Owenite thought by carrying Owen's notions on socialism to their logical conclusions with regard to women. Only mutual cooperation could give happiness to both sexes, wrote Thompson, after learning of Owen's ideas. Individual competition, explained Thompson, permits no compensation for women's inferiority of strength and loss of time in gestation. Under individual competition, even an equality of rights does not give women an equal amount of happiness with men, because men still hold the power—men are still the "producers" who can, because of their superior strength and lack of pregnancies and gestation, accumulate more money, and thus more power than women ever can. This power, wrote Thompson, comes from the "present system," which makes women slaves to men, in part by relegating to woman her "ideal" characteristics of meekness, mildness, and passivity. Every quality that could command the respect of others man reserves for himself. Because of this state of affairs, Thompson urged women to "shake off these fetters of individual competition which relegate all women as slaves to the owners of property." Changing unjust laws is not enough, because man's superiority (his power) comes from production and accumulation of individual wealth, possible only in a system that rewards this individual competition to the detriment of women. Eliminate the system, eliminate competition and private property, and then men will not have power over women. Thompson thus latched onto Owen's vision of communities as his means of liberating women: it was the only way he saw to undo the "present system"—centuries of patriarchal power and men's "ownership" of women.[22]

Together the theories of Robert Owen and William Thompson formed the foundation of thought for the London Cooperative Society, founded in 1824 for "the advocacy of the new Social Science" (W. Brown, 21). In many ways, the London Cooperative was the culmination of Owenite socialistic thought, in that it advocated more potential liberation for women than any other Owenite plan. Like the Edinburgh Society, the London Cooperative Society first opened a trading store and then, with the help of William Thompson, drafted in 1825 a set of articles for an "Association of Mutual Cooperation, Community of Property, and Equal Means of Enjoyment," to be established within fifty miles of London.[23] The articles reflect Owen's theories on an excellent education for youth, the combination of agriculture and manufacturing, the communal rearing of children and sharing of public space, and the alleviation of "drudgery" for women. But because of William Thompson's forceful language and tone, the position of women in the proposed community was quite different from that described in outlines for earlier Owenite societies, including any plans written by Owen himself. According to Article 8, the "rights of women" in the community were to be equal to those of men. To women, "forming half the human race . . . we guarantee eligibility equally with men, to every situation within the community." Women were also guaranteed equal means of acquiring knowledge and social pleasures, equal property, and equal "physical means of enjoyment" with men. In order to ensure that women were allowed the "opportunity of acquiring equal respect and sympathy, by means of equal usefulness with men, and to give them equal facilities with men," the London Cooperative Society promised women complete freedom from domestic work. The cooking, washing, and heating of apartments could be performed, Thompson and the other writers of the articles proposed, "on scientific principles on a large economic scale" for the entire community. All necessary but menial and unpleasant tasks that remained would be performed either by rotation among the adult members or, if no adult volunteered, by the youth of the community.[24]

By combining Owen's communal plan with Thompson's emphasis on the importance of affording women equal respect with men, the London Cooperative Society created, on paper at least, a blueprint for women's liberation. Taking away the domestic work from the women to allow them equal respect and sympathy with men was Thompson's (and Wheeler's) idea. Owen had envisioned the drudgery being performed more efficiently in a communal situation, but he still assumed that women would indeed do "women's work" in the communities. That such work could keep women from being as "useful" or as "respected" as men was the vital element of feminist thought that Thompson added to Owenite theory.

By 1824, Robert Owen had tired of battling with partners at the New

Lanark mills for the educational reforms he still wanted to make, and he was disappointed at seeing his plan constantly modified by well-meaning but, as he believed, misled men such as George Mudie, Abram Combe, and A. J. Hamilton. Frustrated by Parliament's refusal to accept his plan on a national level and discouraged by the moribund Motherwell project, still lacking funds, Owen turned to the New World to realize his dream of a "new, moral world."

Robert Owen was familiar with America's long-standing and successful communal tradition. He had read one traveler's account of his 1811 visit to America's religious communities and had published an essay in 1817 by W. S. Warder on the Shakers. Mudie's *Economist* and the *London Co-operative Magazine* had also published information about American religious experiments. Concerned with American communalism, Owen had corresponded with the Rappites as early as 1820. Writing to Reverend George Rapp, the leader of the Rappite "Harmonie," from New Lanark on August 4, 1820, Owen introduced himself:

> Having heard so much of your Society, and feeling a peculiar interest respecting it, I am induced to open a correspondence with you, in the expectation of procuring a correct account of your establishment. . . . There is a colony here of about 2400 persons, whom I have already placed under new circumstances, preparatory to a still more improved arrangement, from which incalculable advantages to all classes may be expected. I am now in the midst of preparing a further development of the system I have in view, and it will give me pleasure to send you a copy of it, the earliest opportunity after it shall be ready.[25]

Approached by Richard Flower, who had left England some years before to emigrate to the United States, Owen learned of the Rappites' intention to sell their community. After hearing of the ready-made community, some fifteen to twenty-five times the acreage he considered essential, Robert Owen began to believe he could establish his own version of his new world on the Rappites' land. Robert Dale Owen recounts in his autobiography his father's temptation:

> [His] offer tempted my father. Here was a village ready built, a territory capable of supporting tens of thousands in a country where the expression of thought was free, and where people were unsophisticated. I listened with delight to Mr. Flower's account of a frontier life; and when, one morning, my father asked me, "Well, Robert, what say you—New Lanark or Harmony?" I answered without hesitation, "Harmony." (*Threading*, 239–41)

With his son's enthusiasm bolstering his own, Robert Owen, along with his second son, William, and the Edinburgh Owenite Donald Macdonald, traveled to America to inspect the Rappites' community. Sailing to America in the fall of 1824, Robert Owen plunged headfirst into the egalitarian theory his plan had become, leaving behind the successful reforms he had effected as a patriarchal factory owner. While at sea, he read Thompson's just-published *Distribution of Wealth,* which helped to convince him further of the importance of equality, even equality for women. But as we have seen, Thompson, passionately connected to a brilliant, liberated woman, understood emotionally that sexual equality was vital for the happiness of the entire human race. To Owen, a person far more interested in the problems men faced when trapped in loveless, lifelong marriages, sexual equality would always be an abstraction, but an abstraction he would promote in his egalitarian community. Though he agreed with the reasonableness of Thompson's theory, Owen never quite understood Thompson and Wheeler's point.

THE AMERICAN LANDSCAPE

To Robert Owen, the country he was sailing to in the fall of 1824, with its industry, its cheapness of land and quality of soil, and its freedom from governmental interference, was the ideal testing ground for his ideas. America's history was, in effect, the story of rebellion, of small groups searching for freedom and a new start. During the late seventeenth and eighteenth centuries, America had been settled by small, persecuted religious groups who wished either to create a "city upon a hill," which would illustrate how pure believers could form a model society for all to emulate, or to retreat into the hinterlands, where members of the religious group would be undisturbed by governmental regulations. Many groups, of course, wished to do both.

As Robert Owen came to America, religious, not secular, groups dominated America's communal landscape. Yet, in spite of their religious nature, these American communities shared some of Owen's aims. Religious communitarians were searching, as was Owen, for a place where all could live in equality. The people who lived in America's religious communities gave up the quest for power and money to establish a community where all worked and lived for one another's good, without financial concerns. At the same time, America's religious communitarians were willing, in the words of Oneida Community patriarch John Humphrey Noyes, to extend the "little man-wife circle" of the nuclear family to create a dependence upon the entire group, rather than have their allegiances bound up in separate families. To America's religious communards, the happiness of the entire group took precedence over the happiness of a particular individual. Robert Owen spoke of achieving the same attitude in his community.

Unlike Robert Owen, though, most of the leaders of American religious communities were willing to sacrifice sexual passion in order to obtain group cohesion. Group celibacy, a common method of purifying individuals, kept members' energy and passion directed outward to group activities and to the group's benefit. The deeply religious men and women who populated America's sectarian communities understood their experiences to be transitory: earthly life was just a testing ground for a superior, everlasting world. Self-sacrifice was the mode to help them transcend the temporal and prepare themselves for life after death. For community women, self-sacrifice was particularly important because, as descendants of Eve and her original sin, women were doomed to serve men and remain subordinate. The Judeo-Christian tradition, bound as it was in a Hebraic hierarchical tradition, only reinforced all women's subservience.

Most of the religious communities that had emigrated to America before 1825 were divided into two types: foreign-speaking groups such as the Ephrata Cloister, the Moravian Brethren, and the Rappites; and the English-speaking Shakers.[26] The Rappites, with whom Owen had corresponded, are representative of the foreign-speaking communities. Led by patriarchal leader George Rapp from their previous settlement in Pennsylvania, over eight hundred German peasants arrived at the shores of the Wabash River in 1815. They had chosen, according to George Lockwood, American communalism as their escape from the "vice and infidelity" of eighteenth-century Germany (27). Although the humid, malaria-infested forests and lowlands would, within nine years, cause them to sell their land to Robert Owen, during their decade in Indiana the practically dressed religious patriots built homes and a woolen factory, improved the land, and raised a large surplus of produce. Women, like men, worked hard at physical labor in the fields, as well as at household tasks. From 1807, two years after they arrived from Germany, the Rappites in America were celibate, basing their decision on Rapp's teachings. Celibacy, Rapp believed, was necessary for resurrection and for a "community of equality."[27] Celibacy in the Rappite "Harmonie" only helped to reinforce the temporal nature of life on earth, and the sacrifices and duties required of individual men and women to prepare themselves for life after death. Woman's particular roles as helpmate and prime sacrificer were all part of her place in the Christian communal tradition. As one Rappite woman wrote, "we are too few girls for so many men, but we work gladly."[28]

The Shakers, a small celibate group who emigrated to New York in 1774, became, within fifty years, the most populous of the sectarian communities in nineteenth-century America. Instead of keeping to themselves, as did the Rappites, who were insulated by a foreign tongue, the Shaker missionaries converted countless Americans to their celibate, yet passionate, version of utopia. By 1800, most Shaker groups were made up of Americans who still lived in their own neighborhoods but by then were living communally instead of in isolated, individual families. Beginning in Kentucky around 1800, the Shaker revivals caused the most intense religious excitement ever known in America, according to communitarian historian Mark Holloway (69). Many of the people listening to Shaker evangelists became imbued with religious and/or communal spirit. Certainly the Shakers created a climate in the first quarter of the nineteenth century that was ideal for religious community building. By 1830, Shaker communalism had reached the height of its popularity with over five thousand Americans living in Shaker communities.

Eagerly awaiting the docking of Owen's boat in New York in November 1824 were members of The New York Society for Promoting Communities, organized in 1818 or 1819 by Cornelius Blatchly, a New York physician who had been influenced by the Shakers and their emphasis on communal life. Uninterested in Shaker celibacy, Blatchly allied himself with Robert Owen by including Owen's "New View of Society" with his own essay "The Evils of Exclusive Wealth" and an essay on the Harmonists in his 1822 book, *An Essay on Common Wealths.* Like the Shakers and Owen, Blatchly's group promoted the formation of communities, or "common wealths." Blatchly had written in 1822 of the "evils" of a society based on the principle of the getting and keeping of private property. Like Owen, he wrote that "equality" was impossible when exclusive rights and property existed and when, to keep this property, "men enslave blacks from Africa, declare wars, etc." (24). Although the slavery question was an issue Robert Owen had not yet considered, Blatchly's belief in the importance of equality and the necessity of creating communities to obtain it was quite similar to Owen's.

The constitution for the group's "common wealth" did reiterate some of Owen's most important ideas: that children have their "principles and characters . . . formed for them," that equality cannot exist "except in an enlightened, liberal, philanthropic and pious common wealth," and that a community of common property could alleviate the ills of "self-love" and "inequality." But all these "Owenite" tenets were framed within a structure of belief in God. The first paragraph of the constitution of the New York Society for Promoting Communities reads:

> We, the subscribers, do adopt the following constitution, because we believe that all saints are born of one spirit; that all men are made of one blood; and that being brethren by nature and grace, we ought to dwell together in the unity of the Spirit of God, and community of interest in this world. For in the unity of the Spirit, is the bond of peace, and every virtue and happiness; and in a pure community of wealth, the blessings of life are enjoyed inclusively, and without that selfishness and love of money and covetousness, that is the root of all evil. (Blatchly, 61)

This constitution for a "religious community" provides a link between Owenite ideas and the celibate religious communities established in America.

Also bridging the gap between the sectarian celibate communities and Owen's secular community was the Coal Creek Community, which was located close to Owen's New Harmony in place (Fountain County, Indiana) and in time (begun in 1816). The Coal Creek Community, established by

James Dorsey, an Ohio minister, was similar to Blatchly's New York group, with its Owenite emphasis on education and character development but its traditionally religious focus. Coal Creek members professed to believe, like Owen, in "useful knowledge" and in the rearing of children as one family, but, unlike Owen, they also professed to believe in God. The Coal Creek constitution promised an equal education to its boys and girls but excluded from girls' education "those things that are peculiarly adapted to the male sex."[29] Both Blatchly's society and Dorsey's Coal Creek did deal with women's equality to some extent in their communal constitutions, but their discussions centered on the lack of education available to women, a non-threatening topic that did not necessitate thinking about women in any but the most traditional ways and that easily fit in with the Judeo-Christian tradition.

Influenced by the Shakers and by Blatchly's society were numerous Americans searching for their own ideal community, often having been inspired by Shaker missionaries. One such utopian venturer, Paul Brown, who was soon to join Robert Owen's New Harmony, attended some of the New York Society's meetings in the early 1820s and reports that the society did form at least one community that settled in Virginia around 1821 (*Twelve Months*, 5). Although Brown had spoken as early as 1817 on the importance of forming rational communities, of sharing property in common, and of educating people apart from the "fantastical speculations of the priest-hood," he was discouraged by the lack of secular communal attempts in America and his inability to find fellow freethinkers. He looked to Owen to help unify Americans such as himself, people in search of a true com-munity of property. Upon hearing that Owen had landed in New York, Brown quickly wrote to him: "Here is one argument which you had not in Britain, i.e. immense tracts of unoccupied soil are easily obtained in our western states. . . . Inquired much for your works, but could find none—was edified by some extracts made by Dr. Blatchley [sic]. You will see for yourself the deficiencies in what attempts have been made towards estab-lishments of commonwealths" (*Twelve Months*, 5). Brown hoped that Owen's arrival would correct the lack of "rational" communities of common property in America.

To Owen, the religious communities served as an inspiration but not as a model for his own communal impulse. His notion of equality for all people was based on a different premise from theirs, namely, the Enlightenment's concept of the importance of individual rights. Because the religious-based American communities reassumed the apostolic tradition of giving up all worldly things and joining all property in common, members of the com-munities believed, as they were taught in the Bible, that communism would take care of all inequalities in daily life, and any inequalities that were not taken care of were not important. Owen, unconcerned with biblical prom-ises, sought the equality that a community of property would bring but without the concomitant self-sacrifice. He saw no contradiction between his belief in the importance of individual rights and his aim for an egalitarian community based on all property held in common.

Besides the sectarian emigrating communities and the religious reform-oriented communities that gave America its long-standing communal tradition, another type of "community" populated the western American landscape, providing a different sort of backdrop for Owen's experiment. The frontier village had for over two centuries served as a physical or psychological refuge for many Europeans seeking to escape from overcrowded or depressed conditions or to begin life over again. Certainly the emigrating sectarian groups thought of America in this way, but so did individuals who wanted to begin life afresh in a new country. This impulse, the same as the Rappites' and the Shakers', but without the concomitant religious underpinnings, led to the establishment of frontier settlements that concerned themselves not with living communally (one of the reasons for coming to America was the availability of good, cheap land, after all) but with reform attempts.

One of these settlements, the town of Albion in southeastern Illinois, provides an interesting counterpoint to the community Owen would begin at New Harmony. Established by George Flower in 1818, Albion was a place where physical survival was the first priority but where reform impulses were also important. George Flower, whose father would travel to Scotland to offer Owen the Rappites' community, had settled in Albion with no particular goal in mind outside of physical survival and starting over in a land of plenty. Albion was conceived of not to change the world, but just to be a better place to live in it. Yet, at the same time, George Flower held utopian reform impulses that would make him sympathetic to Owen's nearby New Harmony and would lead him to leave Albion to help Frances Wright begin an Owenite community in Tennessee in the mid-1820s.

In 1816 Englishman George Flower left his home (and, apparently, a wife and two children) to travel to America, arriving with the appropriate letter of introduction to Thomas Jefferson from General Lafayette.[30] As was Owen after him, George Flower was invited to the homes of America's elite—Thomas Jefferson at Poplar Forest and Monticello; Dr. Priestley on the Susquehanna; Thomas Bakewell in Pittsburgh; Thomas Rotch in Kendal, Ohio; General Andrew Jackson in Nashville. As a member of the English educated class he was welcomed, his conversation appreciated. While in Philadelphia, Flower heard that his English friend Morris Birkbeck, with whom he had traveled in France, had just arrived in America. Flower joined the Birkbeck party (consisting of Birkbeck's two sons, two daughters, servants, and one Eliza Andrews, age twenty-five, a daughter of a minister), and he and Birkbeck together decided, as Flower remembers it in his autobiography, to "go west," though "exactly where was uncertain" (*History,* 49). In Cincinnati they heard of the availability of land in Illinois and chose their destination. On the way to Illinois, George Flower married Eliza Andrews, after she had turned Birkbeck down.

The party's destination, the Boltenhouse Prairie in uninhabited Illinois, was a wilderness that had housed non-Indian settlers less than a year. The Flowers and Birkbecks found themselves overwhelmed by their physical conditions. George Flower writes:

> It is impossible for any one living in old countries, where the common conveniences of life have been accumulating for centuries and ages, to understand the situation of an individual or small family when first alighting in the prairies without even indirect aid from art and cultivation common to all in a civilized country. The poorest man in an old country thinks nothing of a road or path, or a drink of water from a well. He is the owner or occupier of some small sort of a house, maybe a small college, but even he can shut his door against a storm. . . . Not so here. (110–11)

Perhaps in response to this physical deprivation, Morris Birkbeck planned a type of communal living that would retain individual property. He wanted the entire group to live in one large house built on the property of both families, with the property line going through the middle of the house; thus, they could all enjoy the benefits of group living but still maintain their own land. Eliza, uncomfortable with Birkbeck because of his marriage proposal, however, wanted none of these plans: Flower writes that "Mrs. Flower and myself thought it better to live in our own house" (84).

After settling in the prairie, Flower returned to England to bring his father's family over and to publish Birkbeck's essays on the glories of living in Illinois. By March of 1818 two different groups of emigrants totaling some eighty-five men and three women sailed for the English Colony in Illinois. George Flower also returned with his parents, brothers, sisters, and two sons (he does not mention what became of his English wife). Upon Flower's return, he founded Albion, while Birkbeck, who was no longer speaking to him, founded Wanborough—towns only a few miles apart.

George Flower's "colony," though only twenty-five miiles away from Owen's New Harmony, never professed a particular philosophical system or attempted to live communally. Flower's settlement was primarily an outgrowth of the repressive economic conditions in England in the second decade of the nineteenth century. George's father, Richard, recently arrived at Albion, wrote in 1820 that most of the people who had emigrated to America from England "are those who have diminished their former fortunes; persons who have received good education, but are unable to sustain their stations in England."[31]

The town of Albion was a far more typical town than was the community Owen would create at New Harmony, but George Flower was not a typical man. He was certainly hard working, forging the community out of a forest in the expanses of the western frontier, far from the civilized world of eastern seaboard cities. He was also an eminently practical man. Personally unconcerned with religion, Flower nevertheless decided to create worship services on Sundays in Albion after hearing that rumors of its nonreligious nature circulated throughout the East, preventing many people from coming to join the community.

At the same time, when he was caught up in a cause, Flower could be an impractical man, as when he left Albion in 1826 to join in Frances Wright's attempt to free America's slaves by establishing an Owenite community in Tennessee (see chapter 4). Long before he met Wright, Flower was interested in freeing America's slaves. He writes at length in his autobiography of the horrors of slavery and its effect in the "free state" of Illinois. Seeing no hope for just treatment of the free colored people "living on my lands . . . I proposed that they should go to Haiti" (265). He asked the then-president of Haiti, General Boyer, for asylum for his free blacks, about thirty in number. They arrived in June of 1823, and their settlement was so successful that the Haitian government encouraged other free blacks to emigrate by offering fourteen dollars per head for passage—an inducement Flower would remember when he and Wright created their community in 1826.

Despite George Flower's dedication to the freedom of the blacks living in Illinois, Albion itself was never more than a small western township that housed a number of English people who, for numerous economic reasons, wanted or needed to leave their home. The rigorous work entailed in clearing the countryside, planting the crops, and obtaining the basics allowed little time for ideals and no time to consider such a thing as sexual equality. In the writings of both George Flower and his father, Richard, women are mentioned only in the context of complaints that there aren't enough unmarried women in America to be servants: "Marriage here takes place so frequently that we are certainly in want of female servants," writes Richard Flower, for the third time in two letters. The philosophical underpinnings of the town of Albion, made up primarily of Englishmen who had to leave their native land, and of New Harmony, only twenty-five miles away, could not have been more diverse, but their physical realities, including a population of English-speaking people who for one reason or another objected to living together in one house, were strikingly similar.

Within the American communal tradition, Robert Owen's vision of a utopian community for everyone seemed fantastic. To most people at other western outposts like Albion and Wanborough, simply living off the rugged, uncultivated land was struggle enough. To leaders of religious utopias, the notion of seeking egalitarianism without the Christian apostolic tradition as a foundation was perplexing. Owen's promise of equality without a spirit of sacrifice, without realizing that this world was only a testing ground for a better world, confounded the leaders of religious utopias. According to William Owen's account, when his father was asked by Quakers for whom he was establishing his communities—"for Quakers?, or Jews? or what?"—the Quakers could only shake their heads in amazement when Owen answered that his community was open to all sects, to nonbelievers as well as believers. When asked if he would forbid marriage, Owen said no and was told, "there will be continual quarrels."[32] Owen's claims were equally fantastic to the mainstream culture, which had been titillated by, but was certainly not concerned with, celibate foreign peasants dressed in strange, utilitarian costumes and living communally in the far outposts of their country.

As Robert Owen landed in New York City in November of 1824, he was confident that what he called the "prejudices of the old world" were being left behind.[33] Neither he nor anyone else could have anticipated the tenacity with which people (himself included) held onto their prejudices, especially when they concerned one of the foundations of the patriarchal system: the family and woman's subordinate place in it.

CHAPTER

2

THE PROMISE OF EQUALITY

Our Object, like that of all sentient beings, is
happiness. Our principles are Equality of
Rights, uninfluenced by sex or condition in
all adults.

—Constitution of the New Harmony
Community

Arriving in America, Robert Owen was completely caught up in his own and Thompson's egalitarian rhetoric. Only "full and complete equality," preached Owen, carried to its "full extent in practice," could carry the human race "onward toward the highest degrees of perfection."[1] Owen's vision of an egalitarian world formed the idealistic basis for the promises, the constitutions, the "official words" emanating from New Harmony and the other Owenite communities that sprang up throughout the United States in 1825 and 1826. For Robert Owen, as well as for other reformers who flocked to one or the other of the emerging Owenite communities, the idea of equality was all important.

Owen's most important critics have all noted, some with scorn, Owen's dedication to equality. Charles Fourier, born one year later than Owen but destined not to be read by anyone in America but Owenites until the 1840s, labeled Owen a "believer in complete equality," an idea he found to be antithetical to happiness. J. F. C. Harrison writes that despite the vagueness surrounding Owen's notions of economic and social equality, he agrees with Owen's contemporaries that "ideas of equality were somehow built into the foundations of Owenism." Frank Manuel, coauthor of *Utopian Thought in the Western World*, goes even further; he writes specifically about the most intriguing type of equality promised for New Harmony and the other burgeoning Owenite communities: "For the townships, Owen advocated sexual equality pure and simple in education, rights, privileges, and personal liberty. In this pure democracy there would be no motive for sexual crime, and sexual disease would soon be eradicated. Virtually all marital difficulties would dissolve."[2]

37

The interest in Robert Owen and the egalitarian utopia he was bringing to America peaked during Owen's first months in the New World. Speaking eloquently on equality as well as other subjects dear to his heart, Robert Owen took America by storm: newspapers, especially those in the cities he visited, followed his every movement, his every word. Perhaps it was his impassioned belief in a "system" that promised equality to all people; perhaps it was his linguistic flamboyance, an excessive oratorical style familiar to a people used to evangelical preaching during the Second Great Awakening; or perhaps it was the charismatic quality of his oration that initially captured his audience's attention. But whatever caused their interest, Owen entranced the people of America with his promises and his personality.

Owen's first weeks in America in early November 1824 were marked by a whirlwind of activities and meetings with industrialists, politicians, educators, and communitarians. Just as on the boat to the New World, where Owen had lost no time telling the other passengers about the importance of education with "sensible signs,"[3] in New York City, Owen met with many of the town's most important people, including banker Charles Wilkes, manufacturer Jeremiah Thompson, and professor of moral philosophy at Columbia College, John McVickar.[4]

Others, like Dr. Cornelius Blatchly, the president of the New York Society for Promoting Communities, called upon Owen immediately. Men such as George Houston, who had been incarcerated for two years in Newgate for "publishing his opinions," sought out Owen as well (DDMac, 182). During his brief stay in New York, Owen traveled to Albany, where he called on former New York governor DeWitt Clinton, who gave him letters of introduction to General Jackson and Thomas Jefferson. He also visited the Shaker establishment close by at Watervliet in order to observe the orderly community, which operated not with money or bargaining but with exchange of produce, based on the principle of equal quantities of labor (DDMac, 191). While learning from the Shakers and Blatchly how the American communities functioned, Owen at the same time had the opportunity to meet with some of the "principal people" of New York in small groups, explain his plan, and receive from them appropriate letters of introduction to high-positioned people in other American cities. With such a propitious beginning, Owen, in the words of Arthur Bestor, "could hardly fail to make an impression upon the American public."[5]

From New York on his way to inspect the Rappites' "Harmonie," Owen arrived in Philadelphia on November 19, 1824, and, as in New York, called upon the town's leading educators and scientists. Here too, people knew of Owen before he arrived. William Maclure, a wealthy merchant-turned-scientist and educational reformer, had, only a few months before Owen's trip to America, visited New Lanark to study Owen's school, where he had found his days "the most pleasant of my life." In London on August 25,

1824, Maclure had written his impressions of Owen's Scottish experiment to a colleague in Philadelphia:

> I spent 3 or 4 days, the most pleasant of my life, at New Lanark con-
> templating the vast improvement in society effected by Mr. Robert Owen's
> courage and perserverance in spite of an inveterate and malignant opposi-
> tion. I never saw so many men, women and children with happy and
> contented countenances, nor so orderly, cheerfull and sober a society
> without any coertion or physical constraint. . . . All the children are
> taught from 2 years old and upwards in natural history, geography, statis-
> tics &c, and proves that knowledge is not only power but wealth, as Mr. O.
> makes more twist in his mils than the same number of hands in any other
> mill, and so superior that it draws a premium in the market. It gives me
> courage to undertake my Experimental farming Schools, seeing how he
> has succeeded against a powerfull combination of both church and state,
> and considering the field of moral experiment in the United States to be
> the finest in the Globe. (M/F, 307)

Eight years older than Owen, Maclure had a similar background. As early as 1805 Maclure had visited Heinrich Pestalozzi's school in Switzer-land and had become converted to "useful" education. The following year he brought to Philadelphia one of Pestalozzi's coworkers, Joseph Neef, to establish America's first Pestalozzian school. In the early 1820s he also sponsored two Parisian Pestalozzian teachers, Marie Duclos Fretageot and William Phiquepal d'Arusmont, allowing them to transfer their schools to Philadelphia. Like Owen, Maclure had made his fortune in Scotland and then turned to educational reform on the Continent, subsequently bringing the best he could find in useful education to America, while Owen, who had also visited Switzerland in search of the best methods to use at his New Lanark school, incorporated progressive educational ideas in his Scottish school. Both men believed that the happiness of mankind was the end goal of a society, and both agreed that achieving that happiness necessitated dividing property equally and making available the sources of knowledge to all people. Maclure's letter to his scientific colleague Benjamin Silliman of Yale University in 1822 sounds as if it had been written by Owen: "You will perceive the consequence I attach to an almost equal division of property, knowledge, and power, as the only firm foundation of freedom which includes the happiness of mankind" (M/F, 294). After meeting Owen for the second time, in London just before Owen's first departure for America, Maclure wrote with great enthusiasm:

> Mr. Robert Owen of New Lanark is now here [London] and intends
> making the United States the theatre of his future experiments on the
> facility of rendering the human species happy. . . . Nothing on earth can
> give more satisfaction and pleasure than the certainty [that] the only man
> in Europe who has a proper idea of mankind and the use he ought to make

of his faculties is going to join the finest and most rational Society on the Globe. (M/F, 309)

As early as 1822 Maclure's Parisian Pestalozzian teacher Marie Fretageot and the Philadelphian reform-minded physician Dr. Philip Price had favorably discussed Owen, with Price being "much pleased" with Mr. Owen's system (M/F, 304). In Philadelphia, Owen called on his convert, the "celebrated teacher" Marie Fretageot, as well as her scientific colleagues such as Thomas Say, the librarian at the Academy of Natural Science, and Charles-Alexandre Lesueur, the naturalist and artist (DDMac, 207–209). Owen read their proposals for a socialist community to be formed near Philadelphia (DWOwen, 32). His reception, as in New York, was enthusiastic. As Fretageot wrote to William Maclure immediately after Owen's visit: "You have no idea what pleasure I felt when I was talking by the side of a man whose actions and principles are so much in harmony with mine" (M/F, 312).

The rest of Owen's trip west to Indiana was marked by similar experiences: Owen would visit a town's intellectual and political leaders, would speak to small, select groups in the evenings about his plan—often to people who were already aware of his New Lanark reforms—and would repeat his promises to create a new social system at the Rappite Harmonie. In Washington, D.C., Owen met with John Quincy Adams and President James Monroe. In Pittsburgh, he called on Benjamin Bakewell, a leading industrialist, and he also met George Rapp, the patriarchal leader of the Rappites, who returned to his nearby new community, Economy, with Owen's party. Pittsburgh, like Philadelphia, was full of people interested in Owen and his notion of communal living. A Pittsburgh friend of the Rapps fretted that efforts would be made to induce Owen to locate his community in the Pittsburgh area, instead of purchasing the Rappite Harmonie in Indiana. That many people were interested in Owen was clear from the Rappites' nervous correspondent: "his system of communities . . . is well thought of by many. . . . he will find many persons of science and standing in the United States to aid and associate with him."[6] By the time Owen reached Harmonie on December 16, 1824, everyone reading newspapers in the United States knew that Robert Owen of New Lanark, Scotland, was seriously considering purchasing the Rappites' community to establish a new social system.

Owen spent less than three weeks at Harmonie, but it was time enough for him to sign an agreement to purchase the Rappite community for the sum of $125,000, to be paid in installments until 1831.[7] While in the area Owen could not resist the opportunity to talk about his soon-to-be "New" Harmony. Visiting George Flower in Albion during the last week in December, Owen spoke to two hundred Albion and Wanborough residents on December 26, and to about seventy again on December 30. Owen, pleased to be talking to fellow English settlers, as far away from home as he was, told his listeners that New Harmony would serve as a "temporary residence" for an association of people while they were acquiring the habits necessary to live in a community of equality.[8]

After signing the ownership papers on January 3, 1825, Robert Owen left his newfound community almost immediately to return to the East to promote the experiment that would take place in New Harmony as soon as the Rappites had left and he was able to convince enough people to venture to utopia. His trip this time was marked not just by meetings with small groups of people who were already familiar with his name but also by two national addresses he delivered to Congress on February 25 and March 7, 1825. In his February speech, Owen spoke abstractly but eloquently of his plan to remove the cause of evil in the world; in March, he attempted to illustrate to his audience exactly what New Harmony would eventually look like through the use of a picture of his famous parallelogram. Never modest, Owen lectured with his usual fervor and sense of assurance, proclaiming the great advantages of his system. As he said to Congress in February 1825, "The subject which I shall endeavor to explain is, without exception, the most important that can be presented to the human mind; and, if I have been enabled to take a right view of it, then are changes at hand greater than all the changes which have hitherto occurred in the affairs of mankind."[9]

Owen's answer, both to eliminating the causes of evil in the world and to creating the greatest happiness for the greatest number, was his utopian plan of rational, egalitarian living in a community with all things held in common. Owen explained in grandiose ways how his ideal community eventually would house five thousand people and include a school, an academy, a university, stores, and plentiful gardens. The domestic accommodations would be ventilated, supplied with gas lights, and would have hot or cold water available by "merely turning a cock or moving a slide." All the occupants would find their apartments cooled in warm weather and warmed in cool weather. Technological advances, "mechanical and chemical operations," would provide the service, not servants or "drudges" (*NHG*, May 16, 1827). The only "rules and regulations" for the Preliminary Society were simple principles that Owen had formulated in the early 1820s: that the community should consist of persons who had agreed to cooperate with their labor and skill; that the community should produce within itself a complete supply of the necessities of life; and that a permanent village in the shape of Owen's parallelogram should be started as soon as possible, complete with "proper training and education from birth [for] each child" (*NHG*, May 16, 1827).

No one, not even Owen himself, took very seriously his almost parenthetical demurring during his addresses to Congress that he had "no wish to lead the way" (*NHG*, May 16, 1827). Obviously this was a man who knew what the world needed to save it; this was a man who knew his own mind, who knew "his" plan, and who was charismatic enough to convince hundreds of people to leave their jobs, their home towns, to venture to utopia.

Always the recruiter, Owen's lectures to Congress, and also his speeches in cities along the boat journey taking him back to New Harmony in the spring of 1825, included powerfully persuasive invitations to Americans to join the Preliminary Society about to form at New Harmony. This Preliminary Society, which Owen predicted would last from two to three years, would prepare people to live in a community of equality. Like the Shaker missionaries before him, Owen converted many Americans to his communal ideas through the promise of equality in communal living, but, unlike the Shakers, Owen promised a utopia for everybody.

As Owen was preaching his utopian promises to Congress in February and March of 1825 and picking up recruits along his lecture trail through New York, Philadelphia, Pittsburgh, and Cincinnati, the Rappite Harmonie was evolving into the New Harmony that would receive those converted by Owen's evangelical preaching of a secular utopia. During the spring of 1825, the Rappites moved slowly from the community, in accord with the plan that they leave some members behind to teach the Owenites how to plant the necessary crops and how to run the cotton mill and continue production of soap, candles, dyes, boots, and pottery. At the time Owen purchased it, Harmonie was a functioning community with forty-five frame and one hundred log buildings, a spacious church, a school, and a steam-driven mill that had produced for the Rappites cotton and woolen clothing held in high repute throughout the country.[10]

Leading an anticipatory existence in New Harmony during this transition time when Robert Owen himself was absent, lecturing in Washington, D.C., and in various cities throughout the East and Midwest, were Robert Owen's traveling companions—his second son, William, as well as Donald Macdonald. Macdonald, one of Owen's first disciples, who had joined the Edinburgh Practical Society in 1821 and accompanied Owen to Ireland in 1822, is a fascinating study of a dedicated, idealistic Owenite reformer. A complete convert to communitarian egalitarianism, Macdonald followed Owen to America to help him establish his New Harmony, a world without artificial class lines.

On his way to New Harmony, on the Ohio River with Robert Owen, Macdonald had noticed a poor family living in a log house, complaining of sickness, cold, and isolation. After leaving this family, too poor to share their supplies with the people on the boat, Macdonald wrote in his diary of the advantages an Owenite community of common interest could give a family such as this one: "This is a country rich in natural advantages, single families live in low circumstances, and enjoy none of those comforts which they would so easily secure to themselves, were they to settle together in larger numbers having a common interest, and bringing the arts to their aid and intelligent and experienced managers to organize their associations" (237). But Macdonald was attracted to Owenism for more reasons than because it provided necessities for poor families; he was also attracted to its principle of a classless, egalitarian society. During his first month alone in New Harmony he thought about the relationship between equality and associationism, especially in the particular conditions of America, where there were few domestic servants: "Surely, if Equality be a good principle of society, the proper practice to be followed in a country where it prevails is to unite in associations, in each of which all the children should be educated together in the best manner, and taught in early life to wait upon the old, with the prospect of being waited upon in their turn when they were advanced in years" (DDMac, 283). In Macdonald's mind, the "servants" doing the drudgery of a society would be the children—an idea similar to that found in the plan of the London Cooperative Society, a plan Macdonald was probably familiar with.

While awaiting the elder Owen's return, Macdonald spent much of his time as an emissary of Owenism, visiting the local gentry—particularly the Flowers in Albion and Morris Birkbeck in Wanborough—to discuss Owen's communal ideology. At the same time, he began to receive numerous visitors to New Harmony, such as the Scottish woman Frances Wright, author of *View of Manners and Society*, a popular travel book published in 1822, and her sister, Camilla. The sisters were on their way from Washington, D.C., where they had probably heard Robert Owen speak, to New Orleans, where they were to meet General Lafayette. Though Macdonald describes the Wright sisters in only a perfunctory note, young William Owen wrote more fully in his diary about his first impression of the woman who was to become the most important disseminator of Owenism in America. He noted that her manners were "free" and "unusual in a woman," but that she improved upon acquaintance (128). While talking to both local residents and visitors, Macdonald also attempted to translate Owen's (and his) communal ideologies into practice by writing with William Owen the Articles of Association for the Preliminary Society.

Returning to New Harmony in April of 1825, fresh from his oratorical successes in Washington, D.C., Robert Owen was full of revolutionary zeal, his enthusiasm knowing no bounds. Writing to William Allen, his former partner at the New Lanark mills, Owen used his eloquently optimistic language to illustrate how ready America seemed to accept his new state of society: "The whole of this country is ready to commence a new empire upon the principle of public property and to discard private property and the anchorite assumption that man can form his own character as the foundation of the root of all evil. For years past every thing seems to have been preparing in an unaccountable and most remarkable manner for my arrival."[11]

Owen lost no time in expounding to his new community the glories that lay ahead for those who accepted communal life based on egalitarianism. He spoke movingly to the people beginning to arrive in large numbers in the late spring of 1825:

> I am come to this country, to introduce an entire new state of society; to change it from the ignorant, selfish system, to an enlightened, social system. . . .
>
> After [the New Harmony residents] have had an opportunity of witnessing how much more happiness may be experienced under arrangements in which inequality will be unknown, they will soon be reconciled to the change, and wish of their own accord to possess the full benefits of equality. . . . There will be no *personal* inequality, or gradations of rank or station; all will be equal in their condition, and I shall never consider myself one step higher, nor any better, than any other individual. . . . We shall speedily lose every idea of personal inequality, except that which naturally arises from age and experience. Ardently . . . I long for the arrival of that period, when there shall be no artificial inequality among the whole human race.[12]

Though Owen admitted that this first community was but a Preliminary Society, a "half-way house" necessary to effect the change from single families with separate interests to a community with one interest, he still hoped that any temporary inequality in accommodations or food would soon be eliminated.[13]

It is no surprise that Robert Owen's preoccupation with the abstraction of "equality" permeated his speeches about and at his community. The Constitution of the Preliminary Society that Robert Owen read to his followers on May 1, 1825, written by his son William and Donald Macdonald during his absence, promised that the members of the New Harmony Community were to be "all of the same rank, no artificial inequality being acknowledged; precedence to be given only to age and experience." The result of this equality would be, the constitution continues, "the greatest amount of happiness" for all members. This happiness would be open to all: "persons of all ages and descriptions."[14]

The benefits accorded to members also reflected Owen's and Macdonald's emphasis on the importance of equality. Members of the Preliminary Society would receive "such living, advantages, conduct, and education for their children, as this Society, and the present state of New Harmony, afford," and "the living shall be upon equal terms for all." Old, sick, and injured members would be taken care of, but healthy adults would have a credit and debit account at the community store, where they would be charged with what they received and credited for their labor. Children of members, who were to remain living with their parents unless the parents preferred placing their children in the boarding school, would be educated at the day school.

Such rhetoric helped to convert innumerable Americans to Owen's secular gospel mission: over a thousand people flocked to an obscure corner of southwestern Indiana to become part of Owen's Preliminary Society. Although it is difficult to classify all the people who came to New Harmony during its first few months of existence, many of the community's first residents belonged to one or the other of two very different types. One group, composed of families usually led by a husband, came to New Harmony to partake of a second chance at life. As with many of the English settlers at Albion or Wanborough, these families' previous "situations" had not worked out, or life in England or America had been too hard for them. The Pears family, consisting of Thomas and Sarah, both forty, with seven children ranging in age from fourteen months to eighteen years, are a perfect example of this type. Sarah Pears, niece of Benjamin Bakewell's wife (whom Owen had visited in Pittsburgh), and her husband liked what they heard about the Preliminary Society forming at New Harmony. They had previously tried to run a gristmill in Kentucky but had lost money and returned to Pittsburgh. There they heard (or heard of) Robert Owen, extolling the benefits of communal living. The Pears family, like other families with failed business ventures, saw life at New Harmony as a way (perhaps an easy way) to live a "good" life. Attracted by the prospects of a four- to five-hour workday (Pears, 73) and a free excellent education for their numerous children, who probably had not had much chance for education at a Kentucky gristmill, they arrived in May 1825 with the first group of people to settle in the community, in time to hear Owen speak before he left again in early June for a six-month absence from New Harmony. Owen's powerful rhetoric strongly influenced Thomas Pears. He wrote in his first letter back home to Pittsburgh, "I have just returned from hearing Mr. Owen and I am then always in the hills. I do not know how it is—he is not an orator, but here he appears to have the power of managing the feeling of all at his will."[15]

A second group of people moving to New Harmony were also moved by Owen's promises, but they were specifically attracted to his egalitarian and libertarian rhetoric. Many of nineteenth-century America's most important reformers, such as Frances Wright, Josiah Warren, and Robert Dale Owen, first experienced communal life at New Harmony and used the New Harmony experiment to help them formulate their own ideas about utopian living. Like Donald Macdonald, who had accompanied Owen to New Harmony, many of these reformers were willing to give up their jobs—running lamp-making factories or preaching in the Universalist church or serving as postmaster of an Ohio town—in order to join the great experiment about to begin in New Harmony. Others, such as Paul Brown, had been reformers in search of a community their whole life. Still others, such as the wealthy Price family from Philadelphia, had been interested in Owenism for years and were among the earliest settlers in the Preliminary Society.[16] These reform-minded people formed the ideological core of writers and teachers at New Harmony during its first year of existence, writing enthusiastic letters back home about communal life, preparing articles for the *New Harmony Gazette*, and evolving into what amounted to the community's intellectual elite.

William Pelham, age sixty-six when he arrived in New Harmony, was one of the oldest of the reform-minded men and women who came to New Harmony.[17] Born in 1759 in Virginia, Pelham had been a surgeon during the American Revolution and a frequent traveler to England. Around 1800 he opened a bookstore in Boston; later he moved to Philadelphia. There his son was a pupil in Joseph Neef's Pestalozzian school. In 1816, having acquired land in Ohio, Pelham moved to Zanesville, where he became an editor of the *Ohio Republic* and, the following year, postmaster. A freethinking man, having little use for organized religion, Pelham was immediately attracted to Robert Owen's ideas. Writing to Owen at New Harmony in December of 1824 to inquire about the establishment about to begin there, Pelham was so pleased with William Owen's response that he decided to move to the community because of its "Principle of complete equality." William Owen's letter that so moved Pelham reads in part:

> It is proposed that a Society be formed here, on the Principle of united production and consumption, to be composed of persons practicing all the most useful occupations necessary to the well being of a complete establishment, to whom lodgings, food, clothing, attendance during sickness and a good education for their children will be secured. The profits to accumulate in order to form a new Community on the Principle of complete equality, as soon as a sufficient sum shall be realized. (Pelham, January 22, 1825)

Arriving in August of 1825 at New Harmony, Pelham was not disappointed in the community. He wrote to his adult son in September that "I have become a Harmonite and mean to spend the remainder of my days in this abode of peace and quietness. I have experienced no disappointment. . . . I did expect to find myself relieves [sic] from a most disagreeable state of life, and be able to mix with my fellow citizens without fear or imposition—without being subject to ill humor and unjust censures and suspicions—and this expectation has been realized" (September 8, 1825).

Pelham was taken with Owen, both before he ventured to New Harmony and after he had had a chance to meet him and talk with him. He wrote to his son on February 8, 1826, shortly after meeting Owen for the first time: "He [Owen] is an extraordinary man—a wonderful man—such a one indeed as the world has never before seen. His wisdom, his comprehensive mind, his practical knowledge, but above all, his openness, candor and sincerity, have no parallel in ancient or modern history."

Also taken with Owen was Paul Brown, a communitarian who had wandered America in search of a perfect community his entire life. A single man, like William Pelham, but with no children, Paul Brown's passion was his cause—finding complete equality. Brown had long been interested in communalism and free thought. He wrote to Owen of his own lectures in New York as early as 1817 on "sentiments [that] were gratifying to all free thinkers" (*Twelve Months*, 4). Two years after Brown's first New York lecture, he wrote that the New York Society for Promoting Communities had begun publishing some of Robert Owen's writing in their pamphlet. Intrigued by Owen's ideas, Brown attended some of the New York Society's meetings but did not join the "colony" formed in Virginia about a year later. He did, however, try to join a community "organized on [Owen's] principles" in Kentucky in 1822, but, walking around the state, he could not find the community.

Upon reading Owen's two lectures to Congress in the spring of 1825, Brown considered joining New Harmony but was hesitant because the Preliminary Society was not based on absolute common property and because he had an "obligation" to journey to Tennessee by the end of the summer. In his travels through Pennsylvania, Ohio, and Kentucky, Brown heard of Owen constantly. One man he met, whose son had been in the neighborhood of New Harmony, reported to Brown: "If you see Owen, tell him I intend to be with him (at Harmony) next winter. Tell him *my heart is there*, and I intend to be there with my family next winter" (*Twelve Months*, 8). Even in Tennessee, Robert Owen was the main subject of talk. When Brown read the *New Harmony Gazette* of February 5, 1826, proclaiming a complete Community of Equality, with all things in common, he could wait no longer, leaving Tennessee to journey to New Harmony.

Younger reformers were equally attracted to Owen's plans. Both Josiah Warren and Robert Jennings gave up their professions in order to move to New Harmony. Born in Boston in 1798, Warren moved to Cincinnati, where he operated a lamp factory. When in 1824 Robert Owen lectured in Cincinnati, the twenty-six-year-old Warren became so enamored of Owen's ideas that he sold his profitable business and moved himself and his family to New Harmony, where he became the conductor of New Harmony's orchestra. There he learned and adopted the labor-cost definition of value, as well as many of Robert Owen's most important theories on how a person's character is shaped by environment. Warren, like so many of the reformers populating New Harmony, also accepted Owen's belief in the importance of individual liberties.

Robert Jennings, like Josiah Warren, joined the New Harmony community because of Owen's ideas. A "failed" Unitarian minister, Jennings, at the age of thirty, was more suited to free thought and the kind of "preaching" that he quickly learned to perform at New Harmony than he was to traditional Christian preaching. Living in Philadelphia in 1825, Jennings undoubtedly met Owen (or heard of him) when Owen visited his city. Equally obsessed with the notion of equality and its importance in life, Jennings and his wife joined the community just as it was beginning in May of 1825. Once at New Harmony, Jennings quickly became part of the intellectual elite, often preaching on Sunday mornings. William Pelham relates that Jennings's main message in the New Harmony pulpit was the importance of equality. Pelham says that Jennings, whose language sounded much like Owen's, often ascended to the pulpit to expatiate on the "indispensable necessity of establishing the principle of equality as the basis of liberty." When he was not lecturing in the pulpit on some of Owen's most important doctrines, Jennings also assumed some of the editorial duties of the *New Harmony Gazette*.[18]

All the reformers, represented by such men as William Pelham, Paul Brown, Josiah Warren, and Robert Jennings, reflected in some way Owen's belief that "full and complete equality . . . is the pure principle of democracy, that can alone carry the human race onward toward the highest degrees of perfection" (Manuel, *Utopian Thought*, 692). This group of reformers was, like Owen, interested in creating a city on a hill, a place to show the world what could be done. Their concerns were necessarily different from the majority of people who came to New Harmony not as reformers but as people searching for a second beginning.

The New Harmony Preliminary Society attracted much attention in the United States in 1825. In addition to the dedicated reformers and married couples looking for a new start in life, a variety of drifters, idlers, and curious wanderers ventured to southwestern Indiana to become part of New Harmony. Life in the backwoods utopia during its first summer was rugged and full of hardships, as Robert Owen had predicted in his address to his community in late April. Even though the Rappites had left a completely functioning community, incoming settlers did not necessarily have the skills to continue all the industries. By September the woolen factory was still not functioning, and the cotton factory was not meeting its expenses. At the same time, the workers' lack of experience at farming created untended gardens and shortages of produce. Thomas Pears wrote to relatives in Pittsburgh that "the hogs have been our Lords and Masters this year in field and garden" (26), leaving the New Harmony residents without any vegetables. By the beginning of the first winter in New Harmony, residents found themselves out of a great many necessities including sugar, coffee, sewing cotton, thread, paper, materials needed to build housing, and all bedding.[19]

Incoming residents found only the bare necessities in their housing as well. When the Pears family arrived in late April, for example, they were given a house containing "three rooms, and a kitchen which is about the size of [a] little room over the passage. In this little tenement, our family and that of Mr. Pearson . . . are all crowded, except that we have a room for the boys in a house occupied by a Mrs. Grant" (Pears, 17). William Pelham's first residence was no better; he wrote about his unfinished room that "will do for the present, [but] as the cold weather advances we shall have to shift our quarters or be frozen to death" (Pelham, September 7, 1825).

Yet, for the reform-minded settlers at least, there was the advantage of the union of kindred spirits, of association with people whose beliefs were similar to theirs. Wrote William Pelham shortly after arriving at New Harmony:

I am at length *free*—my body is at my own command, and I enjoy mental liberty, after having long been deprived of it. I can speak my sentiments without fear of any bad consequences, and others do the same—here are no political or religious quarrels, though there is a great diversity of opinion in matters of religion. Each one says what he thinks, and mutual respect for the sentiments of each other seems to pervade all our intercourse. (September 8, 1825)

For such people the free, open discourse, the lectures on a variety of subjects, especially religion, and the lack of the "priesthood" made the New Harmony experience worth the effort of living in a desolate corner of Indiana. The intellectual stimulation made up for deprivation in food and living conditions. From the midst of nowhere sprang a community with schools, a weekly newspaper, an orchestra, and weekly balls. But better even than the activities and companionship were the promises that New Harmony would become a complete Community of Equality.

New Harmony's hardships were exacerbated by the fact that Robert Owen was not present during the settlers' first summer and fall. In early June 1825, Owen along with Macdonald left New Harmony to return to New Lanark and to prepare for the New Harmony experiment. They retraced their steps, stopping through Louisville, Cincinnati, and Pittsburgh and then took a coach through upstate New York. Owen rode his tide of popularity on this trip, as he had on his earlier trip to Harmonie. William Maclure wrote to Marie Fretageot from New York two days before Owen sailed for England, "Every one that he has met approves of his plans and even the priests seems [sic] to him to favor them" (M/F, 323).

On October 1, 1825, the very day the *New Harmony Gazette* began publication, Owen, Macdonald, and Owen's eldest son, Robert Dale Owen, sailed from Liverpool back to New Harmony.[20] For Robert Dale Owen, left at New Lanark to tend to business, time had passed far too slowly during the months his father and younger brother had been in America creating New Harmony. Born in 1801, Robert Dale grew up at Braxfield, the Owen family home in New Lanark. He attended a Pestalozzian school in Switzerland from 1818 to 1822 and returned to teach in the New Lanark schools. A dedicated youthful utopian, Robert Dale Owen had longed to come to New Harmony with his father the year before, but he remained behind to run the mills. He was quite ready to love America—after one week in the United States he declared his intention of becoming an American citizen (RDO-TJ, 176)—and to undergo any hardship to prepare himself for the living conditions at New Harmony. His rough trip to Indiana prepared him, he believed, better than anything else could have for any upcoming hardships; he wrote in his travel journal on December 10, 1825: "I find that this way of life becomes me well. I am exposed to heat, cold, and also the hardships much more than otherwise, but I am truly already stronger and more vigorous. I believe I could not have a better preparation for Harmony and it will probably also be that way with the others" (241).

As soon as they arrived in America, Robert Owen and his companions heard that New Harmony was already overcrowded. To complaints that some of the new members of New Harmony were "indolent," Robert Dale, ever the youthful optimist, responded:

> Dr. Price . . . came in and gave us the latest news of Harmony. Things were, in general, favorable, though the impression here is, that a number of the members are indolent and that this has created very great dissatisfaction among the rest; and that in short the establishment, in a pecuniary point of view, is in a fair way to go to pieces. I dare say there is *some* truth in regard to these complaints, though they are no doubt much exaggerated. (*RDO-TJ*, 229)

Robert Owen, despite reports of some dissatisfaction in New Harmony and a letter from William reporting a lack of accommodations for any new members ("it will be impossible to give them homes, or even rooms," young Owen advised his father in a December 16 letter), was nevertheless optimistic. To Owen, who had hoped that five hundred people would join the Preliminary Society during its first two or three years, the news that over a thousand people were already at New Harmony awaiting his return was most welcome. At the same time, Owen heard that an Owenite society was forming in Philadelphia (DDMac, 308) and that other reformers, such as Frances Wright, by this time "a complete convert to the System" (DDMac, 309), and George Flower were in New York attending to the preparations necessary to begin Wright's own community later in the spring in Tennessee.

In Philadelphia, Owen found even more converts, converts who would be vitally important to the development of New Harmony. When Owen had made his first trip through Philadelphia a year before, he had visited, among others, Marie Fretageot, the Owen devotee and reform-oriented teacher who had relocated her Paris Pestalozzian school in Philadelphia with William Maclure's backing. When he returned to the East shortly after purchasing New Harmony, Owen visited Philadelphia and Fretageot again, as numerous people from Philadelphia such as the Price family were preparing to depart for New Harmony. The more Fretageot heard of Owen's scheme, the more she liked him—he was, she wrote Maclure on March 28, 1825, "the best man explaining a plan which is the best calculated for human happiness" (M/F, 317). She urged Maclure to think about modifying his own plans to establish some schools in the West after hearing more about Owen's, because she agreed with Owen that "the more good means are united the more the effects are powerful, but whe[n] scattered they do little or no effect" (M/F, 314). She wrote Maclure on March 9, 1825, after reading Owen's February 25 speech to Congress: "The more I know of that man, of his plan and of his high sense, the more I am convinced that we will join in his undertaking" (M/F, 316).

Although William Maclure's ideas on educational reform differed from Owen's, he decided to join Owen in New Harmony to "unite the good means," as Owen and Fretageot had suggested. Maclure was a scientist, and his plans for education emphasized establishing a school where research and teaching could both be supported and could support each other. He hoped that the best research would make the best teachers and vice versa. Accordingly, Maclure's influence encouraged many of Philadelphia's most important research scientists to leave the city and go with him and his Pestalozzian teachers, William Phiquepal and Marie Fretageot, to New Harmony, where they established the forerunner of the soon-to-be-popular research university of late nineteenth-century America. Accompanying Maclure and the teachers were many members of Philadelphia's intellectual elite, including Thomas Say, Gerard Troost, and Charles-Alexandre Lesueur. Joseph Neef, the first Pestalozzian teacher Maclure had brought to Philadelphia, was no longer living there because of opposition to his antireligious principles. Heading a boarding school in Kentucky, Neef left his employment to come to New Harmony at Maclure's request. At the same time, Maclure's friend Benjamin Silliman of Yale, the founder of the *American Journal of Science,* publicized the new "research center in the west."[21] Such a collection of great minds seemed to ensure that New Harmony would become a place where the promised equality would become a reality.

While many of the great minds of Philadelphia were preparing to relocate their scientific studies and schools in New Harmony, members of the Philadelphia Owenite society, which Macdonald had heard about when he and the Owens arrived in New York, were busy forming a local Owenite community. On December 17, 1825, the *Niles Weekly Register* announced the beginning of "another cooperative community with families of Wilmington and Delaware." The new society was to be located forty miles from Philadelphia, in "the Great Valley." Two weeks later the *Niles Weekly Register* reported that two hundred families had associated under the title "The Friendly Association for Mutual Interests" and had recently purchased the Valley Forge works, with large tracts of land adjacent, for immediate occupancy and improvement. One of the subscribers was William Maclure, even though he had no intention of living in Valley Forge. The members of the Friendly Association drew up a preamble and constitution on January 19, 1826. The intention of the members was clear from their constitution: "The location being fixed at Valley Forge . . . we will commence erecting a commodious establishment . . . and complete the building of a village for the permanent and *equal* accommodation of all the Members, on a plan similar to that presented by *Robert Owen.*"[22]

As the Friendly Association was forming in December of 1825, William

Maclure, Marie Fretageot, and their scientific and educational colleagues including William Say, Charles Lesueur, Phiquepal, and several of Fretageot's and Phiquepal's students joined Robert Owen, his son, and Donald Macdonald on the boat to New Harmony. This "Boatload of Knowledge," so labeled by Sarah Pears when they arrived in New Harmony, embodied all the hope of what New Harmony was to become. During the long voyage—longer than normal because ice on the Ohio River caused the boat to be grounded for four weeks—the New Harmonites read Fourier and prepared themselves for life in Indiana.[23]

The arrival of the Boatload of Knowledge was New Harmony's greatest moment; the institution of wide-scale reforms seemed eminently attainable now that a group of nationally renowned thinkers had come to locate their schools and scientific research at New Harmony. With Robert Owen's return, too, came unbounded optimism for New Harmony's future as more than an out-of-the-way western outpost full of too many different kinds of people and empty of necessities. Encouraged by his son's and Macdonald's accomplishments, Owen hastened to turn the Preliminary Society into a full-fledged Community of Equality. Owen justified his rationale for eliminating the two- to three-year preparation period that he had earlier believed necessary for the Preliminary Society in the following ways:

> [New Harmony] had been managed in my absence much better, considering the new and extraordinary circumstances in which the parties were placed, than any one who had a knowledge of human nature would have anticipated. . . . I had expected [the Preliminary Society's problems] to be much more formidable than any which have yet occurred. . . . For, in one short year, this mass of confusion, and in many instances, of bad and irregular habits, has been formed into a Community of mutual cooperation and equality.[24]

Robert Owen may indeed have found New Harmony in better shape than he was expecting (William Pelham wrote that Owen had heard upon his arrival in New York that New Harmony was broken up and the members all departed), but the arrival of William Maclure, a man as rich as Owen and with an equally significant reputation as a reformer, and his scientific colleagues in the Boatload was surely another impetus to set up the true Community of Equality as soon as possible. Also, Owen had just returned from visiting the British Owenite community Orbiston, and, surmises Owenite scholar Arthur Bestor, he wished his own community at New Harmony to be the *first* Community of Equality (*Backwoods,* 170).

The movement to turn New Harmony into a Community of Equality could not have been quicker. Only one day after the arrival of the Boatload, during a period described by a New Harmony member as "a state of constant excitement" (Pelham, January 27, 1826), a former resident of George Flower's Albion moved that the Preliminary Society cease and the final community be formed (Pears, 56). The following day the community chose a committee of seven men to draft the new constitution; the elected men included Warner Lewis, the oldest resident of New Harmony; Judge Wattles, the Albion resident who moved that the Community of Equality begin; J. Whitby, a Shaker, recently moved to New Harmony; William Owen, Donald Macdonald, Robert Jennings, and Robert Dale Owen, who had just arrived in New Harmony two days before. Though Robert Owen received the highest number of votes, he and William Maclure were "excused" from serving on the committee.[25] By February 6 the elected coterie had created a constitution worthy of the about-to-emerge Community of Equality at New Harmony, Indiana. The constitution was carried unanimously and the new Community of Equality went into effect on March 5, 1826 (Pears, 59).

The "principles" of the constitution, listed here in the order they occur in the document, reveal Robert Owen's egalitarian premises:

Our Object, like that of all sentient beings, is happiness.

Our Principles are

Equality of Rights, uninfluenced by sex or condition, in all adults:

Equality of Duties, modified by physical and mental conformation:

Cooperative Union, in the business and amusements of life:

Community of Property:

Freedom, of speech and action:

Sincerity, in our proceedings:

Kindness, in our actions:

Courtesy, in all our intercourse:

Order, in all our arrangements:

Preservation of Health:

Acquisition of Knowledge:

The Practice of Economy, or of producing and using the best of every thing in the most beneficial manner:

Obedience to the Laws of the country in which we live.

The rhetoric of the constitution befit a Community of Equality. No longer, as in the constitution of the Preliminary Society, was any kind of inequality sanctioned. The document specified clearly that the first principle of association was "equality of rights uninfluenced by sex or condition in all adults" as well as "equality of duties, modified by physical and mental conformation." In the full-fledged Community of Equality all members would be "one family," with "similar food, clothing, and education, as near as can be, furnished for all"; each member was to "render his or her best services for the good of the whole"; and the "whole" would consist of people who had chosen to live under a community of property.[26]

Along with the equality promised in the constitution, the Articles of Union and Cooperation specified more examples of the freedoms and benefits, as well as the rules and regulations, of the community. The "primary object of the community" was to give "the best physical, moral and intellectual education to all its members." At the same time, each member would "enjoy the most perfect freedom on all subjects of knowledge and opinion, especially on the subject of religion." There was to be no "secrecy or exclusion" within the community, and all misunderstandings were to be adjusted within the community. But most revolutionary was the following article: all members, male *and* female, over the age of twenty-one were charged with "the power of making laws" for the community.

New Harmony's new constitution reflected Robert Owen's and the other Owenite reformers' preoccupation with the importance of equality. Equality was, Owen lectured repeatedly, the only foundation for communal life. He spoke to his community in the late spring of 1826, saying, "a community cannot exist without a community spirit. To produce this spirit, equality and common property are necessary; and these principles require that all the members of the community should be put, as speedily as local circumstances will admit, into the same condition . . . and that all should have the best facilities for acquiring knowledge and becoming intelligent."[27]

What kept people from achieving equality were the forces that promoted ignorance, said Owen—specifically, private property, irrational systems of religion, and marriage. In a forceful speech delivered at New Harmony on July 4, 1826, he proposed that all three needed to be "destroyed," because each supported the others. Private property, lectured Owen, prepared the seeds for all the evils inherent in ownership, including the privations of the industrious and the indolence of the idle. Religion, a type of superstition, destroyed the judgment and made human beings mere slaves. Marriage allowed men to select the most desirable women and thus enslave them, in fact making these women a part of their private property. Women, inexperienced and without property, bartered their feelings and affections for "wealth, trappings, and power." This "formidable Trinity," wrote Owen, was "the only Demon, or Devil, that ever has, or, most likely, ever will torment the human race." The only escape from this "Devil" was, according to Owen, a community of property where no one would own anything and marriage would be based on a partnership of equals. Only when true equals, in wealth, education, and condition, married could there be a "virtuous and happy connection." Owen said: "When . . . the parties are on a perfect equality in wealth, condition and education, and intimately acquainted with each other's thoughts and feelings before marriage; and when no motive whatever exists but genuine affection to induce the parties to unite; it is most likely that marriages so formed would be more permanent than they have ever yet been."[28]

The whole point of New Harmony and many of the other Owenite communities, according to Robert Owen and the other Owenite reformers, was to create this multifaceted equality, essential both to communal success and to individual happiness in marriage. The primary benefit of a separate, intentional community was that it could eliminate all three of the world's greatest evils at once: private property could be abolished at one fell swoop, the power of the priesthood reduced to nothing under the teachings and preaching of the rational lecturers in the New Harmony "church," and women—given the right to vote and other rights and responsibilities equal to men's—would no longer be forced to marry for support and thus would no longer be subjected to anyone.

But Robert Owen and the other reformers understood that in order to achieve this sought-after equality, people's beliefs, attitudes, and customs had to be changed, both by formal education, informal lectures, and essays and editorials in *The New Harmony Gazette,* and by replacing the old, outmoded customs with new ones. It was Robert Owen's and the other reformers' job to lead the way toward equality.

At New Harmony, in order to create "new" customs as well as to create pleasure in the rugged surroundings, many organized activities brightened up the isolated community. Almost every evening there was some kind of event: on Mondays, parade and drill; on Tuesdays, dancing in a large brick building near the church, where people could "find an excellent band of music, and amuse themselves till nine o'clock." On Wednesdays was the public meeting in the church, where "everyone gives his opinion freely." On Fridays was a concert; on Saturdays there were debates and ball playing. Life, even during the first few months of the community, could be "quite gay," according to the young people who participated in the balls and concerts. And there were many "agreeable people here," wrote Sarah Pears in a letter she sent back home (17). All these amusements, as well as the working days, were regulated for the inhabitants: at 5:00 A.M. the bell was rung to arise; at 7:15 A.M. breakfast was served in the boarding houses and tavern; at 12:15 P.M. was dinner, and at 6:00, supper.[29]

Reforms, as well as regulated days, were also effected in the community to help create new habits and customs that would allow everyone to accept Owen's egalitarian ideals. In keeping with Robert Owen's belief about religion, the Sabbath was not a holy day; rather, it was a day of recreation, visiting, or listening to William Owen or Robert Jennings read Robert Owen's tracts or William Thompson's *Distribution of Wealth.*[30] Robert Owen did not forbid any evangelists from stopping in New Harmony and preaching to his people, but often, after traditional sermons in the New Harmony church, former minister Robert Jennings would preach Owen's new egalitarianism. William Pelham relates one such occasion:

A Baptist minister came into the town and announced his intention of delivering a discourse in the evening in the Church. Accordingly, a large congregation assembled, and listened to him with great attention. He is certainly one of their first rate preachers, and he managed his matters with much address. The next evening . . . Mr. Jennings delivered a lecture in the same place, and ably demonstrated the sandy foundation of the ingenious gentleman's arguments, without any pointed allusion to him or his arguments. At the close of the lecture my gentleman thought proper to make a rejoinder, tho nothing had been said of him or his doctrines, but he did not seem to be in so good a humor as he was the evening before— although he had previously preformed [sic] the marriage ceremony for a young couple—especially when this young couple retired with their friends into the Hall to enjoy the pleasures of music and dancing instead of listening to his rejoinder. (September 7, 1825)

Pelham notes in his letters that on a given Sunday Jennings might talk about William Thompson, agreeing with him that the "evils of society may be traced to the unequal and unjust division of property, and that this again may be attributed to the principle of individual competition" (October 10, 1825). He explains how Jennings illustrated that "equality is the parent of liberty and justice; without a full enjoyment of which, mankind cannot be otherwise than unhappy" (September 11, 1825). Other times he writes of Jennings's talk about the "indispensable necessity of establishing the principle of equality as the basis of liberty" (September 19, 1825), or records that on October 3, 1825, Jennings delivered "an excellent discourse on Equality;—showing that it was essential to the happiness of society, as all arbitrary distinctions and partialities not founded on real merit, and all distinctions arising from extravagance in dress and external appearance have no solid foundation." To those like Pelham and Jennings, who had joined New Harmony because of its egalitarian underpinnings and who longed for a time when "plainness of manners and plainness of dress" would become the norm, New Harmony provided the discourse requisite for utopian living.

In fact, one of the first reforms at New Harmony was the institution of a new plain dress for the community. William Pelham writes in early October of 1825 of hearing that at a regular Tuesday night dance a number of the community women appeared in a new "uniform" made of inexpensive, American-made material. Although few of the married women in the community wore the new dress, many of the younger women adopted the more practical clothing.[31] This new costume consisted of pants and a tunic, a practical unisex outfit that would suit men or women. Men wore wide, full pantaloons buttoned over a boy's jacket without a collar and bound around the waist with a wide belt made of black-and-white striped cotton. Women also wore the wide trousers but with an overjacket reaching the knees.[32]

Another reform in accord with Owen's beliefs that was quickly enacted at

New Harmony was the prohibition of hard liquor. Pelham writes that "no member of the community can obtain any ardent spirit either at the Tavern or the store, without a certificate from the Doctor that it is needed as a medicine—a regulation that would be very useful in Zanesville as well as here." A visitor to the community in April 1826 noticed the same thing: "Mr. Owen has forbidden distilling also, as well as the use of ardent spirits."[33] Although the regulation forbade strong spirits, some members of the community did imbibe, at least during the time of Robert Owen's absence. Thomas Pears admits in a September 29, 1825, letter that "I drink whisky here, for we have nothing else. I sometimes used it too freely, but never in business hours" (36).

But the reform most important to Owen was schooling, because he believed that people's values and personalities were formed for them, not by them. He saw no better way to achieve an egalitarian society than to teach its principles in the schools, thus shaping the children's characters for them in the mold of a new, moral world, where all children would grow up to be rational adults, making decisions based not on superstition or hypocrisy but on the truth of their own senses. Owen established both a day school and a boarding school based on Pestalozzi's ideas about "useful" education. Though most of the community children did not live in the boarding school, those who did, reports Thomas Pears, appeared "contented and improved" (26). The community children attended the day school and found life in New Harmony to be "quite gay."[34] The visiting Duke Bernhard commented, as had visitors at New Lanark, on the children's "healthy look . . . [they] are cheerful and lively, and by no means bashful."

With the arrival of the Boatload of Knowledge and all its educators—William Maclure, Marie Fretageot, Joseph Neef, and William Phiquepal—the formal education at New Harmony began to approximate Robert Owen's dreams for it. William Maclure, the world-renowned educator who brought what appeared to be the whole of the intellectual elite of Philadelphia to New Harmony, agreed with Owen on the importance of equality. Writing to a French journal on the same day Owen gave his infamous July Fourth speech lambasting private property, religion, and marriage, Maclure said of Owenism, "The System spreads daily. This perfect equality offers a charm which outweighs every idea of fortune and ambition, and the simple thought of working for his food renders each of the members of our great cooperative family more happy than the ardent thirst and often deceitful prospect of gain can in Old Society."[35]

Like Owen, Maclure wanted his schools to be the vehicle through which children would learn about egalitarian living. From his first day in New Harmony, Maclure spoke of the importance of "equality by rights" in his schools (*NHG*, May 17, 1826). In a letter Maclure wrote from New Harmony in March 1826, he told of the success of his schools after only two months: "We have nearly 400 children belonging to the society, besides strangers from the different parts of the Union. The girls are taught the same things as the boys, by Madam Fretageot, and are classed, alternately, to work in the cotton and woolen mills, and in washing, cooking, &c. (for no servants are permitted in the society, and every one must do something for himself)" (M/F, 331). Maclure wrote to his friend Benjamin Silliman that in other schools, "youth of both sexes have been unjustly treated" with useless activities, but he promised that "the schools here will be on such a scale . . . as to constitute them the first in the Union for every species of useful knowledge."[36]

Also like Owen, Maclure proposed giving boys and girls the same useful education because he believed that the prejudices that caused "half our species" to live in a "degraded state" had to be eradicated. To improve society, Maclure suggested that women's education be placed "on a par . . . with the men['s]"; then women would be able to fill "all places of honor and profit" (Opinions, 479–80). In the old, immoral world, women were prevented "by the oppression of men, from being useful either to themselves or others. . . ." How simple to improve mankind by educating women, who were presently "confined to their physical accomplishments, and their mental faculties so much neglected" (Opinions, 64).

For adults in the communities who might be in need of changing their own beliefs and actions, Robert Owen and other reformers spent a considerable time lecturing and writing on how to change manners, old habits, and outdated thoughts. Speaking every chance he had, Owen promulgated his ideas about what was wrong with the old world, stressing the importance of equality and how his system could achieve it. Owen, Jennings, and other New Harmony reformers such as Robert Dale Owen, William Pelham, and visitor Frances Wright wrote numerous essays for the New Harmony Gazette, a weekly publication that circulated throughout the United States, to convince New Harmony members and other readers of the importance of cultivating new customs and habits. In its first two years of publication, from October 1825 to October 1827, the Gazette published many articles on the new ways of thinking that Owen's Social System would foster. The reformers often wrote of the importance of equality, many times addressing themselves specifically to the topic of women's equal place in the New Moral World.

The importance of a good education, that all-encompassing equalizer in Robert Owen's schema that was intended to alleviate unreasonable customs and unthinking practices, is constantly reiterated in the ideological tracts that all the editors published with great regularity in the Gazette. It was, according to Owen's Articles of Cooperation, a "primary object of the community to give the best physical, moral and intellectual education to all its members" (NHG, February 15, 1826).

With education would come new customs, new habits that would create equality between the sexes. The anonymous author of "Mental Capacities of Females," an article in the Gazette of March 29, 1826, finds it not "at all surprising, that females seldom shone very conspicuously on the stage of life," because "man withheld from them that rank and influence, which their sex demanded, and which nature intended." The argument continues when the author blames the inadequate training women receive for their lack of knowledge: "woman has a mind equal in every respect to man; though it may, and often does, lie under partial neglect, it by no means implies that women have not adequate understandings, or that they can never be brought to the same perfection as those of the male sex." The argument concludes with examples of the accomplishments that would be possible if women were allowed to develop their mental capabilities, because in the past, women have "governed states—presided at councils—adjusted disputes; they have headed armies. . . . The female mind has been found capable of reasoning on the hypothesis of Locke—of commenting on the various positions of Reid—and of expatiating on a proposition of Euclid . . . this, can woman do—this, woman has done."

Another unsigned lead article ridicules, in the rational, Enlightenment-like rhetoric found so often in the writing of the New Harmony reformers, the absurd customs women have been taught to accept. "Females," this article on "Fashion" begins, have always "imagined themselves much more dependent upon public opinion, whether rational or irrational in its dictates, than men. Yet, there appears no just cause or reason why a woman should sacrifice her better judgment to that of her neighbors, any more than her self-styled lord and master is called upon to sacrifice his." Blasting away at cultural conditioning that limits women to passive roles, the author points out that

> Independence of character is considered unfeminine, and the right of female self-judgment, though it be recognized in theory by the voice of reason, is yet condemned in practice by the voice of the public. . . . And what is the consequence? This—that a foolish habit, or an irrational custom, or a silly practice, once adopted among the fair sex, is perpetuated from generation to generation, because, forsooth, though females may imitate folly, they may not originate reason. (*NHG*, November 29, 1826)

The tirade continues by berating the stupidity of permanently diminishing the capacity of the chest through the use of "fashionable" stomach boards and tight lacings. Three weeks later, in a follow-up article "for the Ladies," the standards of the Chinese are criticized: "It does certainly seem a strange perversion of nature to admire female feet contracted to deformity" (*NHG*, December 20, 1826).

These articles, the reformers surely hoped, would create new attitudes, and thus new behavior, in New Harmony members as well as in other readers who might wish to come to New Harmony. What the constitution did not accomplish and what reforms did not accomplish, they hoped lecturing and writing would. They hoped to change the human race, particularly women, who had been the sex with limited access to education. When they saw changed behavior, the New Harmony reformers were inordinately pleased. When a young married woman from New Harmony went to Kentucky, she boarded in the same house William Maclure happened to be visiting. He noted with great pride that she "insisted on washing, ironing &c all her own and her husband's cloths [sic] as she was accustomed to do at Harmony" (M/F, 370). Such new habits of doing for herself (and her family) instead of expecting servants to take care of her were noteworthy to Maclure, who believed some of New Harmony's egalitarian training was beginning to take hold.

One of the greatest successes at New Harmony was the Owenites' ability to spread the news of their great experiment taking place in the Indiana backwoods. Robert Owen particularly was gifted in attracting men and women to his new system. Wherever Owen stopped as he traveled in America, he met and converted followers to his system. Whether he met his converts by accident, sitting in a coach crossing New York state, or by preaching to them in large crowds in Washington, D.C., Cincinnati, Pittsburgh, or Philadelphia, the end result was the same: many Americans wanted to join the venture at New Harmony or to try their own hand at creating a "Community of Equality."

Certainly, such emulation was nothing new for Owen. In Scotland A. J. Hamilton and Abram Combe had begun an "Owenite" community without Owen. Other British followers, such as George Mudie, had extracted the idea of the benefits of community from Owenite thought, even though Mudie himself abhorred the notion of a community of property. In America the same impulses occurred, particularly the impulse to extract from Owenism a specific aspect of Owenite thought. Like George Mudie, a number of reformers in America were attracted to the economic benefits of communal living but did not wish to advocate a community of property or "egalitarian" living. Their communities, when established, had little that was "Owenite" in them. Two examples will illustrate these adjunct Owenite communities that sprang up in the mid-1820s.[37]

In the summer of 1825 Joseph Davis (brother of Jefferson) chanced to find the gregarious Owen in his stagecoach crossing Pennsylvania and New York as Owen traveled from New Harmony to New York on his way back to England. Davis, already familiar with Owen's theories, decided, after talking with Owen, to establish his own version of an Owenite community in Vicksburg, Mississippi, in 1827. Davis's community, "Davis Bend," was a model plantation where for over thirty years the slave-owning Davis educated his slaves and encouraged them to participate in profit sharing. Davis Bend continued to function with a benevolent master-slave relationship until the Civil War. After the war, Benjamin Montgomery, a former slave and Davis's protégé, purchased the estate to run as a black cooperative community until Davis's death in 1870. Even then the experiment was not over: Isaiah Montgomery, Benjamin's second son, established his own cooperative community, Mound Bayou, near Memphis in 1887, which was to last another twenty-five years.

Though neither Davis Bend nor Mound Bayou was "Owenite" in intention, it was Owen's vision of the importance of cooperative communities that fused with Davis's desire to help his slaves while improving his own finances. Introducing free-enterprise incentives to slaves was a long way from Robert Owen's objectives at New Harmony, but not such a distance from his original communal plans for his workers at New Lanark. One of Owen's selling points for his communal plans in 1816–17 was the fact that rich landowners could profit by giving their land to the landless poor to work. Certainly creating a model community that provided workers with comfortable cottages, reasonable working conditions, and schools for their children was an undertaking close to Owen's heart. Davis's version of communalism, however, never did contain either of Owen's most important demands for communal life—community of property and equality of status. In these two communities no one spoke of equality, at least in part because the population consisted of slaves and master.[38]

Also influenced by Robert Owen enough to attempt his own version of an Owenite community was William Hall, a resident of Birkbeck's Wanborough across the Wabash in Illinois. Born in England in 1773, Hall emigrated to Wanborough in 1821 for the same reason many married men brought their families to New Harmony: he needed to provide a better life for his wife and nine children. Although he had been the owner of a watermill in England, Hall had difficulty providing for his family; at the same time, he wanted to escape "Oppression, Tyranny, Hypocrisy, & Misery which prevailed in England."[39] After hearing Robert Owen speak at Albion twice in late December 1824, Hall went to New Harmony for three days in mid-January and "spent our time very pleasantly in ye society of Capn. Macdonald and W. Owen."[40] In July 1825 Hall announced in his journal that he had held a meeting at his house with six members of Wanborough to start "a Society to be styled the Wanborough Joint Stock Society" (244). Unable to accept Owen's views of religion, education, or women's rights, Hall nonetheless fashioned a community that provided equal economic benefits for all members after expenses were paid. Women were never mentioned in the Wanborough Constitution, and it is clear that they could not be "members" of the society; only men, at the age of twenty-one, were allowed that privilege.[41] By using Owen's ideas, as Davis had, to create a cooperative community with members benefiting from one another's work, Hall extracted from Owenism just what he wanted, leaving the social schemes for the Owenites in New Harmony.

Other people, such as Frances Wright (the subject of chapter 4), Daniel Roe, and Samuel Underhill, though, are more pertinent to this study because all of them formed, or helped to create, an Owenite community in the 1820s, replete with the requisite demands for a Community of Equality

based on common property and increased rights for society's discriminated-against groups such as slaves or women. While it is impossible to know how many people began their own Owenite communities in the mid-1820s, we do know of at least seven attempts, with several more Owenite societies formed that never became full-fledged communities. Owenite communities that sprang up in 1825 and 1826, local offshoots of Owenite thought, promised most of the same things as did New Harmony; their difference from New Harmony stems primarily from the fact that the leaders of these communities were not "foreign," as was Robert Owen, but were, with the exception of Frances Wright, Americans who, intrigued and excited by the promises of Owenism, believed that forming an intentional community with local people would be their answer to heaven on earth.

Few scholars have studied these fascinating communities, perhaps because they agree with William Hinds, who wrote that "it is unnecessary to give in detail the history of the other communistic experiments in this country owing their origin to the labors and principles of Robert Owen. Their lives were short and devoid of special interest" (150). Or perhaps scholars have found details of these little-known communities hard to locate because much of the information published about them has been erroneous. The first collected material on these communities came from the research of A. J. Macdonald, an admirer and disciple of Robert Owen who came to America in 1842 and spent the next twelve years visiting all the communities he could locate, gathering documents as well as oral stories that were not always accurate. Many Owenite scholars have accepted the existence of the nine Owenite communities that Macdonald "uncovered"; unfortunately, Macdonald's nine communities—Yellow Springs, Nashoba, Blue Spring, Forrestville, Haverstraw, Coxsackie, Kendal, Franklin, and the Co-Operative Society—did not all exist as separate entities. The Franklin Community, for example, *was* the Haverstraw Community, and the Forestville experiment, which Macdonald spelled "Forrestville," took place not in Greene County, Indiana, as Macdonald believed, but in Greene County, New York, and it was alternatively called Coxsackie. The Co-Operative Society, formed by Benjamin Bakewell, who hosted Owen when he visited Pittsburgh, never established a community, though its members did publish a constitution and looked for land. The Friendly Association for Mutual Interests at Valley Forge *did* establish a community.[42] Thus we are actually left with seven other Owenite communities in addition to New Harmony established in 1825 and 1826 that lasted long enough, or had literate enough members, to leave records of their existence. Yet these seven communities—Yellow Springs, the Friendly Association for Mutual Interests, Franklin, Forestville, Blue Spring, Nashoba, and Kendal—left information that supplements and reinforces the New Harmony experience, illustrating just how pervasive Owen's call for communities of equality was.

The first of these Owenite communities created on American soil by American reformers was the Yellow Springs Community, located in Greene

County, Ohio. As Robert Owen lectured to a large Cincinnati audience on March 11, 1825, Daniel Roe, a minister of a local Swedenborg church, heard him talk about the advantages of his "system." Trying to find out more about the subject, Roe and two friends went with Owen when he returned to New Harmony and stayed for four days in April 1825. When Owen returned to Cincinnati in June of the same year, he found that Roe and his parishioners, known to be "intelligent, liberal, generous, cultivated men and women . . . many of whom were wealthy and highly educated" (Mac Ms, 304), had already made arrangements to begin the "Yellow Springs" community. In July Roe and over seventy-five families, including professional men, teachers, merchants, mechanics, farmers, and a few common laborers, journeyed north to Greene County, Ohio, where they purchased more than eight hundred acres of land for their experiment. They formed an Owenite community "in imitation of that of Mr. Owen, the basis of which is community of interest" (*NHG*, November 23, 1825). They agreed that all additional property they might acquire by either labor or purchase would be "added to the common trust for the benefit of each and all."[43]

By the spring of 1826, Owenite enthusiasm had spread throughout Indiana and Illinois. Numerous people living in Flower's Albion and George Birkbeck's Wanborough joined New Harmony or became members of William Hall's Wanborough Joint Stock Company. At the same time, one hundred miles to the north of New Harmony, a new Owenite community, the Blue Spring Community, came into being. The Blue Spring Community patterned itself after New Harmony in many ways but originated differently. The Blue Spring Community was not founded as the Friendly Association at Valley Forge or Yellow Springs had been—by an Owenite Society growing into a communal movement where people left their homes and journeyed to a new place. Rather the Blue Spring Community consisted of twenty-nine original members, who had lived in and around the area and who, swayed by Owen's prophecies, decided to abandon individualized farming and join together communally. In January of 1826 they purchased the land for the community; on April 10 twenty people, eleven men and nine women, signed the original constitution; less than a month later nine more people signed the constitution. Unlike many of the members of New Harmony, the Blue Spring communitarians were religious, as all had been members of the Church of Christ. Paraphrasing Robert Owen, the leaders at Blue Spring proclaim in the Preamble to their constitution that they will "remedy the ills inflicted on mankind by the poverty and the ignorance of the individual system of society."[44] The *New Harmony Gazette* of January 31, 1827, reports that the community was off to a good start and tells of visits between the groups: "we have recently received a visit from two members of the Blue Spring Community . . . who inform us that their society there proceeds harmoniously and prosperously."

Also in the spring of 1826 New Harmony reformers and other Owenite followers founded two Owenite communities in the Hudson River Valley.

The first New York community to be established was the Franklin Community at Haverstraw, founded on "Mr. Owen's Principles" by several New York freethinkers, including George Houston, who had been one of Robert Owen's first visitors in New York City; Henry Fay, a lawyer known for defending the freethinkers in New York; and Jacob Peterson, who held the deed to the property. Joining these three men at Franklin was New Harmonite Robert Jennings, who left New Harmony April 10, 1826, in order to become the president of Franklin.[45] The New York founders of the community wrote a constitution dated March 1826 and then publicized the experiment soon to take place, hoping to encourage membership. Reverend Abner Kneeland, a minister who would go to jail for blasphemy in the 1830s, actively encouraged participation in the community from his pulpit in New York.[46] On April 28, the men agreed to purchase land from Major Suffern at Haverstraw, and by May 1 people were already showing up in Haverstraw ready to join the communal venture. By June 23, the purchase was complete and a new communal dining room was under way.[47]

After the Franklin Community broke up in Ocotber, some of its members, including Jacob Peterson, journeyed eighty miles north to Coxsackie, in Greene County, New York, where they united with people already settled there to form a new community, the Forestville Community. Originally organized by Samuel Underhill with four families and thirty-one people on December 16, 1825, the Forestville Community had published a constitution by March 1826 and membership had grown to more than sixty persons.[48]

Samuel Underhill, the driving force behind the Forestville Community, was, in many ways, a quintessential American Owenite reformer. Born in 1796, the son of a conservative New York farmer who took his son out of school because of rumors that the schoolmaster was a Deist, Underhill first became a schoolmaster himself, then a physician. Always interested in discovering a community of like spirits, Underhill joined the Quakers in 1821 but was excommunicated from the Society of Friends, according to Underhill, "for a difference of opinion only."[49] Severed from the Quakers and a "sceptic," Underhill searched for other ways of obtaining the community he desired. When he, like Paul Brown, read Cornelius Blatchly's pamphlet published by the New York Society for Promoting Communities, he was "awakened" to Robert Owen's social system. To the antireligious Underhill, Owen's ideas matched his need for a community of equality without religious underpinnings. Living in Coxsackie, New York, with a wife and children, and with several brothers nearby, Underhill started his community in the same way the founders of the Blue Spring Community in Indiana did: with people living in the area who decided to cooperate in order to enjoy better lives. An experienced worker both with the stone hammer and at the sawmill, Underhill believed in the importance of common property. He wrote to Robert Owen in May of 1828 explaining that "no community can prosper unless each member is profitably engaged. . . . for a member to have private funds by which he is enabled to dress or live better than others . . . is a curse" (RO Papers, #126). The community that Underhill forged had 325 acres, two sawmills, a gristmill, carding machines, and a tannery. Like Franklin, Forestville's principles were "purely republican," with no established religion (*NHG*, November 7, 1827). Unlike New Harmony, the Forestville Community required that all candidates for membership produce satisfactory evidence that they be persons of good moral character, sober, and industrious. Underhill wrote that a member could be of any religion, be it Baptist, Methodist, Universalist, Deist, or any other, "provided he or she be a genuine good moralist" (*NHG*, November 7, 1827).

Other New Harmony reformers besides Robert Jennings were also promoting Owenism around the country. Both Paul Brown and Josiah Warren reputedly visited northeast Ohio in the spring of 1826, and their missionary message helped to begin yet another Owenite community, the Friendly Association for Mutual Interests at Kendal. Like Blue Spring and Forestville, the Friendly Association for Mutual Interests at Kendal originated with stable, mutually acquainted families who were united in their Quaker religion. Most of the original members of Kendal had lived in close proximity to one another for years before the establishment of the community, and the first draft of the constitution was signed by men from the same families who had been members of the Kendal Society of Friends. From March to May 1826, members of the Kendal Community drafted a preamble and a constitution in order to form "an organization founded upon the principles set forth by Robert Owen."[50]

In the late fall of 1827, Samuel Underhill and twenty-seven people from the Forestville Community continued their search for egalitarian communal living by joining the Kendal Community. Their arrival at Kendal illustrates the circularity of the Owenite movement in America in the mid-1820s. Inspired by New Harmonites Paul Brown and Josiah Warren, the Kendal Community was supplemented with Samuel Underhill and his contingent from Coxsackie, which had, in turn, been reinforced by members from the Franklin Community, which had itself received its president from New Harmony.

Like that of New Harmony, the constitutions of these other Owenite communities promised equality: they guaranteed a community of property where men and women could live as equals. The Friendly Association of Valley Forge is a case in point. Their constitution, found as an appendix to the 1826 Philadelphia edition of John Gray's *A Lecture on Human Happiness*, is adapted from the London Cooperative Society's constitution, and thus is quite specific in proposing equality for both sexes: the Friendly Association's constitution requires that members be accommodated equally, and that both "MEN and WOMEN" be appointed as the twelve managers who would make the regulations and bylaws. Like the other Owenite constitutions, the constitution of the Friendly Association promised the community's children a useful education that combined practice with theory; they "discouraged" the use, vending, and distilling of ardent spirits, while pledging that the religious opinions of the members would not be "interfered" with. They also promised the "female part of the company" equal access to "the pleasures of social intercourse and the acquisition of knowledge."

Likewise, the Blue Spring Community promised equality in its constitution, proposing that "all the members of the community shall be equal in rights and privileges according to their ages" (BS Const. Article 18th). Children were to receive a "superior" education, and, as at New Harmony, they were to be taught as "one family" so each child could develop into a "rational being" (Preamble and Article 19th). The Franklin Constitution offered "a community of interest and an equality of rights by which happiness would be secured to industrious families," as well as promising every member the "utmost freedom" in religion (M'Knight, 8). The Kendal Constitution, though declaring the "Great first cause and Creator of all things" as its underlying principle, does lay out the groundwork for political equality between the sexes. The second article reads: "The location of the company having been chosen by the general concurrence of the adult members of the community, they shall hold stated meetings consisting of men and women, by whom all rules and regulations shall be made and before whom all the business of the company shall be laid." Furthermore, after the arrival of the Underhill party from Coxsackie, the reports from the meetings of the Kendal Community reveal that wives of members, upon signing the constitution, were considered to be members also (passed on April 27, 1828).[51]

Similarly, these other communities, especially Franklin and Yellow Springs, were, like New Harmony, devoted to social change, especially change that altered women's "false and vicious" position in the mainstream culture. Franklin was, from its onset, a radical place, a collection of New York freethinkers, with one of the most liberal of the New Harmony reformers, Robert Jennings, acting as president. Unlike at New Harmony, where Methodist ministers shared a pulpit with Robert Jennings, the leaders at Franklin formed their own church—the Church of Reason— which encouraged labor on the Sabbath and promulgated Robert Owen's "more extreme views on marriage" (M'Knight). Franklin leaders wished to follow Owen's ideas on separating children from their parents and educating them to understand reason, even to the point of forbidding the teaching of Bible stories; "works of nature" were to be taught instead, by young women rather than parents. As at New Harmony, there was an emphasis on educational projects such as public lectures, while weekly dances, balls, and other amusements were also offered. Jennings encouraged women to wear the "New Harmony" pantalettes, a practical kind of bloomers, combined with an overcoat reaching only the knees (M'Knight, 15). At Franklin every member was to "enjoy the utmost freedom on all subjects of knowledge, especially religion." Marriage, according to one resident's description of the constitution, was regarded as "slavery."

Also like New Harmony, the Yellow Springs Community planned schools that would teach all things useful, except religion; instituted dances, public lectures, and pleasant exercises; and ignored Christianity by having walks, rides, and plays on the Sabbath (Mac Ms, 304). The Yellow Springs Community, like Franklin, tried to create the foundation for truly egalitarian living. Contemporary records illustrate that everyone entered into the new system with enthusiasm. Men who had never before "labored with their hands devoted themselves to agriculture. . . . Ministers of the gospel guided the plow." Also, as in any communal group venturing into a wilderness, "service" was reputed to be "the order of the day" for the women of the community as well. Women who had seldom seen the inside of their own kitchens went into the common eating house and made themselves useful among pots and kettles. Refined young women who had all their lives been waited upon took their turns in waiting upon others.[52]

Although the equality that Robert Owen preached was always an abstraction, the concrete reforms and constitutions that the Owenite communities established in 1825–27 were anything but abstract. Women, considered in Owenite thought to be the oppressed sex, nominally gained equal rights with men in the Owenite communities. Politically, this concept translated into women being given constitutional guarantees that allowed even married women to vote in public meetings. Socially, such a policy meant that women were given new, practical clothing to wear that would not restrict their movements or injure their internal organs, and were taught new egalitarian habits whereby they, not servants, would cook, wash and iron, and milk the cows. In the schools, boys and girls would learn the same subjects, preparing them to be equals as adults. The rhetoric was all there— in the constitutions, in the *Gazette,* in the letters the reformers wrote to outsiders, in the speeches Owen and his reformers made. It was simply waiting to be implemented.

CHAPTER

3

THE COLLAPSE OF THE COMMUNITIES
The Ideology of Gender and the "Woman Problem"

> What a pity . . . that the kitchen, and the house-work generally, cannot be left out of our system altogether! It is odd enough that the kind of labor which falls to the lot of women is just that which chiefly distinguished artificial life--the life of degenerated mortals—from the life of Paradise. Eve had no dinner-pot, and no clothes to mend, and no washing day.
>
> —Coverdale speaking in *The Blithedale Romance*

Regardless of the Owenite constitutional promises and the reformers' enthusiasm, the Communities of Equality that formed at New Harmony and elsewhere in America in the mid-1820s did not live up to their dreamers' hopes, and all disbanded within two to three years. In none of the communities did equality of any sort become realized.

In all ways except the passion of the founders, the stories of the Owenite communities in the 1820s in America read like case studies on how not to begin an intentional community. Instead of Owen's parallelogram, complete with running water, heated and cooled apartments, and two separate rooms for each adult, new recruits found log cabins, mosquitoes, and empty fields. Particularly for the communities like New Harmony, Franklin, and Yellow Springs—communities made up of people who had never lived together before—the reality of what members were used to and what they found in the wilderness was enough to discourage all but the most devoted disciples. Life at New Harmony, or any Owenite community, was

68

remarkably similar to satirist "Peter Puffin's" view of New Harmony in his 1825 work "Heaven on Earth," a play populated by characters such as Mr. Plausible, who chooses rich people to go to New Harmony and who believes in "no distinctions based on sex, colour, or property" (11). The final act of the play places all the characters in Harmony, living in log houses, freezing and miserable.[1]

Given the intractable problems associated with beginning a community—the hardships before the crops are planted and the industries running smoothly, as well as the dissension among the members—having a charismatic leader who will guide the community through its initial phases, solve conflicts, and keep members' minds on the glorious future rather than the dismal present is vitally important. That Owen spent less than two months of the first year in New Harmony only exacerbated its problems. Arriving in January of 1825 to sign the agreement to purchase the lands and buildings, Owen left a few days later to return to Washington, D.C., and to lecture in other cities along the way. After returning to New Harmony in April, Owen remained only until the beginning of June, when he returned to Great Britain to gather more converts and supplies and to take care of business at New Lanark. Morale sagged lower and lower in New Harmony as the first winter approached and Robert Owen did not.

But even when he returned in early January of 1826, Owen, instead of attempting to solve the economic and social problems besieging the community, chose instead to believe that the Preliminary Society had already removed the cause of society's evils. Thus Owen created a Community of Equality on the spot, disregarding all the evidence before his eyes that his community was not ready for such a move.

Less than a year earlier, Owen had insisted in his March 2, 1825, speech to Congress that potential New Harmony members had to agree to cooperate with their labor and skill, that they needed to produce within the community all necessary food and supplies, and that they should begin immediately to build a planned Owenite community as illustrated by his parallelogram model, with buildings, gardens, and pleasure grounds. These requisites, in fact, were the first premises of Owen's "Rules and Regulations" for a successful community; yet none of these requirements had been met at New Harmony at the time Owen dissolved the Preliminary Society to establish a Community of Equality. The people who came to New Harmony could not even operate all the Rappite industries, let alone build a complex, technologically advanced model village spacious enough to house a potential five thousand utopian dwellers. Of the over one thousand people moving to New Harmony, many were ready to begin a new moral world but had no skills for farming Indiana swamplands; others, with necessary skills, were ready to begin life anew by prospering economically but were not interested in Owen's social experiment. Some cared neither for a new moral world nor for working.

Compounding the economic problems and the lack of cohesion among members was Owen's willingness to allow a sudden fracturing of New Harmony into splinter groups. On February 15, 1826, at the same time the Community of Equality was forming, Owen gave some choice land to a group of New Harmony members who were religious backwoodsmen wanting to form their own community. They named this division Macluria, in tribute to the recently arrived educator, whose negative opinion of religion had obviously not come to their attention. Whether the group split off for "religious reasons" or self-interest is debatable, but one New Harmony resident believed that "the former was the ostensible, the latter the real reason, I suppose" (Pears, 78). In early March a second defection took place among the English farmers, the "best farmers," according to Thomas Pears. Robert Owen again granted this offshoot some 1,400 acres of choice land. The formation of such factions encouraged William Maclure, desiring more autonomy in his schools, to propose yet another modification in the communal structure—three independent communities, an Agricultural and Pastoral Society, a Mechanic and Manufacturing Society, and the School of Education Society, which Owen also approved. Trying to accede to all the disparate groups' demands, Owen succeeded only in turning what was intended to be a unified community into warring camps. The Owenites had, in the words of William Owen, "attempted too much at once."[2]

Not only was Owen unable to unite the many factions of people living in New Harmony, he also could not provide a common focus for the idealistic reformers living there. Reform-minded men and women such as Donald Macdonald, William Maclure, Marie Fretageot, and Paul Brown were all committed to the Owenite system or at least to some aspect of it, but they all had their own notions about just what constituted a "Community of Equality." Paul Brown, for example, wanted the community to live up to its rhetoric about sharing property; Donald Macdonald wanted to decide issues by consensus at "family"-like group meetings; William Maclure wanted autonomy to run excellent schools.

Because Owen did not provide a focus for all the communitarian idealists living at New Harmony, they often worked at odds with one another instead of cooperating. William Maclure, who believed in his educational cause above all others, had a different first priority from Owen. To Maclure, educational reform was a community's *raison d'être;* to Robert Owen, on the other hand, education was a stepping stone to mature communitarian thinking—necessary, but essentially a handmaiden to the community. The longer Maclure resided at New Harmony, the more he became frustrated with Owen's ideas on education. In the summer of 1826, Maclure wrote about Owen's ranting in "big vague and undefined words" (M/F 365); by the fall, he said outright that Owen was "wrong-headed on education," (M/F 367); and by the following spring he related that Owen had "not the smallest idea of a good education" (M/F 385). He wrote to Fretageot from

New Orleans on his opinion of Owen after hearing from her what was happening at New Harmony:

> He is the most obstinate man I ever knew. It's that obstinacy that I fear for our schools. He has not the smallest idea of a good education and will not permit any to flourish within his reach. His parot [*sic*] education to exhibit before strangers as at New Lanark is the whole he knows. He is, like all enthusiazts, determined to carry his point *cout qui cout* [*sic*] and will sacrifice every other consideration for it. (M/F, 385)

Owen also could not provide the leadership needed to sustain his long-time followers such as Donald Macdonald. Just as groups of New Harmony members broke off from Owen's Community of Equality, so disillusioned individuals left as well. Donald Macdonald, one of Robert Owen's staunchest supporters since 1821, an "ardent, generous, intelligent" man who "won universal affection and confidence," abruptly left New Harmony on March 4, one day before the Community of Equality was to begin.[3] Macdonald strongly opposed the new constitution and led attempts to throw it out during the constitutional debates that took place the month before he left. He was "suspicious" of constitutions and wrote to the *New Harmony Gazette* the explanation of his opposition to the new constitution: "We never introduced [constitutions and laws] into the Practical Society [at Edinburgh] and consequently we never disagreed" (February 22, 1826). Macdonald wanted simple communal regulations—a "family meeting" with men, women, and children coming together to express aloud before everyone all they had to say about the running of the community. What he wanted, in effect, was government by consensus. When his ideas were voted down, Macdonald left New Harmony, and his leaving cost the community one of its most devoted utopian thinkers. His farewell "Letter to the Equalites," published in the February 22 *New Harmony Gazette*, illustrates his true utopianism:

> I have wished to teach the Equalites, both by company, conversation, and example, to love and help one another.—I have wished to give them a spirit of industry in producing, and a desire to be careful and economical in consuming. I have wished to point out and explain to them, in the plainest and most friendly manner, what I believe is the best for each to strive to do; and I have endeavored to make them ardently devoted to the pursuit of everything that is useful. . . . But I have not been favored by the confidence of the majority of the Equalites, and must, therefore, plod along, and endeavor to acquire still more experience and influence.

That Robert Owen could sanction Macdonald's departure, as he allowed William Maclure to divide New Harmony into three communities, speaks eloquently of his failure to keep his faithful followers together.

A year after Robert Owen's hasty move to bring about equality at a single stroke by dissolving the Preliminary Society, the communal attempt at New Harmony ended. The other Owenite communities experienced similar endings. Yellow Springs, in Greene County, Ohio, the first of the other Owenite communities to organize, was also the first to disband. Suffering from a lack of housing and mismanagement of available money, by the summer of 1826 Yellow Springs was publishing "appeals" in the local newspaper for financial help. The Friendly Association for Mutual Interests, which had begun in the early spring of 1826, dispersed in only a few months, breaking up by early September 1826, allegedly because a fanatical local minister drove the members away, but more realistically because few of the members were imbued with the "cooperative spirit." The Franklin Community lasted an equally short time: beginning in the spring of 1826, Franklin was dissolved by October 1826, when several members journeyed eighty miles up the Hudson River to Coxsackie, where they united with people already settled there and formed the Forestville Community. The Forestville Community, with too little original capital to escape its debt, the Kendal Community, with too little cash, and the Blue Spring Community all outlasted New Harmony, but none remained a functioning community longer than an extra year, with Forestville splitting up in October of 1827, Blue Spring in 1827 or early 1828, and Kendal in October of 1828.[4]

When New Harmony disbanded in the spring of 1827, everyone pointed fingers at everyone else as the cause of the experiment's demise—except the nonjudgmental *New Harmony Gazette*, which reported that "irreconcilable differences had dissolved the harmony between members." Robert Owen blamed Maclure and his teachers. He said at his departure from New Harmony that although many were not prepared to be members of a Community of Equality, "yet there was much good feeling among the population generally,—and, if the Schools had been in full operation, upon the very superior plan which I had been led to expect . . . [we could] have succeeded in amalgamating the whole into a Community."[5] Later he blamed the Rappites for leaving Harmonie too soon. Most of the New Harmony members, especially those in the Education Society, laid the failure of the community directly on Robert Owen. Teacher Joseph Neef was particularly vehement:

> Your conduct, Sir, is the sole and only source of this abortion. . . . All your multifarious writings, speeches, lectures, addresses, teem with denunciations against individual property, against competition, against inequality. Common property, co-operation, equality, form, according to your doctrine, the true and only basis of social happiness. . . . But it seems that all the various preachers are doomed to be alike in one respect, namely, in making their doctrines disagree with their practice.[6]

Neef focused on one central problem that caused New Harmony's demise: Robert Owen's inability to translate his abstract ideas into reality. While Owen pleaded for equality, inequality was the norm; when Owen promised a healthy economy and full working participation, in reality New Harmony was besieged by economic problems from its inception, caused at least in part by Owen's errors in judgment.

The question we must ask is why neither Robert Owen nor any of the other community leaders was able to bridge this gap between plan and reality. Why, after devoting so much time and money to a project, did Owen do all the wrong things? Why did he antagonize his faithful followers and provide no leadership for the workers? Why did other leaders such as Daniel Roe at Yellow Springs and Robert Jennings at Franklin have the same kind of problems? The answer has to lie at least in part with the ideologies the men brought to their role of leadership. The ways they conceived of themselves, the ways they thought about the world, their relationship to others, all entered into their abilities to be leaders of "communities of equality."

In Robert Owen's case, his personality, his great abilities to "lead the way" conflicted from the onset with the message he was preaching; his personality and his philosophy of egalitarianism had never been compatible. Even though Owen demurred in his first speech to Congress in February of 1825 that he had "no wish to lead the way," his personal history suggests this statement to be blatantly false. In the early 1820s Owen had nothing but disdain both for the British government, which ignored him, and for some of his own disciples like George Mudie, whose modifications of his design were, according to Owen, only muddying his own clear waters of reform. He had even less regard for the women at New Lanark, who couldn't even keep their kitchens clean without his surprise "inspections." Unless he could precisely control the conditions in his proposed communities, he wanted nothing to do with them. Not only had Owen wanted all his life to be in charge and lead the way, but his own previous success had been predicated on inequality. Believing as he did that the character of man was formed for him, not by him, Owen saw his role as teacher, as leader. His experiences as a wealthy factory owner only reinforced his opinion of himself: he had to "give" the workers better working conditions as well as educational opportunities. Being in charge, he could "offer" benefits to them. As a reform-minded factory owner, Owen was remarkably successful. As a director, planner, overseer, Owen could cajole, threaten, give incentives to, and generally overwhelm his poor, uneducated factory workers. Owen's reforms at New Lanark, whether he intended them to do so or not, perpetuated the "old" system by successfully altering it rather than supplanting it.

But by the time that Owen had arrived in America, he was completely caught up in his own and Thompson's egalitarian rhetoric—the natural outgrowth of his evolving beliefs in reform—yet without any realization that that rhetoric lived out would necessitate a very different attitude toward workingmen and toward women. Owen's success had come from his actions as a benevolent patriarch. His experiences as a factory owner reinforced his beliefs that badly educated workingmen needed the paternal benevolence of a wealthy, educated landowner in order to change the conditions of their environment. Working women needed their children taken away from them to be trained "properly." On one hand, he was an effective patriarch conducting his reform in the tradition, as J. F. C. Harrison labels it, of the paternalistic English squire (*Quest*, 49); on the other hand, he desired to create that "perfect equality" he had come to believe was the only foundation for an elevated state of society. The results of these contradictions were a tone of superiority and condescension that angered those whom Owen sought to "save" and an inability on Owen's part to join rhetoric and practice. In egalitarian communities, benevolent patriarchs have no place.

One of the main causes of unhappiness in the Owenite communities was this tension of inequality. In all the communities, economic inequality, not equality, was the norm. During New Harmony's first year the contradictions between what Robert Owen and the other reformers were preaching about egalitarianism and the reality of life in the community became apparent to most of the people there, sowing the seeds for dissolution. Living in primitive conditions in the Indiana wilderness would have been difficult enough if all had been in it together; that some endured economic hardships and others did not caused more grief than the lack of goods itself. Although New Harmony was organized on a joint stock principle, with a "nominal allowance of $1.54 per week" allocated to all members from which they could purchase their necessities at the community store, not everyone was so tightly strapped (Pelham, November 22, 1825). Because the Articles of Association of the Preliminary Society encouraged members to bring capital into the community if they wished, wealthy members lived quite well. Poor members became dissatisfied and resentful when they discovered they had joined a "Community of Equality" in name only. William Pelham, though a staunch supporter of the "new and equal" proposed living arrangements, described a sumptuous supper at one of the wealthier member's houses:

> The table was covered with a profusion of delicacies, excellent coffee, tea, cream, honey, sweetmeats, ham, sausage, &c &c in abundance—But I would not have you to infer that this good cheer is found in every family in New Harmony,—the time has not yet arrived when *all the members* are to fare alike—though I really believe this will be the case in the *new Community*. . . . Now do not . . . imagine we are starved for this is not true, tho our privations are sometimes such as to test the strength of our principles. (January 8, 1826)

Others were not as sanguine; William Maclure was perturbed because Owen allowed "certain aristocratic families [to] have every thing at the store they want, some of them as far as 6 or 8 fine ladies' dresses" (M/F, 376). Paul Brown noted that Robert Owen, who boarded at the tavern, had "luxurious regale . . . copiously provided . . . while the multitude of laboring people who quartered in the large boarding houses, being circumscribed in their rations, were very much in the habit of drinking rye coffee, or rye mixed with store coffee" (25). "A few," he complained, "had wealth, a vast superfluity of possessions more than by the law of nature they had any right to: they would not share it with the people of New Harmony" (29).

Similar tensions between groups of haves and have-nots formed at other Owenite communities as well. At the Friendly Association for Mutual Interests at Valley Forge, the supervisor, James Jones, was reputed to have more pleasant quarters than the rest of the community (J. Reed, 29). Likewise, at Blue Spring, one special man, Colonel Berry, got to go to town in clean clothes on a good horse to learn about prices and fluctuations. A member working the fields on the same hot July day could not understand "the workings of [the] system" when both were supposed to be equal (Duncan, 10, Blue Spring Community Papers).

Owen and his fellow reformers were powerless to unify disparate groups because of their ideologies of both class and sex. At New Harmony, Owen "allowed" certain "aristocratic families" finer dresses at the store because he accepted the notion that the upper classes were more deserving of benefits. They were, after all, his friends and family; he had persuaded many of New Harmony's "elite"—the Prices, Madame Fretageot, Maclure, Thomas Say—to come to New Harmony to continue their work.

That the elite class and the working class had different reasons for coming to New Harmony helped reinforce the separateness and inequality there. Most working-class members of New Harmony were not drawn to community life because of Owen's distinctive ideals; rather they came because of some of the promises Owen made on his lecture trail—particularly those dealing with cooperative work that would ensure greater profits and shorter working days. These people were attracted to the communities because of Owen's specific plans for a shortened workday and good schools for their children. They liked Owen's plan for economic equality but found the promises for other kinds of equality repugnant. Thus the two different groups—workers bent on improving their economic lives and reformers bent on change—remained separate and distinct.

Working-class people both kept to themselves and were perceived as "others" by the elite. Working-class members did not dance at the weekly balls, separating themselves from what one visitor called "the better people." The "better people" kept to themselves as well. One member wrote home: "Oh, if you could see some of these rough uncouth creatures here, I think you would find it hard to look upon them exactly in the light of brothers and sisters. . . . I am sure I cannot in sincerity look upon them as my equals" (Pears, 60). Another member, who had been "enthusiastically attached to Mr. Owen's system," found upon her arrival in New Harmony, that "the highly vaunted equality" was not to her taste and that some of the society were "too low."[7] Duke Bernhard, an aristocratic visitor to New Harmony in April of 1826, wrote how shocked he was to see that "people of education . . . live on the same footing with everyone indiscriminately." Though one might dispute the Duke's premise that everyone did live on the same footing, he related a story that epitomized the class ideology so prevalent in New Harmony. One night, a "young and pretty [and] delicately brought up" woman, Virginia Dupalais from Philadelphia, was singing and playing on the pianoforte when she was told that milking the cows was "her duty." The Duke wrote of how she betook herself, "almost in tears," to this "servile employment, deprecating the new social system, and its so much prized equality" (Bernhard). That one group of people at New Harmony—primarily its intellectual leaders and reformers—thought of most of the necessary work to be done as "servile" boded ill for the establishment of an egalitarian state. Indeed, the Boatload of Knowledge, which brought Virginia Dupalais and her teacher Marie Fretageot to New Harmony, was composed of people who wanted to change the world by teaching and doing research. If someone else could milk the cows (just as Nathaniel Hawthorne escaped from his duty of milking the cows at Brook Farm twenty years later), all the better from their perspective for creating a utopian world.

The tone of condescension toward the working people at New Harmony is never so evident as it is in the letter of one class-conscious visitor, in which he relates to Frederick Rapp the state of affairs at the community. Responding to Rapp's inquiries about the "situation" at New Harmony, he tells him, in a mocking way, of how "washerwomen" voice their opinions:

> A new form of government was produced [at New Harmony], called the perfect system . . . providing that every thing was to be adopted and carried into effect agreable [sic] to the free will of the whole community to be decided by the voice of the whole (male and female) . . . dressed in a costume resembling a feather bed tied with a rope around the middle. . . . but lo! on the first meeting it was discovered that though the washerwomen had left their duds in the tub they had brought with them what they conceived of much more importance, the article commonly called a tongue which when put in motion emitted the Eloquence of Billingsgate with such power and force as to convince the leading satellites that though the system might be perfect the only way to keep its subject so was once more to confine their female orators to their closet or curtain lectures. (Reprinted in *Harmony on the Wabash*, p. xxx)

The letter writer's clear class and gender biases were shared by many of the aristocratic New Harmony residents. Washerwomen, whose tongues put in motion the "eloquence of Billingsgate," the London fish market known for foul and abusive language, needed to be hushed up and "confined to their closets" if the "system" was to remain "perfect." There was no place in New Harmony for a working-class woman's complaints.

The tension between classes and the attitudes of the reformers toward the working classes continued unabated at all the Owenite communities. At Yellow Springs, members argued about the worth of various types of work. A band of musicians insisted that their music was as necessary to the common happiness as food and thus declined to work in the fields or industries. A science teacher believed his service to the community was to lecture, not to work with his hands (Mac Ms, 305). Various groups of laborers debated the value of skilled and unskilled labor, resulting in growing antagonism. One group believed that if the community were to be truly egalitarian, there should be no differentiation between skilled and unskilled work; the skilled laborers disagreed. Daniel Roe, powerless to stop the debates that focused on some of the central issues that a "community of equality" could raise, soon abandoned his enterprise.

At Franklin, former New Harmonite Robert Jennings was equally helpless in dealing with workers who joined his community to benefit themselves economically but who disbelieved in the Owenite social plans. He, along with the community's "directors"—George Houston, its secretary, who had met Owen in New York; Henry Fay, a radical New York lawyer; and Jacob Peterson, who held the deed of the community property—wrote the constitution so as to embody Owen's beliefs about religion, education, and reforms for women. Their sense of mission kept them from enfranchising the mere "workers" at the community. From their perspective, workers who questioned the Owenite mission were a problem. From the perspective of the workers, the community that "enslaved" them was a failure.

One such working couple, James and Eliza M'Knight, joined the Franklin community when it began in May 1826. Out of work, with a child to support, James M'Knight had been attracted to the notices about a community to be formed "by which happiness would be secured to industrious families" ("Discourse," 8). But he was immediately displeased with the community, in part because he believed the nature of the experiment had changed without his knowledge. He had signed one community constitution that he agreed with before leaving New York City for the farmlands near Haverstraw, New York. During his absence, he fumed, "a few members met and adopted a new constitution to suit their views" (4). This new constitution for the Preparatory Society of the Franklin Community was typically Owenite in its promises for each member to be able to enjoy "the utmost freedom in all subjects of knowledge and opinion—especially on the subjects of religion and politics." But for the religious M'Knight family, the "utmost freedom" in religion translated into "downright infidelity and atheism" (5).

M'Knight disliked almost everything about the way the community was

run by the directors. Their ideas on education were Owen's—taking children from their mothers at age two, keeping books away from children
until they were twelve, having children taught by young girls. M'Knight, of
course, disagreed completely:

> How many mothers are there who will part with the children of their
> affections to be brought up in the principles of infidelity, and suffered to
> pursue their own inclinations without any restraint or admonition? Have
> not many of us cause to rejoice that we were ever instructed by a pious and
> affectionate mother? Some, perhaps, remember the tears and prayers of
> their parents for their welfare and happiness. How many can testify that
> the first impressions of religion and virtue upon their minds, were pro-
> duced by the admonitions of a tender mother. (12)

M'Knight was also appalled at "Robert Owen's view of marriage," as
proclaimed at Franklin. That marriage could be dissolved when the union
promised more misery than happiness appeared to M'Knight to be "de-
structive of the foundation of society" (8). He simply disbelieved the constitution, which included a section that proclaimed marriage to be slavery for
man to be bound to his wife or for a wife to be bound to her husband. He
explains in a brief anecdote that a member of the community told the
president, Robert Jennings, that he disapproved of his wife's dancing in the
public ballroom because "the young men squeeze the ladies hands . . . they
sometimes kiss them . . . and *something else* very often takes place." Jennings's indifferent reply—"what of that . . . you must become naturalized
to our *social system*"—did nothing to alleviate M'Knight's fears that he was
living in a den of iniquity (11).

Finally, the new costumes women were encouraged to wear in New
Harmony were also available in Franklin, much to M'Knight's disgust.
M'Knight explains Robert Jennings's position on this new dress, intro-
duced as a reform for community women:

> Mr. Jennings wishes every lady among them to wear a dress similar to that
> of an Indian, (the gown reaching to the knees—with pantalettes on the
> legs.) His wife wears this outlandish costume, as well as several other
> females on the ground. Those who have not seen the antic tricks, both of
> men and women, at their balls and amusements, and their ridiculous
> gestures at other times, can scarcely form any idea of their behaviour. It
> does appear as if it would soon become necessary for the country to build
> a lunatic asylum for them. (15)

For M'Knight, egalitarianism, libertarianism, and free thought were signs
of the devil. Since he could never become a believer in the Owenite system,
his only recourse was to complain, to get sick and become unable to work,
to leave the community, and then to write and lecture about the conditions
of "absolute slavery" that existed at Franklin. In Franklin's short existence,
Robert Jennings never discovered what to do with people like the

M'Knights. He and the other directors needed them to work, but because of his class ideology, Jennings was not prepared actually to listen to their complaints.

Even more pernicious than—but in many ways analogous to—the ideology of class that permeated the communities was the ideology of gender. It was more important than class ideology because it sundered harmony between individuals of the same class as well as between the groups of "elite" reformers and "common" workers. It was not only washerwomen of the working class whose behavior was judged and disparaged by the male leaders, but all women. It was not only working wives who were forced to occupy a certain—and inferior—place in the hierarchy that quickly coalesced as the communities' short lives proceeded; it was also middle- and upper-middle-class women who were used to individual homes, servants or hired workers, and an amount of freedom to do as they wished within their domestic spheres.

The ideology of gender is perhaps the most important factor that kept the reformers' egalitarian rhetoric from being realized in any but minor ways. Because Owen and most of the Owenite reformers unquestioningly accepted the Cult of True Womanhood and its attitude toward women, their abstract promise of "equality," so preponderant in constitutional discourse, was quietly yet firmly denied to women on every level. The very term everyone was using—"equality"—signified to the reformers that women would be "allowed" to work full-time in community industries *as well as* be responsible for their families' domestic services. This rather specious notion of "equality" necessarily threatened the women of the communities— particularly the married women of the middle and upper-middle classes, who came to community life with the same class and gender ideologies that the leaders did. Accepting the same class and gender biases, they did not want to do menial work for the community at large. Believing that their "sacred sphere" was being violated, they vociferously rebelled. For them their deprivation was relative: in their former lives they had been much better off with only domestic duties. At the Owenite communities they had more work to do and less power. Their subsequent unhappiness added to the growing problems surrounding the communities.

The ideology of gender that infused all the communities carried out the precepts of the Cult of True Womanhood, even if these precepts created a mismatching pastiche when mixed with "egalitarian" rhetoric. According to Cult ideology, men *were* powerful, or were believed to be so, and women *were* powerless. To Robert Owen and leaders of the other Owenite communities, despite their words in lectures and essays, men and women were simply unequal. They all accepted the great "given" in early nineteenth-century America: that women were beings with different natures, different roles, different personalities from men, and all of these "differences" signified that Woman was a being who could not possibly equal Man. This

ideology was reflected in every aspect of community life—from the constitutions and community publications to the attitudes toward community
women and the demands on their time.

The very community constitutions that promised complete equality,
"regardless of sex or condition," relegated women to specific tasks and
duties that were sex-bound. In Blue Spring, for example, the employment
of the "female part of the community" was carefully laid out: women's work
consisted of "preparing food and clothing, in the care of dwelling houses
and dormitories, in the management of washing and drying houses, in the
education (in part) of the children, and such other employments as are
suited to the female capacity" (Article 33rd, BS Const). Collecting data from
the children and grandchildren of the Blue Spring members, one historian
has corroborated the constitutional functions for women. In the community, some women did the spinning, weaving, and cooking, while
others washed, set the table, served in the dining room, did chamber work,
and attended to dyeing and making the clothes (Duncan, 9, Blue Spring
Community Papers). Likewise, in the Kendal Community the sexes were
separated and unequal. As the communal structure broke down in the
spring of 1827, members began to receive extra pay for extra work. The
resulting charts allocating money to necessary duties reveal the vast economic differential between "men's" and "women's" work in the community.
While a married male member of Kendal was allowed ten dollars a month
for his regular labor plus extra for any additional labor, a female member
was entitled to only twenty-five cents a day for eight hours of washing or
seventy-five cents a week for "each week's actual labour at housework"
("Minutes," April 19, 1827).

In some ways, it is the Friendly Association for Mutual Interests at Valley
Forge that has the most revealing constitution. The members of the
Friendly Association derived their constitution from the Articles of Agreement of the London Cooperative Society. The London Cooperative Society,
an Owenite group consisting of, among others, William Thompson and
John Gray, proposed an eight-hour day, offered a choice between communal meals in public halls or private meals in individual apartments, and
allowed parents to board their children in "dormitories" if they chose.[8] The
Cooperative Society, with William Thompson writing its constitution, attempted to guarantee equal rights to women in the community. Women's
rights were forcefully set forth in Thompson's rhetoric in Article VIII: "To
women, forming half the human race, equally capable with men of contrib-
uting to the common happiness, and equally capable of individual enjoyment, we guarantee eligibility equally with men. We also guarantee to
them means of acquiring knowledge and social pleasures, and of the
physical means of enjoyment with men."

The Cooperative Society did not stop with just this abstract rhetoric.
They found a practical way to guarantee women's equality: communal child
care, to be provided by "voluntary agents" plus parents, and freedom from

all domestic work for women. According to Article IX of the constitution, the "domestic drudgery of cooking, washing, and of heating apartments . . . will be performed on scientific principles on a large economic scale . . . [in order to] afford [women] an opportunity of acquiring respect and sympathy . . . and give them equal facilities with men, of social intercourse and of acquiring knowledge." Instead of women doing the "drudgery," the youths of the community (ages ten to seventeen) would "repay the adult members for the support and education previously conferred upon them" by performing all "useful and menial" services (Section XV).

The Friendly Association at Valley Forge adopted but tellingly modified many of the Cooperative Society's egalitarian propositions in their own constitution of January 19, 1826. Though the Valley Forge Community promised "equal accommodations to all members," nowhere in the constitution is the importance of women's rights spelled out as it was in the Cooperative Society's constitution. Rather than free women from *all* "domestic drudgery," Article XIX of the Friendly Association's constitution modified the original to read that women "will be relieved *as much as possible* from the *heavier* duties of domestic life," in order for them to "equally enjoy the pleasures of social intercourse, and the acquisition of knowledge" (my emphasis). Eliminated from the Friendly Association's constitution is any reference to "acquiring equal respect"—the prime reason the Cooperative Society gave for eradicating "women's" work in their proposed community. In the American community, domestic work remained women's duty. Only the British Owenite William Thompson had understood the importance of eliminating gender-based occupations. Robert Owen might have agreed intellectually with Thompson, but he was too much imbued with his own patriarchal notions to agree with him on any but an abstract level. Modified reforms in dress or in marriage ceremonies were a safe way to perpetuate the patriarchy in which everyone was living.

The ideology of gender imposed limitations on women not only abstractly, in the Owenite constitutions, but also in the day-to-day life of the communities themselves. At the most elementary level, although both boys and girls had been guaranteed an equal education in most of the Owenite constitutions, such a promise did not become a reality. In part, the frontier conditions of the Owenite communities mitigated against establishing schools of any type, let alone avant-garde Pestalozzian ones complete with supplies and scientific laboratory equipment. The Kendal Community, despite its "resolutions" to establish a school with "useful" education for both boys and girls, never got one under way while the community was functioning.[9] The grand plans the directors had for the Franklin schools, where boys and girls would be taken from their parents at two and taught rational and useful things by young women of the community, were all dissipated when the community disbanded six months after it began. Even in New Harmony, which did begin both a day school and a boarding school, not all of Owen's plans were incorporated. At New Lanark Owen had established schools that educated the children of working-class people. Their education was practical, useful, and pleasurable. But believing that education alone could not overcome the entire old, immoral world, Owen established New Harmony, whereby education would be the handmaiden to a new, reformed society. His plans included housing his schools in his elaborate parallelogram and taking all children from their parents at the age of two to be educated away from their nuclear families. In the short life of New Harmony, no parallelogram was ever built and no children taken away from parents to be educated together.[10] Until the Boatload of Knowledge arrived the community had few teachers who understood or could apply the "new principles." Children over twelve, promised a half-day of schooling, had to forego their lessons to work full time.

When Maclure and his coterie of teachers and scholars arrived in New Harmony in January of 1826, they took over the educational activities in the community and created, in Arthur Bestor's words, a contribution to New Harmony more enduring than Robert Owen's (*Education and Reform*, 297). The Education Society, composed of the Philadelphia educators and a few other New Harmony teachers, was a model of community living, according to Paul Brown, a teacher in the group. He said that the Education Society, one of three divisions of the New Harmony community that Maclure induced Owen to approve, was "more republican" than any of the other "communities" at New Harmony. The members of the Education Society regularly assembled together and, "by a majority of the free and equal suffrages of male and female members, [made] their own laws" (P. Brown, 83). The New Harmony schools lasted longer than the community itself, with Marie Fretageot remaining in New Harmony until 1831, directing the schools.

Although the New Harmony schools after the arrival of Maclure and his teachers were by most accounts "excellent," complete with laboratory equipment, scholar-teachers, and a large number of books, the schools never did live up to their promise "to teach the girls the same thing as the boys." In the first place, William Maclure believed that boys should be taught by men and girls by women. Although Maclure approved of Marie Fretageot's teaching of a coeducational group of very young children (ages two to five) in the "infant school" and teaching them the same things, he did not approve of Fretageot's teaching older boys. Similarly, Maclure believed in women's separate, domestic sphere, where little girls should be trained for their future activities. Thus, girls in the New Harmony schools learned "female employments," while the boys worked in the fields and gardens, at the printing press, and in the bootery. Maclure himself approved of the wise course of teaching the girls the "washing, cooking, & c." His plan of "equal education" never crossed the fixed occupational lines of the sexes. Rather than challenge such givens as women's roles, Maclure proposed that "perhaps all the common occupations of women, such as sewing, cooking, washing, & c can be transformed into an amusement by early habit" (M/F, 331).

Perhaps it was the notion of "useful" education that exacerbated the inequalities in the community schools. Teaching children what would be "useful" for separate adult spheres could only reinforce and perpetuate traditional sex-role behavior by categorizing boys and girls into "appropriate" roles.

If young women were relegated to their own sphere in the New Harmony schools, few adult women found their "proper" spheres enlarged in the community either. By the fall of 1825, the members of the New Harmony Preliminary Society were heatedly debating the constitutional rights for women in the community. Thomas Pears summarized in a letter to his uncle just how the words of New Harmony's constitution—"all" persons "may" vote on community business—were interpreted: "wives of members," he reported, were not to be considered members, and "it was finally decided that they should not vote" (39). Thus married women were not to be included in the Preliminary Society's constitutional framework, which ostensibly guaranteed equality to all members over a certain age. Five months later, the new constitution of New Harmony did, in accordance with its egalitarian rhetoric, given women the right to vote in public meetings, but few women ever took advantage of the opportunity. Paul Brown wrote of a May 1826 Sunday community meeting where "some women" were invited to vote, while others, "not knowing they should have a voice, remain[ed] at home" (19). Sarah Pears wrote to her aunt on women's constitutional rights in New Harmony but added that, despite "ladies being permitted to vote," she had not "as yet availed [herself] of the privilege" (66).

The same kinds of limitations on women's political equality arose in the other Owenite communities as well. In two of the communities the issue of women's voting was settled when members created a separate sphere for women and allowed them to vote in it. In Blue Spring, for example, only male members eighteen and over were considered "legal voters." Women had a separate and unequal realm that allowed them to have a voice only in "domestic matters of their own concern" (Article 7th, BS Const). In the original Kendal Constitution, drafted May 15, 1826, only men could alter or amend the constitution. With the arrival of Samuel Underhill and the Forestville contingent came a vote, in April of 1828, that married women be considered members. The motion passed but in combination with a measure that segregated women by requiring them to meet each week "and report to the Commissioners the wants of the various families which occur in the female department" ("Minutes," April 27, 1828).

Perhaps the best illustration of the ideology of gender is found in the New Harmony community's main publication, the *New Harmony Gazette*. The *Gazette* was not a "news" papers, much to historians' disappointment, except for a brief section, "New Harmony," and its last pages of notices. Rather it was a collection of essays, editorials, and reviews, all promoting Owen's "new moral world." Each week a serialized central essay, usually written by an ideological leader such as Robert Owen, Robert Dale Owen, or Frances Wright opened the paper. Without exception, this lead essay and the following major essays placed prominently at the front of the paper encouraged a true community of equality.

Despite the attempts in the first pages of the paper to criticize customs women had been taught and to posit new assumptions about education, marriage, and divorce that could liberate women from the familial chains binding them to a servile position, the New Harmony reformers, including Robert Owen himself, held unthinking and unanalyzed assumptions about women that meshed nicely with the same assumptions so prevalent in the mainstream culture. Although they might on one occasion speak eloquently for women's rights and for "equality" on some abstract level, the reformers also believed that women were very different beings from men, not "equal partners" in any way. Recall William Maclure's letter to Marie Fretageot about the young women he had met in Kentucky whose acceptance of the "new" system at New Harmony was evidenced by her washing all her husband's and her own clothes. Maclure expressed pleasure that this woman had learned well the egalitarian training she had received at New Harmony. This young woman, though, had only learned her "proper" place in the community: to be a washerwoman and not complain about it. Maclure's "pride" in her actions and his conviction that this woman provided "a better example of some little good in practice growing out of this deluge of theory than anything I have heard" (M/F 370) only reflect how ingrained were his beliefs about women's true natures and roles in society. Similar beliefs held by all the reformers surface as soon as one leaves the front pages of the *Gazette*.

The resulting tension between the rhetoric of equality and its subtle but constant contradiction appears first in the editorial commentary. The earliest editors of the *Gazette*, William Owen and Robert Jennings, say in an afternote to a review of Mary Wollstonecraft's *Vindication of the Rights of Women*:

> It is, we believe, contemplated in Mr. Owen's system, by giving our female population as good an education as our males, to qualify them for every situation in life in which, consistently with their organization, they might be placed. We have several instances on record which demonstrate, that, properly educated, they equal our sex in legislative ability, and in the lighter paths of literature, they probably excel. . . . In the next generation, when our females have from infancy been properly educated, we shall have a fair opportunity of ascertaining whether their general organization is such as to admit of their participation in the legislative proceedings of their country. We think, however, with deference to the opinion of Mrs. W. that this privilege should be limited to single females; for when a woman

marries the man of her choice, her husband becomes her political representative by and with her own consent. (*NHG,* November 23, 1925)

Though young Owen and Jennings admit that women have not had an education comparable to men's in the past, women to them are beings quite different from men. They, after an equal education, will be qualified only for those "situations" in life that are "consistent with their organization"; they are beings who excel in the "lighter paths of literature," who may or may not have the "general organization" that would allow them to cast a ballot—but whether they have this "organization" or not, should they marry, such options will be closed to them.

Because women were "others," they were the sex advised, lectured to, and admonished. Nowhere in the *New Harmony Gazette* were men ever advised; nowhere were there articles on "Men's Natures" or "How to Capture a Wife," but women were advised by the male editors at every turn. Selecting an essay on the importance of a "silent example" being set by women in order to persuade their "obstinate husbands," William Owen and Robert Jennings suggested in an editorial commentary that "the following advice may not be unacceptable to our married females, for whom it is particularly selected." Their advice instructed women to manipulate their husbands by subterfuge: women should never lecture or admonish, rather they should "hint" at a problem; thus "by an artful train of management and unseen persuasions, having at first brought him not to dislike, and at length to be pleased with, that which otherwise he would not have borne to hear of, she would then know how to press and secure this advantage, by approving it as his thought and seconding it as his proposal" (*NHG,* November 5, 1825). Women thus did not need a ballot to cast their opinions; they could express their ideas through manipulating their unsuspecting husbands.

Women were also advised on how to get and keep a husband, despite Robert Owen's theoretical statements on the absurdity of "old world" marriages. During his editorship, William Owen included in the *Gazette* several essays from other newspapers to help counsel women. An article on female beauty noted that in order to "enchain the heart of a husband with those golden fetters which only death can sever," a woman had to be "as beautiful as one of the celestial beings"; furthermore, she must be able to unite the external charms of her person "with her refined accomplishments and sublime sentiments of an elegant mind" (*NHG,* January 15, 1826). Once a woman "enchained" her husband with those golden fetters, she was then advised in "Whisper to a Wife," extracted from *Mrs. Colvin's Weekly Messenger,* of her "sacred and important" duties to fulfill. These duties included asking, "How shall I continue the love I have inspired? How shall I preserve the heart I have won?" The answer to these questions was simple for a self-sacrificing True Woman, if not for an egalitarian-minded New Harmony woman:

Make yourself amiable and pleasing to him. Study your husband's temper and character; and be it your pride and pleasure to conform to his wishes. Check *at once* the *first* advances to contradiction, even of the most *trivial* nature. . . . And the woman, who after a few years are gone by can say, "My husband and I have never yet had a loud and angry debate," is, in my opinion, better entitled to a chaplet of laurels than the hero who has fought on the plains of Waterloo. (*NHG*, December 19, 1827)

The advice given during William Pelham's editorship agreed with that of his brother editors. Pelham patiently explained to his readers that "no anger or irritation ought to be felt toward female members [of the New Harmony community] when they brawl or quarrel, because they have been taught to believe that loud talking is an effectual way of giving force to what they have to urge in their own favor." Pelham quickly added, however, in complete agreement with the "whispers" given to a wife, that "nothing tends more to distort the female character than loud and stormy disputations. It is contrary to the course which nature meant them to pursue" (*NHG*, April 19, 1826). In order to eradicate the "wish of finery and pretty baubles in women," Pelham included in the June 28, 1826, *Gazette* a poetic "Address to the Ladies":

> No more ribbons wear, nore [*sic*] in rich dress appear . . .
> This do without fear, and to all you'll appear
> Fine, charming, true, lovely and clever
> Though the times remain darkish—
> Young men will be sparkish,
> And love you more dearly than ever.

Even in New Harmony men wrote or quoted bad poems to cajole women to cast off their "innate" wish for finery in return for men's love.

Robert Dale Owen, the *Gazette*'s popular editor from October 1826 to May 1827, reiterates his colleagues' attitudes despite his personal commitment to women's rights. As he says in an editorial aimed at the women in the community:

> It is our wish to see the conversation of well-bred women rescued from the vapid commonplace; from uninteresting tattle, from trite and hackneyed communication, from frivolous earnestness, from false sensibility, from a warm interest about things of no moment, and an indifference to topics the most important. . . . Ladies commonly bring into good company minds already too much relaxed by petty pursuits, rather than over-strained by intense application. (*NHG*, March 7, 1827)

Although Owen admits further on in the essay that the "uninteresting tattle" that makes up women's conversations is an effect of socialization and not weak-mindedness, he believes, like his father, that his role as a liberal editor and reformer (and a male) allows him to lead women away from the "things of no moment" that occupy their minds filled with "petty pursuits."

One of the "things of no moment" that Owen criticizes women for participating in is quilting. In disagreeing with a brother editor's praise of a quilting party, the young Owen uses a patronizing tone, just like that of all the editors when addressing women:

> A brother Editor had expressed his "pleasure at an elegant bedquilt made by a Mrs. Carr and containing the extraordinary number of 4,572 pieces." . . . Now ladies, . . . such a contest is, at the best, but a childish one, unworthy of your good sense. We ourselves would be ashamed to engage in any such. . . . We ought at least to be reasonable enough not to encourage by publicity an idle and girlish ambition, which seeks to put as many stitches as possible in a given space, and to spend the greatest possible amount of labor to produce nothing, or, it may be, to create an object fit only to gratify a silly vanity. . . . Scarcely any useful inventions have been made by you: yet your inventive powers are at least equal to ours; and if we had possessed but good sense enough to direct these powers as they ought to have been directed, we should have been able to give publicity to exertions more creditable to your sex and more useful to society than Mrs. Carr's in bed quilting. (*NHG*, November 29, 1826)

Men, it would appear, needed to direct women's inventive powers; otherwise, women would occupy their time with "childish feats" such as quilting—the very domestic tasks that young women were taught in the New Harmony schools to perform, and the very tasks that New Harmony women had to perform for their community to survive. Women at New Harmony were thus ideologically trapped: their "proper" domestic tasks were not, in Robert Dale Owen's eyes at least, a credit to the community, yet they still had to get done. Whether the male editors were advising women to be traditional True Women or advising them to give up their quilting as a "silly vanity," women as a sex were bound to displease some group in the community.

In giving their advice, the *Gazette*'s editors prescribe an immutable "nature" for women, with women depicted as being self-sacrificing influences—the same image so pervasive in the mainstream culture, the image so inimical to equality. The disparity between the reformers' ideal of equality and the unquestioning belief in the vastly different natures of men and women is revealed in the hundreds of brief articles, aphorisms, notices, and poems that constitute the last pages of the *Gazette*. Unlike the articles that make up the front pages of the paper, these brief pieces include no pretense that men and women are or could be equals in any sense. Women are depicted repeatedly here as "bright ornaments" whose "delicacies and peculiarities unfold all their beauty and captivation," while under their beautiful exterior is "tenderness of feeling and charity of sentiment."[11]

The editors of the *Gazette* often chose poetry of well-known women poets—most frequently Sarah Hale or Mrs. Stanley Hemans—to conclude their papers "gracefully." The didactic doggerel taught unambiguous lessons. In an anonymous poem entitled "Woman," reprinted from the *Philadelphia Album*, woman's self-sacrificing nature is romanticized in typical singsong couplets:

> Pain, peril, want she fearlessly will bear,
> To dash from men her cup of dark despair;
> And only asks for all her tireless zeal,
> To share his fate, whate'er he feels to feel;
> To breathe in his fond arms her latest breath,
> And murmur out the lov'd one's name in death.
>
> (NHG, August 29, 1827)

In a similar poem, "woman's love" is extolled because it is "unceasing" and "rich with humid springs of truth," but most important, because it "throbs for another's pleasure" (*NHG*, January 15, 1828). Woman's amazing ability to "love with more truth and fervor than men" (*NHG*, January 15, 1828) culminates in a brief aphorism about woman's purpose for living: "A thousand thoughts distract, a thousand passions are a substitute for the devotion of a man; but to love is the purpose—to be loved the consummation—to be faithful the religion of a woman; it is her all in all" (*NHG*, January 3, 1827). Here is the nineteenth century's Cult of True Womanhood expressed in its clearest form, yet it is found not in *Godey's Lady's Book* but in the *New Harmony Gazette*, a journal, in part, dedicated to eradicating "outdated" customs and beliefs about women. As Barbara Welter has described, a True Woman had only two rights—to love and to comfort. All the proposed rights in the world could not hold a candle to woman's "natural" rights—those springing from her nurturing, loving, self-abnegating character.

Woman's unique duties, derived from her innately pure and loving nature, were also spelled out clearly in the latter part of the *New Harmony Gazette*. Always, woman's importance was depicted as coming from her salutary (and passive) influence upon a man or upon society—never from her own initiative, courage, or intelligence. Women "smoothed" men's manners: when women conversed with men, those men, according to brief articles in the *Gazette*, lost "their pedantic, rude, declamatory, or sullen manner" (November 8, 1826), for nothing "serves so much to polish man as the soft intercourse of refined female society" (January 25, 1826). Without a woman's friendship, "our manners have not their proper softness, our morals their purity, and our souls feel an uncomfortable void" (November 22, 1826).

Not only did woman give an individual man's morals "their purity," but her very existence purified the whole culture. But woman had to beware, for even if she possessed a "well-cultivated mind" and was "industrious and economical," should she be "destitute of neatness and taste, she depresses rather than elevates the character of her sex, and poisons, instead of purifying the fountain of domestic and public happiness" (May 10,

1826). The ideal women portrayed by the composite images found throughout the last pages of the *New Harmony Gazette* is aptly exemplified in the brief article "Woman," from the November 5, 1825, *Gazette:*

> She is the purest abstract of nature that can be found in all its works. She is the image of love, purity, and truth; and she lives and moves in all who possess virtuous innocence. Woman ever has, still is, and always will be, the main spring of every masculine achievement—her influence is felt by ALL, from the hero to the clown, from the man to the stripling: and whether she fire a Troy or excite emulation at a game of marbles; whether she influence a court or rule in a dairy, the end, cause and effect, are still the same. We may talk of patriotism—we may prate of fame—but who could feel the one, or seek the other, but for the sake of woman?
>
> Woman! still more interesting when we contemplate her, night and day, watching by the pillow of a friend, administering the healing balm, sustaining the drooping head on her sympathizing bosom, and wiping the clammy dews of death from the sunken cheek—it is such a scene lovely Woman shrines unrivalled and constrains man to pay homage due to angels of humanity.

This imagery of "True Womanhood" was all-pervasive. A telling letter appeared in the March 7, 1827, *Gazette,* just as the community of New Harmony was dissolving:

> I will not undertake to controvert your position "that females are, naturally, as capable of acquiring strength of mind and accuracy of perception and of reason as any other sex," but will content myself with suggesting, that the physical difference between the sexes admits that there is a corresponding degree of mental inequality; and, therefore, that it would not deteriorate the aggregate of happiness to retain the most rational parts of that system which was designed to educate them for their respective spheres.
>
> Caroline

Caroline's request for a retention of separate educational spheres is understandable, though it implies that she was a reader of the *Gazette* and not a member of the community, since the New Harmony schools did in fact prepare women and men for their "respective spheres." Caroline's unquestioning assumption of men's and women's mental inequality, though disclaimed and refuted in the main articles and editorial comment in the *Gazette,* is implied over and over again in the briefer articles, poems, and aphorisms in the closing pages of each issue. Certainly a woman who was depicted as a "delicate," "pure," and "self-sacrificing" creature whose only thoughts centered on soothing and comforting those around her had little need for a "rational" education or for increased rights. If, indeed, a woman's goal was to "love and be loved," then she was certainly a different being from one who used intelligence and creativity to forge ahead in the world. Caroline believed overtly, as did Robert Owen and his nineteenth-century colleagues covertly, that woman's "nature" dictated servile occupations, different roles in the family and temperaments for the sexes. Caroline carried these differences to their logical conclusion by using the very Enlightenment-like rhetoric that the reformers used.

If Caroline and her contemporaries at New Harmony could have questioned the unassailable premise that woman was a being with a more pure, more moral nature than man, and that this nature was given to her to influence those around her, then perhaps women could have lived some of the equal rights promised to them in the constitution of the New Harmony Community of Equality.

In their constitutions, in their schools, and in their editorials, the men who acted as the leaders of the Owenite communities effectively limited women's rights without even realizing how one set of their words contradicted another. The obvious effect of this pervasive ideology of gender was to negate the equality that the reformers proposed. However, there was another result: the creation of a "woman problem" that consumed the Owenite communities and helped to lead to their early demises. The women who lived in the Owenite communities—particularly the middle- and upper-middle-class women who read and had been part of an eastern city's cultured elite—also believed the message of the Cult of True Womanhood, but they felt no conflict between two sets of opposing ideas. To them their sphere was the home and family, although much of the domestic work might be done by servants or hired help. When the Owenite egalitarian rhetoric assigned them what they considered to be demeaning roles, many of the women rebelled, and their letters tell of their attempts to break the system and drive their husbands away from the communities. At first glance we might agree with the Owenite reformers who believed that, with more education, these women would also accept the benefits of communal living and agree to commit themselves. However, the ideology of gender imposed upon these women a patriarchal version of "equality," one that insisted upon both "egalitarian" work and a domestic sphere. Like the disaffected James M'Knight at Franklin, women were "slaves" to the will of a system not of their making, though in a more severe and limiting way than M'Knight had experienced. Adult community women were expected to work both in industries and in their homes, creating what we in the twentieth century call a "double day." Responsible for all the communities' domestic services, women had far more work to perform than the men of the communities or than they had had in previous lives.

From the perspective of the unmarried women in the communities, particularly the young women in New Harmony or Yellow Springs, the Owenite experiments offered a plethora of advantages to mitigate such "inconveniences" as cow milking at inopportune times. It offered a "gay" life of weekly balls and concerts and all sorts of interesting, idealistic young men with whom to attend them. The single young women's experience at

New Harmony clearly bears out Tocqueville's theory that single women in early nineteenth-century America were offered far more freedom than their European counterparts. Even older single women who chose to join the communities could bear their increased burden with good humor because they were part of the Owenite mission to change the world and thus believed themselves to be at least potentially imbued with the same power as the male reformers.

The perspective of the middle- and upper-class adult *married* women in the communities, though, was different. To married women who followed their husbands to the communities, the Owenite experiments offered nothing but hard work and, at the same time, threatened their power. Because part of the communities' egalitarian goal was to turn the domestic province from a private into a public one, these women felt deprived of the only sphere of influence—the home—open to them in America in the 1820s.

Sarah Pears, arriving in New Harmony with her optimistic husband and their seven children in the spring of 1825, is a perfect example of a threatened married woman. She left, along with her husband, an epistolary record of her year in New Harmony, ironically now anthologized as *New Harmony: An Adventure in Happiness*—perhaps the most misnamed collection of letters in American history. While she began her "adventure in happiness" with at least faint hope (she says in her first letter home that "we feel perfect confidence in Mr. Owen's sincere desire to promote the happiness of all"), Sarah Pears quickly changed her mind when she understood her and her daughters' role in the community. Her oldest daughter she described as "poorly" because of an illness she caught washing clothes for the community. Sarah lamented that "all the hard work falls upon her and it is more than she can bear. We had hoped she would have been rather relieved from her heavy labor than otherwise by coming here, but at present it is far from the case" (18). Interestingly, the complaint came not from eighteen-year-old Maria, the person doing the "heavy labor," who found Harmony to be "quite gay"; rather it came from her mother, a person without a place in communal life.

Sarah Pears quickly dismissed any hope that communal living would improve her life, and her letters record her growing disillusionment and depression, often resulting in her feeling "poorly." As Carroll Smith-Rosenberg has found in her study of the ailments of nineteenth-century American women, illness often represented the only legitimate rebellion women could engage in to escape from their prescribed, heaven-ordained "duties."[12] Set into a foreign environment with few amenities and an abysmal climate, given more work to do than in her previous life in Pittsburgh, Sarah Pears rebelled in the only way available to her. She became ill, too ill to "take her turn" at the cooking or washing, and she complained not to the hierarchy of the community, with positive suggestions for improving communal life, but to her aunt, safely removed in Pittsburgh.

At first Sarah Pears told her aunt that, "sick and debilitated in body, distressed and disappointed in mind, oppressed by extreme heat night and day such as I never before experienced, I felt utterly incapable of writing" (33). She complained that she could hardly get enough sleep. Then she wrote of feeling "excessively stupid and dull," and, finally, "hopeless."[13] As she herself felt worse, she viewed the events of the community from her increasingly pessimistic perspective. By the time Owen again returned to New Harmony in January 1826, after almost a six months' absence, Sarah Pears was confident that she "would never be able to perform what he expects" (60). New Harmony had taken away all the comforts of her life and replaced them with a rhetoric of equality but with a practice of inequality. Since New Harmony had none of the technological advances that Robert Owen advocated for getting the drudgery done, it was Sarah and her daughters who were to perform the drudgery.

The letters of other Owenite women substantiate Sarah Pears's fear of too much work to do. Marie Fretageot was a dedicated professional woman at New Harmony, in some ways the complete opposite of a Sarah Pears. In the early 1820s, with the help of her good friend William Maclure, Fretageot had established one of the finest and first Pestalozzian schools in the United States in Philadelphia. Fretageot's description of her subsequent hectic life at New Harmony helps to justify Sarah Pears's complaints. Fretageot listed her daily activities in one of her many letters to Maclure, who, like Owen, spent much of his time away from the community: "My school is going on pretty well. . . . I get up regularly at four o'clock." Her duties combined her professional pursuits as well as her "female duties," so that she was the busiest teacher in the community. From 4:00 A.M. until 6:30 A.M. Fretageot taught "twelve young men" who boarded with her; from 9:00 to 11:00 A.M. she instructed all of the children under twelve. After dinner she taught the smaller children again from 2:00 to 4:00 P.M. and once more received the twelve young men plus all the children above twelve from 6:00 to 8:00 P.M. The other hours, she said, "I am occupied cooking for the whole family. I may say that I have but very little the occasion of wearing out the chairs of the house, having not a single female to help me" (M/F, 391).

While her male colleagues were responsible for only a select group of older students, Fretageot taught all of the younger children as well as her "twelve young men," for whom she also had to cook and clean. The male teachers in the new Harmony school—Robert Dale Owen, William Maclure, Paul Brown—wrote of their casual days at New Harmony and of their many trips away from the community, but Fretageot left no comparable carefree epistles. She was continually in New Harmony working in some capacity "like a slave" and remaining to direct the schools until 1831, long after Owen's communal enterprise had been abandoned (M/F, 383).

Women were expected to perform the same kind of herculean tasks in other Owenite communities as well. In Franklin, Eliza M'Knight, the wife of the disgruntled James M'Knight, was as unhappy as her husband with the community life but for more concrete reasons. Her complaints were founded, in part, on the overwhelming amount of work a woman in an Owenite community had to perform. As M'Knight relates: "Twelve members boarded at our house and my wife, though a delicate woman, cooked for them, until she became so worn out with fatigue that I was obliged to hire a girl to assist her. She was told this trouble would be over as soon as the public dining room could be finished" (9). However, when the room was completed, Robert Jennings then instructed Eliza to "go to the public kitchen" and cook for everyone, despite his promises to her for a "resting spell."

But it was not just the excessive work that bothered the community women; they were also distressed about the kind of work they were required to do and the fact that they had no free time. As Sarah Pears writes about her duties at New Harmony: "My strength, which never was great and is much diminished since I came here, is unequal to taking my turn in the kitchen, which I find it is required that all should do by turns for six weeks together. No one is to be favored above the rest, as all are to be in a state of perfect equality" (60). Sarah's ironic restatement of Owen's theory that "all are to be in a state of perfect equality" gains its force from her own knowledge that the "all" required to take turns in the kitchen are only the women of the community, not the "all" who will be in the state of perfect equality.

Women in the Owenite communities were offered "regular employment," in accordance with Owen's theory that women would not be economically dependent upon men if they had livelihoods themselves. In theory, Owen's ideas sounded liberating for women, but in the patriarchal Owenite communities what happened in practice was that women who did work in "regular" positions then had to spend their "free" time doing traditional "female" work. For example, working women in New Harmony had to spend Sunday, the day the men relaxed, doing the washing, ironing, and other "female tasks." As Sarah Pears reveals in one of her letters home:

> Indeed the day [Sunday] here is only used as a day of recreation, visiting and amusement, military operations, and with some few of work. Those ladies who are in regular employment, having no time allowed them, have some excuse for washing, ironing, and doing their own sewing on the Sabbath. Every Sunday evening there is a meeting at which Mr. Owen reads over the particulars of the expenditures of the Society, and the amount of work performed by each occupation, and also the names of the workmen and women, with the characters attached to each. (83)

Whereas the men needed to perform only one service for the community, the women who worked "equally" alongside the men in communal enterprises discovered that their work was not over at the end of the working day or week; they were still responsible for their family's food, clothes, and dwelling place.

Sarah Pears and her friends, other married women who had come to New Harmony with their husbands, actively disliked New Harmony and spent much of their free time plotting their own private rebellions. Robert Owen's "reforms" to institute egalitarianism threatened their sense of themselves as dignified women in charge of their sacred homes. Simple dress reform became, to these women, representative of all that was bad in the Owenite communities. Railing against the new "costume" for women, a practical petticoat that Owen and other reformers prescribed for women's wear, Sarah Pears declared "absolute war against [it] . . . both for myself and my daughters" (42). In her last letter from New Harmony Sarah Pears described the new costume she opposed:

> I wish I felt in sufficient spirits to give you a description of the new costume which Mr. Owen has been trying very hard to introduce, and which has actually been adopted by several of the beaux and belles. The female dress is a pair of undertrowsers tied round the ankles over which is an exceedingly full slip reaching to the knees, though some have been so extravagant as to make them rather longer, and also to have the sleeves long. (82)

For married women, the communities were inimical to good living and common sense. In part, of course, many women were unprepared for the sheer amount of physical labor necessary to survive in a primitive community. In part, they were isolated from their families, far from loved ones and relatives who might help with child care and sewing. Many of the married women were quite miserable even on the way to New Harmony. Robert Dale Owen noticed on only the second day of his trip with the "Boatload of Knowledge" that "some of the ladies of our party" were already impatient and "dissatisfied, the more so because they almost can't do anything for themselves." Two days later the "ladies" were exhausted and without patience: "they complained publicly about their unhappy lot and did not want to believe me when I told them I felt quite well and found the journey to be above all quite amusing." The following day the ladies were "becoming even more disgusted, particularly S.T. [Sarah Turner] who cried this morning during breakfast." To the young Owen, the trip was a lark, a "good education for her [Sarah Turner] and for all of us." Not surprisingly, the young Owen believed that the women who fared well were the young, single ones, not the married, complaining ones.[14]

As James M'Knight had felt in Franklin, married women in the Owenite communities believed themselves to be powerless, and it was this feeling of powerlessness, even more than the hard physical labor, that caused their anguish and led to the communities' "woman problem." At New Harmony, Sarah Pears labeled the Preliminary Society, in which a married woman had no voice, a "despotism . . . it makes my blood boil within me to think that the citizens of a free and independent nation should be collected here to be made slaves of" (40). Just like James M'Knight, Sarah Pears was on the "outside" of the ruling elite and thus she continually referred to her position in the community as "a slave." But unlike M'Knight, Sarah did not write a scathing essay publicizing all the problems in an Owenite community; she vented her anger only privately—to her husband and children and to her aunt. Although she and her husband were supposed to be equal members of the community, Sarah knew that she was not. She also knew it was not her place to criticize openly.

Other married women also complained of the overregulation of their days and their time, and their lack of power to do as they wished. Lydia and Alma Eveleth wrote to Sarah Pears just as New Harmony was breaking up in the spring of 1827 to tell her, with glee, that "now, we can do as we please" (Pears, 88). Some of the women at Franklin once inquired whether they could go to church on Sunday morning but were told that "we have church in the dining room, every Sunday morning, at the usual hour." The required Sunday morning "services" consisted of a public recounting of work that had been accomplished during the week: "The members' names are first called over, beginning with the ladies. 'Well, Mrs. A. How many pairs of stockings have you knit during the week? Mrs. B. What sewing have you done? Mrs. C. What members have you washed for?—how many dozen clothes in all? Mrs. D. how much wool have you spun?' This is the way the *ladies* are obliged to spend the Sabbath morning" (M'Knight, 14).

Married women, especially those with children, had much to feel powerless about in the communities. The conditions in "the West" were difficult, at best, with little fresh food and dwindling commodities, including medical supplies and milk. As a mother of a fourteen-month-old when she came to New Harmony, Sarah Pears watched helplessly as the infants of two of her friends died—"young Mrs. Grant" lost her five-month-old baby, Sarah wrote to her aunt (34), and at the same time Mrs. Pearson's seven-month-old died while living at the Pears's house. Her striking imagery reflected her helplessness and subsequent alienation. She wrote that she heard "very little more of the old world than if I were an inhabitant of a different planet. I believe there are papers at the reading room, but only the male part of the community have as yet assumed the privilege of reading them" (53). Another time she wrote of being "out of humanity's reach" (41). Even when it came to such mundane daily activities as reading the newspapers that reached New Harmony from the "civilized" world, Sarah Pears was excluded.

For women like Sarah Pears, the hardships caused by frontier living coupled with excessive hard work and a lack of power led to depression and sickness. But the final blow that caused them to convince their husbands to leave the communities was losing their power in "their" sphere of influence to raise their children. Responding to rumors about the new schools in New Harmony shortly after the arrival of the Boatload of Knowledge (a term she had coined), Sarah Pears gloomily forecast: "all our elder children . . . are to be taken away from us, [and] are to be placed in large boarding houses. . . . Instead of our own dear children each housekeeper is to receive two more families, one of which will have a child under two years old. The rest will be at boarding school" (72–73). Sarah realized that when her children left her, her role, her purpose would be gone and she would no longer be able to "tell them to do anything. They will be completely taken from under my control" (74). The thought of having someone else, someone "wrong" taking her children from her and raising them, caused her great distress. As she said to her aunt, "it is impossible to express how completely miserable I am. . . . I know were I to consider this world only, I would rather, far rather, that Mr. Owen would shoot me through the head" (72–73). Reacting intensely against the imminent breakup of her family, Mrs. Pears implored her aunt: "Can you . . . conceive of anything so absurd as breaking up and dividing families in order to make them more comfortable? Comfort! Name not the word in Harmony, or at least in the Community of Harmony. And Equality!—It would be a total anomaly!" (73).

In Franklin, Eliza M'Knight felt the same passion as Sarah Pears did that someone else, someone "wrong" would be raising her children in a community where her value was only that of a cook and domestic worker. When Eliza was teaching her son his Bible lessons one Sunday, Henry Fay, the secretary of the community, said with a sneer: "How ridiculous it is to be teaching children such a *bundle of lies!*" This conversation had such an effect on her son that he said to his mother the next day, "what use is there in my learning the Bible, if it is all lies?" (M'Knight, 14). The outraged Eliza M'Knight approached Robert Jennings, and asked him if he would instruct children to believe in the Bible. When Jennings told her that the Bible was full of "superstitious notions" and that children had to be separated from other children and parents who might give them "erroneous notions" because they have been deluded by "priestcraft and foolish creeds," Eliza responded fiercely, "I have heard enough. . . . I see you are determined to destroy the youth with your infidelity. But I can assure you that you will not have *my* children to corrupt" (M'Knight, 12). True to her word, Eliza convinced her husband to leave the community immediately, even though James was hesitant to depart before he received pay for the work he had done. Eliza, adamant, told him she would rather beg for her bread than remain in Franklin.

What "equality" translated into for women like Sarah Pears and Eliza M'Knight was working hard plus giving up the power of being in charge of "their" home or child. This elimination of their one role—the True Woman in charge of her separate sphere—with no role to take its place created intense bitterness for married women living under Owen's "system."

By the summer of 1826 New Harmony's problems with women like Sarah Pears had spread, and even the community leaders had to address the "woman problem" because it threatened community cohesion and commitment. William Maclure mentioned the "discontent and dissatisfaction" of the community women in a letter to Fretageot, while proposing that this discontent could be alleviated if all women were made to do the "drudgery":

> Even in our small society certain ladies by not doing any of the drudgery caused the discontent and dissatisfaction which is doing 100 times more harm than all their labor at lessons can possibly do good; for it is clear that if one is exemp[t] from the hard labor when they have time, all has the same right; and it's too soon for the women of the society to understand the utility of education. Untill they do, all must participate of what is called manual labor, that is Cooking, Washing &C. . . . (M/F, 376)

William Pelham's son wrote to his father that the women in New Harmony "sometimes cannot agree among themselves who is cook" (June 10, 1827). Even Robert Owen had to acknowledge the "woman problem" and to confront the women's charge that their labor was "too onerous."[15] Just as Maclure was writing to Fretageot of the numbers of married women who had lately left New Harmony (August 21, 1826), Robert Owen was addressing his problem-plagued community in August 1826 on the "real cause" of the women's difficulty in performing their domestic duties: the reason, he said, was that they "talk too much." Owen explains in his typical, rational, patriarchal style:

> Female labor in a community would certainly under proper arrangements be lighter than it can ever be in individual society. Perhaps the true cause of the evil complained of, may be, that, when females who have heretofore been strangers to each other meet together in order to cooperate in some domestic labor, they spend time in talking, which should be devoted exclusively to work. Now they cannot talk and work too. . . . I can discover no other cause than the one assigned, why female cooperative labor should be more onerous than their individual and unaided exertions in individual society have been. (NHG, August 30, 1826)

Certainly in a community where true equality existed, female labor would be "lighter than it ever could be in individual society," but in a community where "equality" meant that women could have full-time employment as well as responsibility for their own family's domestic requirements, women's work was not "lightened." The cooking, cleaning, ironing, and sewing for the entire community fell to the women. Rather than being "relieved" of work, as was New Harmony's goal through the use of advanced technology, women often found their labor increased. Concomitantly, the men of New Harmony had a great variety of occupations open to them, and many of the men changed positions frequently, while others did nothing at all for long periods of time. William Maclure, William

Pelham, and Robert Dale Owen all left epistolary records of their own sporadic and changeable work histories. But since everyone had to eat and wear clothes every day, since children had to be fed and taken care of all the time, and since requisite daily domestic services fell to the women, they had little variety in their work, and less opportunity than men to shirk their duties.

By insulting the communal women, as he must have when he attributed the women's problems to their "talking too much," Owen only convinced them that communal life was not possible for them. As it was, his ideas, which included his wish to dissolve the nuclear family, threatened women's traditional sphere without replacing it with anything but more work to perform. Indeed, the "woman problem" at New Harmony stemmed not from "too much talking" but rather from too much work and from the leaders' inability to think of women except as unquestioning servers to the needs of men.

The "woman problem" that plagued New Harmony found its way into other communities as well. At Franklin, one nameless married woman, who discovered that "it was impossible to be happy in such a place," refused to let her husband pay the three hundred dollars he had subscribed to the community (M'Knight, 15). Eliza M'Knight, after great anguish, convinced her husband to leave the community. Unexpectedly seeing M'Knight a few days after he had withdrawn from the community, Robert Jennings told him he was "a fool" to have been "led away by your wife." M'Knight responded that he did not wish to remain in a situation "where my wife was unhappy." Jennings, less attuned to his own wife's needs, responded: "As to *my* wife . . . I don't mind what she says, if she is not satisfied she may take herself away" (M'Knight, 13). Jennings's response to his community's "woman problem" was to propose that future Owenite communities allow only unmarried people as members. As he said to the departing James M'Knight, "we have seen the impropriety of having married people among us; for the future we are determined to admit none but young men and women, as our social system will do better with them than with married folk; we shall also collect a number of orphan children who will know nothing of any other state of society than that which we are endeavouring to establish" (M'Knight, 13).

In Blue Spring, married women were equally unhappy. Women who had lived private lives in Indiana's farm country found themselves participating in a "Community of Equality," where they were expected to share labor and eat at a common table. As oral tradition has it, the women of the community did not like the common table. Women at the foot of the table believed, so it is said, that the coffee tasted like "too much Wabash"—i.e., too much Wabash River—by the time it reached them. Likewise, each woman suspected that her chores were the hard ones while other community women had easier chores. Some women feared that other members' husbands and children had better clothes and food than theirs. The climax of the conflict reputedly occurred when the women of the community disagreed as to the color to dye their husbands' homespun jeans. Each stubborn, adamant wife refused to compromise, and, according to one man recording the community's oral history, another utopian venture toppled. Though the perspective viewing the "stubborn" women is distinctly a male one, we can nonetheless see that at Blue Spring, as at New Harmony or Franklin, women's bickering within their spheres reflected their powerlessness.[16]

In the Yellow Springs Community unmarried women were as dissatisfied as the married women in other communities. Unmarried women had a different stake in communal life from most of the married women who came to the communities because of their husbands' wishes; unmarried women came to be part of the great experiment in egalitarianism. At Yellow Springs, the women's dissatisfactions, also exacerbated by the extraordinary amount of work they had to do, stemmed from the lack of sexual equality they found in communal life. According to legend, young unmarried women who in Cincinnati had cultivated "an attractive spirit of meekness" left their homes to join Yellow Springs and there insisted "upon equality." This insistence reputedly distracted these young women from their innate submissiveness, their self-abnegation, their untiring service. Soon the community disbanded because, according to the "leading minds," a "community of social equality . . . is impossible" (Mac Ms, 305). The equality proposed by the Owenites to ennoble all human beings was dysfunctional. Somebody had to perform the ceaseless domestic tasks so necessary for communal survival; if women were going to insist upon real "equality," then the communities might not run smoothly.

It is an ironic commentary that the experiment besieged with the fewest recorded "woman problems" was Kendal, the one Owenite community that made no promises about egalitarian living, at least in its first year. Though the community was founded "upon the principles set forth by Robert Owen," it was a community, like Blue Spring, populated during its first year by religious people who had lived and worshiped together long before they became interested in Owen's system. Perhaps one of the reasons Kendal lasted longer than any of the other Owenite communities, besides its common religious bond, was the absence of egalitarian tension. The questions that came up in every other Owenite community—what was "equality" and who was to be "equal"—simply never arose in Kendal during its first year of existence. Thus it resembled more a traditional religious utopia than an Owenite one.

Because of its religious background, the Kendal Community's first principle was not equality but, instead, "Love to the Great First Cause and Creator of all Things" (Preamble, K Const). Egalitarian discourse was conspicuously absent from the constitution. Though members of the community, women had no voting privileges (Article 20, K Const). The Kendal schools proposed no egalitarian education for both sexes. Boys were to learn "agriculture and some one mechanical art," while girls were to be taught "in a manner suitable to their sex, and that guardian care and protection extended to them that their situation may require" (Minutes, August 19, 1826).

With the arrival in the fall of 1827 of the "sceptic" Samuel Underhill and his coterie from the Forestville Community, egalitarian rhetoric began replacing religious references in the notes from the weekly meetings. At the December 15, 1827, meeting the membership petitions of the Under-hills, the Macys, the Fosdicks, and others from Forestville were accepted. Two weeks later the monthly "wages" for work done were suspended. By March of 1828 the Kendal members had approved a revised constitution. By April they voted that married women could become members upon signing the constitution. Robert Owen noted a thriving community when he visited in July of 1828.

Only after this egalitarian thrust did Kendal begin to have a "woman problem," just like the other Owenite communities. Samuel Underhill wrote to Robert Owen in May of 1828, inviting him to visit the community and sharing with him his thoughts about how Owenite communities could succeed. He noted that "men have been greatly devoted to the undertak-ing," but at the same time, "it has often happened that their wives were most bitterly opposed." Underhill expressed his dismay over this problem, which he credited to women's lack of education: "This is a sore evil and owes its existence to a want of acquaintance with the difficulties of individ-ual life and. . . to their [women] being cruelly kept in the background of intelligence" (RO Papers, #126). Underhill, was of course, correct; women in the 1820s had indeed been "kept in the background of intelligence." This lack of "mental pursuits" was one of the reasons for women's disaffection with the experiments. William Thompson, writing in 1824, best summed up what happened when women were not educated to the same principles as men. He wrote that the alienation of women from "mental pursuits necessarily throws all their exertions into the physical line—beauty, dress, manners, arts, etc." Because of their ignorance, Thompson wrote, women become selfish and wish to "bring down to their own level the . . . aspira-tions for knowledge of men. Whatever *not them* man sets his heart upon is with them *a rival*" (*Inquiry*, 299).

Yet, at the same time, Thompson and Underhill, like other Owenite reformers, assumed that education alone would eradicate "woman prob-lems." Perhaps with better education more women might have ventured to the Owenite experiments as potential reformers, but for those married women who tagged along because their husbands were enthused by Owen's system, a better education would not necessarily have given them a place in communal life; they would still have been "others," the sex that was promised equality yet lectured to and advised.

According to one Kendal resident, it was only a freakish summer fever in 1828, which killed the heads of seven families, that ended the experiment at

Kendal, but according to the records of the community meetings, what truly destroyed the community was the members' inability to get along. In the fall of 1828 all the former Forestville members asked to be released from the community, one after the other. They moved less than half a mile away to Massillion, to retreat to individual families. The equality that they had sought, that they had encouraged after they joined the community, could not be realized.

Although the Owenite communities established in the United States in the mid-1820s all stressed the importance of women's rights and promised equality for both men and women, all of them limited women's participation in some way. New Harmony and the other American Owenite communities claimed to have "equal educational opportunities" for both sexes, but employed gender-based training, because "useful" education meant training children for their future roles in life. Although women were expected to work "equally" with the men, the ideology of gender translated the notion of "equality" into more work for the women.

The message that comes from these Owenite communities is clear. Whether Woman was depicted as a self-sacrificing server, as in the *New Harmony Gazette*, or as the selfish cause of a community's collapse, she was a being entirely different from rational man. Neither of these abstract and extreme definitions rendered her a human being, a person who would participate fully in egalitarian living. Real-life women in the communities found themselves expected to perform all the ceaseless domestic tasks, but without the concomitant power associated with "their" sphere in the outside world. The powerless women devised tactics like those of the powerless in any age: dissimulation, illness, covert criticism written in letters "home," or "talking too much." Unable, or unwilling, to change the community, perhaps knowing that they did not have the power to effect change, these women vented their hostilities within their private families. Unable to own any part of the community, women urged their men to leave community life. Being a woman in utopia meant performing endless "women's" work so that the makers and doers of utopia could get on with their attempts to change the world—without altering in any way the politics of a patriarchal system.

Robert Owen (courtesy of the Library of Congress)

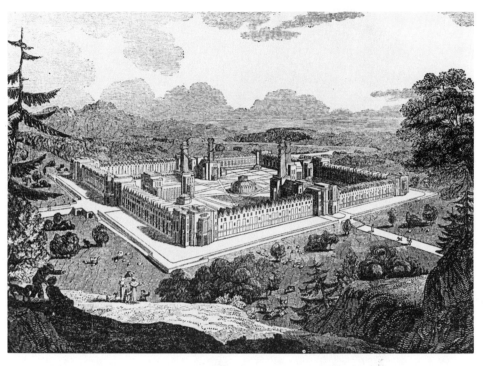

Robert Owen's parallelogram (courtesy of the Library of Congress)

William Maclure (courtesy of the Library of Congress)

Madame Marie Fretageot (courtesy of the New Harmony Workingmen's Institute)

Community House No. 2 at New Harmony, site of the school (courtesy of the Library of Congress)

Robert Dale Owen (courtesy of the Library of Congress)

Frances Wright, by Henry Inman (courtesy of The New York Historical
Society, New York City)

Camilla Wright (courtesy of Kenneth Dale Owen)

George Flower (courtesy of the Library of Congress)

Eliza Flower (courtesy of the Chicago Historical Society)

Thomas Steel's sketches of a log cabin that was in the vicinity of Equality Community and of the house he owned after leaving community (courtesy of the State Historical Society of Wisconsin)

CHAPTER
4

FRANCES WRIGHT
A Woman in Utopia

Frances Wright was the first woman in this
country who spoke on the equality of the
sexes. She had indeed a hard task before
her. . . . She had to break up the time-hard-
ened soil of conservatism, and her reward
was sure—the same reward that is always
bestowed upon those who are in the vanguard of any great movement. She was subjected to public odium, slander, and
persecution.

—Ernestine Rose at the tenth National
Woman's Rights Convention (1859)

For if contemporary women do now attempt
the pen with energy and authority, they are
able to do so only because their eighteenth-
and nineteenth-century foremothers strug-
gled in isolation that felt like illness, alienation that felt like madness, obscurity that felt
like paralysis to overcome the anxiety of authorship that was endemic to their literary
subculture.

—Gilbert and Gubar, *The Madwoman
in the Attic* (1979)

Most of the women members in the Owenite experiments were wives of
men who had joined the communities, and for that fact alone, the communities were not "theirs." In New Harmony as in the other Owenite communities women were primarily viewed as outsiders or interlopers. As J. F. C.
Harrison tellingly writes in his *Quest for the New Moral World:* "If the
[Owenite] communities are surveyed as a whole the total membership
embraces a wide range of social status and occupation. Retired phi-
lanthropists, business men, professionals, intellectuals, farmers, skilled

111

artisans, and labourers—together *with their wives and children* can be found" (184, my emphasis). To Harrison, as well as to many of the people living in the Owenite communities, women, particularly married women, were not even considered to be members, despite their constitutional guarantees. Always women were the objects of action—of advice, of encouragement, of chastisement—not the doers and planners of action. As we have seen in the previous chapter, this lack of power over even their domestic sphere, coupled with extraordinary amounts of enforced work, caused much bitterness among community women.

Few women escaped being such objects in nineteenth-century life, even in utopian communites created as "communities of equality." That one woman tried to create her own community of equality rather than being an object in someone else's speaks to her extraordinary perseverance and dedication. Frances Wright, one of the most despised women of the nineteenth century, and one of the least remembered in the twentieth,[1] attempted even more than Owen: she designed and began a community to end slavery in America. After her community ended, Wright became the most important extender of Owenite thought as she remained dedicated to Owenite principles for her lifetime.

Frances Wright came to her ideas much the same way Robert Owen did, first by being a reformer in her own right, then by using the idea of a community of property as the vehicle by which her reforms could be realized, and finally by focusing on reforms that would increase women's individual rights. She was predisposed to the notion of reform as a young, highly intelligent woman who rejected the role British society had set for her in the 1820s. Born in Scotland in 1795 of a bluestocking mother and a liberal father who admired Thomas Paine, she was orphaned before she was three. Raised by her aunt, Frances Campbell, who subscribed to quite traditional ideas on proper girls' behavior, Wright early on initiated her pattern of rebellion. As she turned eighteen, Wright, with her younger sister, Camilla, left her aunt's home in southern England, where she had lived since early childhood, and returned to Glasgow, to live with her father's uncle, James Mylne. There, from 1814 through 1818, she lived with the same people who had stimulated Robert Owen when he was in New Lanark; her great-uncle was Owen's acquaintance, if not friend. Mylne, like Owen, believed in the utilitarian premise that happiness for the greatest number was the greatest good, and that reason would show the way to obtain this happiness. His wife, the former Agnes Millar, was the daughter of John Millar, a man who counted among his friends Adam Smith, David Hume, and others closely associated with the Scottish Enlightenment. Millar, like others, including Wright's father, supported the principles of the American and French revolutions.

In this ambience Frances lived for five years, surrounded by supportive mother surrogates (her great-aunt Agnes and specifically her aunt's sister-in-law Robina Craig Millar) and brilliant men. She sought their advice, read what they gave her, and spent her time writing. She wrote tragic drama (one play survives, *Altorph*) and a treatise on Greek philosophy, *A Few Days in Athens*. That she took herself seriously was wholly unusual in the early nineteenth century. But even serious reading and writing were not enough for Fanny, who shared her father's and great-uncle's love of the principles of *fraternité* and *égalité*. She had her own need to visit "a young country inhabited by freemen" (Wright, *Biography,* 14). As soon as both she and her sister were of age, Wright set off with Camilla for the potential freedom of America, which she had read of and heard about from Robina Millar. The summer of 1818 found the two young women sailing for America.

Wright's first trip to America was full of successes. Introduced to a banker, Charles Wilkes, who helped her with her finances, and to the Garnett family, including the three daughters who remained her good friends for over a decade, Wright was feted by wealthy New York society. Her influential new friends helped her get her play *Altorph* produced on Broadway in February of 1819, though she had to keep the play's female authorship a secret, which displeased her. Fascinated by America, Fanny wrote an epistolary record of her experiences there from 1818 to 1820, *Views of Society and Manners in America*, which was to become her most popular book. Its writing provided her with her first occasion to synthesize the issues that had occupied her mind in Glasgow during the previous two years and were to become so important in her life.

Both her great-uncle James Mylne and her great-great-uncle Millar had been fervently opposed to the slave trade. In her book, the first recordings of her reform thought, she sees the horrors of slavery from an outsider's point of view and thus she brings the fresh perspective of a young woman's horror to an old American problem. As she writes just returned from America: "When my thoughts turn to America the crying sin of her slavery weighs upon my heart; there are moments when this foul blot so defaces to my mind's eye all the beauty of her character that I turn with disgust from her, and in her from the last and only nation on the globe to wch my soul clings with affection, pride and hope" (F. Wright to Garnett Sisters, October 1820, G-P Collection).

Wright also brings a fresh perspective to another "problem" she writes of in her book, but in discussing this issue she sees it as an insider, not an outsider. Specifically, Wright was fascinated with the rearing and educating of women and wrote of problems in women's education in the early nine-teenth century from a firsthand point of view. Having had access to fine private libraries since she was a child, Wright realized early that education was a key to changing women's role in society. It was, along with the abolition of slavery, her prime concern, and it would be for life. Having studied the same Enlightenment figures as Robert Owen, Wright compre-hended the same thing Owen did—that women's inferior education and social conditioning led to inferior adult lives. Wright understood the prob-lem, though, from her own personal history, being a female not allowed to attend Glasgow University. Thus she specifically devoted part of her book to the rearing of young women. Women's education, claimed Wright in her book, "has been slightly attended to." If women have ambition, she wrote, "the road to honorable distinction is shut against them," and if they have intellect, "it is broken down by sufferings, bodily and mental" (22, 222).

In Great Britain from 1820 to 1824, Wright continued to develop her ideas on the importance of education and human liberty. Because of her illustrious family and because of her own initiative and growing fame as a critic of Tory England, she had instant connections with many of the great thinkers of the 1820s. An outspoken young woman with a brilliant mind, she formed friendships with two of the most important men in Europe—Jeremy Bentham and General Lafayette. Though her relationship with Bentham appears to have been innocuous, her relationship with the general was more complicated. From the first moment she met him—she initiated the meeting by going, uninvited, to his chateau in France—she encouraged a passionate relationship, much to the horror of his family, who noted that he was old enough to be her father. She proposed to him, then suggested that he adopt her as his legal daughter; she (and her sister as well) often referred to him as "Father," all the time giving him lively companionship and learning from him. Their intimacy, whether that of friends or lovers, helped give her more intellectual confidence as she wrote and planned grand schemes for liberating the world. When Lafayette sailed for America in 1824, Wright and her sister were close behind. Though propriety did not allow them to travel together, wherever the general visited, Fanny and Cam would appear a few days later and join him.

From her first letter to her friends the Garnett sisters, shortly after her second arrival in the United States, Wright's growing hatred of slavery occupied much of her time. Influenced by General Lafayette's own pet reform scheme to liberate his slaves in French Guiana, Wright saw, on this second trip to America, more flaws in the New World. Spending seven out of nine months in slave states, where she saw slavery first-hand, Wright discovered the hypocrisy of the white elite: "I see already that we shall find here as in Norfolk much pleasing and polished society—but my thoughts and feelings ever wander from it contrasting the condition of the proud and accomplished master with [that of] the debased and injured slave [to whom] that master's will is law—Amid all the politeness I see and attention I receive my heart is sick" (F. Wright to J. Garnett, October 30, 1825, G-P Collection).

The more she saw of slavery, the more Wright became personally involved in the issue, taking the idea of eradicating slavery as her own and removing herself from her uncles' ideas and the general's plans. Her thoughts and inquiries during her second visit to America were "engrossed by & directed almost exclusively to, the subject of slavery" (F. Wright to J. Garnett, June 8, 1825, G-P Collection). Visiting Thomas Jefferson at Monticello in November 1824, Wright heard of his plan to emancipate his slaves and learned that "Hayti" offered a "safe and convenient haven" for the blacks in the United States. There she also became aware of Jefferson's antipathy to the amalgamation of the races—as she says, "the prejudice whether absurd or the contrary against a mixture of the two colors is so deeply rooted in the American mind that emancipation without expatriation (if indeed the word be applicable) seems impossible" (F. Wright to J. Garnett, November 12, 1824, G-P Collection). Yet Wright could also see that Jefferson was not doing anything to implement his plans for slaves' emancipation.

The catalyst that moved Wright to action came in February of 1825 in Washington, D.C., when Robert Owen spoke to Congress. After hearing Owen talk about his new moral world and the possibilities inherent in communalism (or hearing of his talk), Wright and her sister visited New Harmony in March on their way to New Orleans to meet Lafayette. Fanny was greatly impressed with the industriousness of the Rappites still working in New Harmony and with the Owenite promises of a Community of Equality to come. Meeting George Flower at New Harmony, Wright and her sister rode on horseback to his home in Albion, Illinois, where they learned that Flower had been instrumental in helping some free blacks emigrate to Haiti during the early 1820s when many blacks were captured by unscrupulous backwoodsmen to sell into slavery. They also heard about a project in Edwardsville, where Edward Coles had purchased a large tract of land upon which he taught slaves he freed how to work for themselves.

On her second trip to New Harmony to see "Mr. Owen and his plan in operation," Wright decided to create an intentional community where blacks could "work out" their freedom while, at the same time, they and their children could become educated and be prepared for life as free men and women (F. Wright to J. Garnett, April 12, 1825, G-P Collection). As she says in a letter to her friend Julia Garnett, "it was not until I visited for the second time the settlement of Harmonie in Indiana, considered attentively the practice of its original German proprietors, together with the system now commenced by Mr. Owen that I distinctly conceived the only scheme wch I believe capable of being rendered *general* and consequently efficient in its effects" (June 8, 1825, G-P Collection).

Despite the fact that, later in her life, Wright would disavow Robert Owen's influence upon her, her letters to the Garnett sisters and her writing at the time reveal her and Camilla's growing enthusiasm for Owen's "plan" to save the world, and they illustrate just how Owenite Wright's own version of utopia was. Sharing with Owen an identical background in the Scottish Enlightenment and common acquaintances in Glasgow, Wright accepted his rationale for beginning a community. "After considering his [Frederick Rapp's] system & practice together with those of Mr. Owen . . . [and seeing] that the effects of united labor are . . . so greatly exceeding those of individual labor," she realized that if individual labor could not "stand in competition with united labor in a free state how much less cd it do so within the regions of slavery" (F. Wright to J. Garnett, June 8, 1825, G-P Collection). In accord with Owen's logic, she wrote, as her great-uncle had taught her, that "men are virtuous, in proportion as they are happy, and happy in proportion as they are free," but that "freedom" is "but a chimera" without "equality." Finally, she concluded, as had Owen before her, that "equality may be best, perhaps only obtained by a union of interests and cooperation in labor" (*NHG*, January 30, 1828).[2]

The more Wright saw Robert Owen, the more she wanted to pattern her community after his. After becoming acquainted with Owen's ideas, Wright detoured from her prescribed path to New Orleans to meet General Lafayette. Both times she visited New Harmony in the spring of 1825 she was impressed with the possibility that communal life could work better than any other plan to liberate people, particularly slaves. Like Owen before her, Wright was not interested in plans she had heard from Jefferson or even from Flower simply to send blacks to Haiti—as Owen hadn't been interested in helping poor people by giving them money. Her fascination with Owen's communal life was that it promised, according to Owen at least, a way for poor, landless people to benefit from their own labor. Likewise, Wright believed slaves could work their way to freedom in a painless way. Her plans, on paper at least, looked promising. She wrote to Julia:

> [Having] already ascertained that [in] 4 to 6 years [it] is considered a good negro will work out his value. Four years wd certainly suffice on our improved system—Commencing at this calculation with 100 slaves in 50 years 188,800 parents, with the children born during that period wd be redeemed.—Two such establishments wd shorten the term for the redemption of the same no to 29—four such to 16 & 1/2 years—exceeding the whole no of slaves in Kentucky in the year 1820. (June 8, 1825, G-P Collection)

At the same time, Wright wrote to Julia that she wanted to visit Mr. Owen's "Society" a third time because he "is working miracles and promises fair to revolutionize a 2d time the North as I pray we may do the South" (June 8, 1825, G-P Collection).

Camilla too, was much taken with Robert Owen. Content with following her sister wherever she went, Cam wrote letters to the Garnett sisters that inevitably reflected Fanny's perspective. She wrote to Julia of the "truth" of Owen's ideas and, indirectly, of why her sister had begun an Owenite community:

> The principles advocated by Owen are to change the face of the world as surely as the sun shines in the heavens—this is my calm opinion it does not rest upon the man but on the principles with wch that man stands connected—these principles have been mine ever since I learnt to think & in opening to you the secret projects of Owen. I shall have to open also my

own mind—Not even to you did I ever disclose some opinions in wch I never expected to find sympathy, or conceived they could ever form more than a theory—Owen has discovered the means of connecting the theory with practice. One word opened to me a new world—reconciled me with life, & gave me hopes for the human race as high as my former despair had been deep. (December 8, 1826, G-P Collection)

Should they ever become destitute, Camilla believed that New Harmony would be their "resource and resting place & one that I could look to with infinite satisfaction" (January 10, 1826, G-P Collection). Wright agreed with her sister's perception of Owen's "system" and added: "poor human life—what is it worth unless Owen can mend it!" (to J. Garnett, April 11, 1826, G-P Collection).

Before beginning her community to liberate America's slaves, Wright asked many important men for advice. First, of course, she sought General Lafayette's "permission and approval" (F. Wright to J. Garnett, June 8, 1825, G-P Collection). Lafayette did give her his "blessing" but cautioned her as to the dangers involved in opposing southern whites. In some ways Fanny saw herself carrying out the general's plan but in a manner that she believed could work. As she wrote to Julia, "I am perhaps the only indivl (with the exception of the beloved Gen), who cd enter on or carry thro such an undertaking" (June 8, 1825, G-P Collection).

Other men, though, did not give her their "blessings" as easily. DeWitt Clinton, the governor of New York from 1817 to 1823 and again from 1825 to 1828, sidestepped her adroitly when he told her that she "had given him a more correct view of the whole surface of Southern slavery than he had previously rec'd. That the plan [presented] to his mind was so new and promised apparently in its results to influence so importantly the future destinies of a large portion of the country that he wished before giving me his opinion to weigh and digest the matter at leisure" (F. Wright to J. Garnett, June 8, 1825, G-P Collection). Wright also sought the help of General Andrew Jackson, whose residence near Nashville, Tennessee, would help deteremine the location of the community, "shd he prove favourable" (F. Wright to J. Garnett, June 8, 1825, G-P Collection). At the same time, other important men, such as Charles Wilkes, overtly disapproved of Fanny's plan but were charmed by her enthusiasm for such an idealistic project. Wilkes wrote to the Wright sisters in the winter of 1826: "I am assured you wd not have rested in peace without making the experiment & tho' I have no belief whatever in its success I sincerely wish you all the satisfaction your ardor & enthusiasm in a good tho' hopeless cause so well deserve" (C. Wright to J. Garnett, January 10, 1826, G-P Collection). Wilkes believed Fanny's attempt to save the world to be an amusing pastime for a wealthy dilettante.

Wright found some supporters at New Harmony, where she met numerous people who promised to help her begin her communal venture. She wrote to Julia that "a very amiable young man" who had conducted schools similar to Owen's at New Lanark "engaged me immedly his services as schoolmaster," while another person volunteered himself as physician. At the same time, Flower, who Wright says was "working night and day in the cause of the negro," promised to engage to supply all the stock and help direct the new establishment.[3]

In October of 1825 Wright began publicizing her "Plan for the Gradual Abolition of Slavery" anonymously in the abolitionist journal, *The Genius of Universal Emancipation.* By using "united labor," her advertisement read, slaves would be able to work for their liberation. On December 10, Benjamin Lundy, the editor of *The Genius,* revealed that the plan was Miss Wright's and that she would have the assistance of George Flower. By mid-December Wright had purchased 320 acres of land in southwestern Tennessee on the Wolf River some fifteen miles from Memphis. The land, according to Wright, was "gently undulating and hilly what is called thro'out the great western valley *rolling.*" Sleeping with "my saddle for a pillow," Wright traveled by horseback, sometimes up to forty miles a day, to oversee the construction of houses on her land, which she placed within a quarter of a mile from the bank of the Wolf River. With the arrival of Flower's wife and children and Camilla Wright in late February 1826, as well as donated slaves (a mother and six daughters from South Carolina) and eight purchased slaves (five men and three women), who would work until they had earned their freedom, Frances Wright's experiment, the Nashoba Community, began.[4]

As at New Harmony, Nashoba began full of hope and expectation for what it would accomplish. Pleased that she had received at least one donation from a wealthy Quaker merchant in New York to help her outfit her store, and expecting any day a carpenter, blacksmith, and shoemaker, Wright overlooked, in her first optimistic months at Nashoba, the fact that she had to use more than a third of her inheritance to cover her starting-up expenses. She wrote to Julia of her pleasure with their recruits—namely James Richardson, an ex-medical student whom they "found" in Memphis recovering from a long illness. Wright believed Richardson would make an excellent assistant to help conduct the community's business because of his "invaluable qualities," particularly "prudence," and his accurate attention to business details. That he possessed a "finely cultivated mind" along with "every liberal and generous opinion and sentiment" was only an added bonus (F. Wright to J. Garnett, April 11, 1826, G-P Collection). Though the community began small, Wright hoped for an orderly, pleasurable existence. She planned to construct a washhouse and bathhouse on the river, to start a dairy, and, "in time," to "open some beautiful wooded pastures and retired walks extending our meadows along the . . . watery bottoms" (F. Wright to J. Garnett, April 11, 1826, G-P Collection).

As Wright conceived it, equality would be the norm at Nashoba, both for blacks and for women. Like New Harmony, Nashoba had as its "one great end" the liberty and equality of all its members (*NHG*, February 6, 1828). Like New Harmony, Nashoba was founded on the principle of community of property. Nashoba also intended to provide a school for its children, with teachers and equipment promised by William Maclure. But unlike New Harmony, the Nashoba school included black children in its plans, and Nashoba's laborers were slaves working for their emancipation. The community's admission requirements were also to be much stricter than New Harmony's. Wright proposed that at Nashoba, the admission of a husband did not guarantee the admission of a wife, nor did the admission of a wife insure the admission of her husband; rather "each individual must pass through a separate trial and be received or rejected on the strength of his or her merits or demerits."[5] Perhaps learning a lesson from the Owenites in New Harmony, Wright specified that all potential members be told not to seek Nashoba with a notion of superintending the work of others. Young men were recommended to apply themselves to a useful trade such as carpentry, bricklaying, or farming. Young women were "equally recommended" to acquire a previous knowledge of some useful employment (*NHG*, February 13, 1828).

Possibly because she was herself a woman in utopia, Frances Wright created, on paper at least, a community attuned to the needs of women. Women's rights were spelled out more explicitly at Nashoba than at any other nineteenth-century community. At Nashoba, Wright dictated that "no woman can forfeit her individual rights or independent existence, and no man assert over her any rights or power whatsoever . . .nor, on the other hand, may any women assert claims to the society or peculiar protection of an individual of the other sex, beyond what mutual inclination dictates and sanctions, while to every individual member of either sex is secured the protection and friendly aid of all" (*NHG*, February 6, 1828). At Nashoba, all young minds were to learn rational thinking in order to discern the absurdity and ignorance abounding in society's laws and opinions about women.

Despite Wright's plans, though, Nashoba, like New Harmony and the other Owenite experiments, failed in many ways to live up to the hopes for it during its four-year existence. The most obvious problems were the same ones that plagued New Harmony and the other Owenite communities: too little money, too little food, and too much to do to maintain civilized life in the middle of "the West." Though Wright had proposed that every member build "himself or herself" a house, after four years Nashoba consisted of only three or four log houses and a few small cabins for the slaves. Milk, butter, cheese, meat, and fresh vegetables were consistently absent from "the common table," where everyone ate. The proposed school, "erected for the children of the establishment; and for the reception, afterwards, of other children from individual society; to be received, without regard to color," never materialized, though the slave children were taught by different members of the community. A visitor to Nashoba in the winter of

1828 wrote that the total Nashoba school population consisted of "three yellow children running wild in the swamps" (F. Trollope to Charles Wilkes, February 14, 1828, G-P Collection).[6]

At Nashoba, unlike at New Harmony, where over a thousand people had flocked to the new community, a further problem exacerbated the economic difficulties—a lack of public interest and subsequent recruits. Both the climate and primitive conditions—mixed, of course, with widespread disapproval of the amalgamation of the races that might be found there—contributed to the lack of public enthusiasm and support for Nashoba. At all times, the community remained "a small circle," with no more than thirty to forty slaves and a handful of white residents. For a time, the "small circle" of Richardson, the Wright sisters, and George and Eliza Flower, as well as the slaves, appeared to be making a success of communal life in Tennessee, but less than a year into the project, the Flower family moved back to Illinois and took with them much of the practical knowledge of farming.

During her first summer in Tennessee, in 1826, Wright became ill with fever, probably malaria, and her recurring illness forced her to take a convalescent trip to Europe the following summer. Her absence, coming in the wake of the Flowers' defection eight months earlier, caused yet another problem for the struggling community. With Wright and George Flower both gone, the community lost its founders' impulses. Left under the care of Camilla; James Richardson, the ex-medical student; and Whitby, the New Harmony recruit, Nashoba turned into a public scandal.

As Wright was sailing to Europe, Richardson gave a copy of the "Nashoba Book," a journalistic account of life at Nashoba, to Benjamin Lundy to publish in its entirety in *The Genius of Universal Emancipation* in late July 1827. Included in this journal was a juicy piece of information: on June 17, 1827, Richardson had informed the slaves that he and "Mam'selle Josephine," a young, attractive daughter of a free black woman recently moved to Nashoba, had begun living together the previous night (*Genius*, July 28, 1827). With the publishing of this account of the long-suspected immorality and miscegenation at Nashoba, public outrage against Wright's "free love colony" sprang up all over the country. The Wright sisters' wealthy and conservative friend, banker Charles Wilkes, wrote to Nashoba asking for an explanation of the incident, which he hoped was "exaggerated," but Camilla responded with vehemence in her sister's absence. Rather than disapproving of Richardson's living arrangement, Camilla wrote to Wilkes that her disapproval was of "the Marriage tie, wh. I regard as not only in the utmost degree irrational, in requiring of two individuals to love each other during life, when they have not the control of their affections for one hour, but in the highest degree pernicious in compelling these individuals to continue united, when the feelings which brought them together have turned to utter aversion." Mr. Richardson's conduct, concluded Camilla, "far from exciting my reprobation, or that of any individual associated here," had the community's sanction and approval.[7]

Camilla's response, in effect, helped close the door on the benevolence of proper society in America. Wilkes, formerly an avid supporter of both Wright sisters, who had patronizingly advised them of the impracticality of establishing a community like Nashoba, now censored them for overstepping proper bounds, and the loss of his support is indicative of the loss of support generally for them. Their relatives and friends wrote one another in horror: James Mylne wrote to Julia Garnett after hearing that Fanny had left Camilla at Nashoba in the company of "negroes in all the debasement of ignorance and slavery" while she went to Europe. Mylne was particularly incensed by Wright's "senseless system" based on a community of property and, even worse in his eyes, on "atheism and intercourse of the sexes unrestrained except by choice of the parties" (August 12, 1827, G-P Collection). Where Fanny and Camilla had been New York's darlings in 1824, they were no longer considered so three years later. Wright's attempts to defuse the issue went unnoticed. She did write Richardson, telling him that she believed the Nashoba papers to be "unfit for publication" and wondered if, perhaps, he had intended the papers to be a private letter. She reminded Richardson that "all principles are liable to misinterpretation but none so much as ours. If good taste and good feeling do not dictate their expression and guide their practice, they will fall into . . . contempt" (August 18, 1827, G-P Collection). None of Wright's efforts succeeded, though, because what Nashoba stood for—a radical restructuring of society—was simply too abhorrent. That this restructuring was suggested by a woman made the message even more unpalatable.

When Wright returned to Nashoba in December 1827, she found it drastically altered. Richardson and Josephine had departed, and her sister was married to Richesson Whitby. Whitby was, by one account at least, "coarse-minded and uneducated," a "surly brute" (F. Trollope to Garnetts, April 27, 1828, G-P Collection). Yet another account says that Whitby was a "great, handsome, coarse animal, without education, decent breeding, or good morals," but that Camilla found him delirious in his cabin and nursed him back to health. Despite his "coarseness," Camilla, according to legend, fell in love with him, though she "awakened from the horrid spell" and later fled from him.[8]

Though Camilla told none of her friends in England the reason for her marriage, she hinted of "circumstances" that were impossible to explain by letter: "the tidings of my union with our associate Richesson Whitby will ere this have reached you and no doubt after the perusal of my phillippic against matrimony will not a little have surprized you.—I shall only observe that the circumstances which induced me to conform to the legal ceremony of marriage were of a very peculiar nature and such as it were impossible to explain by letter" (April 26, 1828, G-P Collection). Frances

Trollope suggested to the Garnett sisters that the reason Camilla married the brutish Whitby had to be an unexpected pregnancy, but there is no evidence that Trollope was correct. Camilla did get pregnant in mid-1828, over six months after she married, and had a son in early 1829.

Back in Nashoba, Wright, by necessity, began to shift her emphasis. The "small circle" of white residents was growing smaller all the time. It was, by the winter of 1828, limited to Whitby, Cam, and Wright herself, with Robert Dale Owen an occasional visitor. The only other visitors were Frances Trollope, three of her children, a servant, and a potential Nashoba schoolmaster who left Nashoba after only a ten-day residence, appalled by the "desolation" of Wright's "forest home" and by Wright's fanaticism (Trollope, *Domestic Manners*, 39).

Though Wright attempted even more reforms at Nashoba than the reformers did at New Harmony or any of the other Owenite communities, she and her "small circle of friends" brought with them to communal life, as did all the Owenite reformers, ideologies that undermined what they were trying to accomplish. At Nashoba, the most obvious ideology—that of race—was operative, ironically, because of Nashoba's idealistic attempt to eradicate slavery. At New Harmony, "people of color" were simply forbidden from becoming members, and thus New Harmony suffered no discrepancy between what was promised to blacks and the reality they found there. Given the purpose of Nashoba—to allow slaves to work their way to freedom while receiving an education—it is not surprising that the white residents held the power while the slaves had as little of it there as they had had elsewhere. While Nashoba's intentions were liberating for slaves, they found themselves still subject to the whim of masters and mistresses. As it worked out, white members could try to implement certain Owenite proposals more easily at Nashoba than at the other Owenite communities because the slaves could not put an end to experimentation by leaving the community.

In New Harmony, Owen's attempts to remove children from their parents failed because of protests by women like Sarah Pears. At Nashoba, the slave children were taken away from their families in order to educate them away from their parents' influence. Shortly after Wright left for her recuperative trip to Europe in the early summer of 1827, Camilla told the slaves that the children would be placed under a free black woman's care and that "all communication between parents and children shall, in future, be prevented, except such as may take place by the permission, and in the presence of, the manager of the children" (*Genius*, July 28, 1827).

Similarly, slaves were reprimanded, told that they were not allowed to receive pay for extra work, and directed to eat meals together in the public rooms instead of with their private families, as they preferred. When one slave, Isabel, complained that a male slave "took liberties with her person," Camilla condemned his behavior, repeating that "we consider the proper basis of all sexual intercourse to be the unconstrained and unrestrained choice of *both* parties" (*Genius,* July 28, 1827). But in what must be considered an overenthusiastic reliance on doctrine over common sense (and a lack of respect for an individual slave woman's need), Camilla refused Isabel's request for a lock for her door because "[our] doctrine which we are determined to enforce . . . will give to every woman a much greater security than any lock can possibly do" (*Genius,* July 28, 1827). It is not surprising that the slaves' response to the egalitarian doctrine was skeptical, as it was imposed upon them in much the same way as other masters' ideas had been. One slave, Dilly, grumbled justifiably about having "so many mistresses." The Owenite response that she was given—that it was good not to be at the mercy of one master or mistress—probably did not make sense to her as she now had to obey several owners rather than one.

Nashoba also suffered from its own version of the "woman problem" that plagued the other Owenite communities. George Flower's departure from Nashoba is a revealing amplification of why families left experimental Owenite communities. The reason Flower left Nashoba is similar to the reason many families left New Harmony: his wife's unhappiness living in the new "system." Fanny and Camilla had liked George Flower instantly when they met him in New Harmony in March of 1825. He was, according to Camilla, "one of the most amiable beings I have ever known, and possessed all the qualifications that go to form an agreeable and intelligent companion" (C. Wright to J. Garnett, January 10, 1826, G-P Collection). His only flaw, "respectability in marriage," the Wright sisters were perfectly happy to overlook.[9]

Frances Wright and George Flower had worked together on the Nashoba project from the beginning. Flower met Wright in New York in July of 1825 to help with the plans for Nashoba and then rode with her to Nashville, Tennessee, in the early fall to meet with Andrew Jackson. From there they rode to Memphis to inspect the land. Flower ordered supplies and in mid-November rode back to Albion to secure additional provisions and to bring his wife, children, and Camilla to the community.

When Wright and Flower were in Tennessee organizing the beginning of the community, Cam stayed in Albion with Eliza Flower and her three children. At the time Camilla wrote glowing letters about Eliza's character; she was

> [an] admirable woman who possesses one of the most noble, generous, and candid minds I have ever known in life. . . . We understand each other perfectly and I believe the person in the world next to her husband she confides in the most, is myself and she is so frank, so open, so candid in her disposition and intercourse. I often tell her that come what will there can never be a misunderstanding [or] concealment between her and me. (To J. Garnett, January 10, 1826, G-P Collection)

At the same time that Camilla extolled her new friend's candidness, she noted that Eliza's affections were "entirely centered in her husband and children and while I admire and esteem her as my friend I do not and shall never feel for her that affection that constitutes real friendship." Less than a year later, Eliza's family-centeredness would cause the Flowers to leave Nashoba, never to return.

Eliza was the interloper at Nashoba, the one person who did not fit in. As Cam wrote to Julia Garnett, after the Flowers had departed: "she is not in any way suited to fill any situation in this establishment nor does she possess a mind calculated to enter into the views connected to it" (December 8, 1826, G-P Collection). Eliza was in the same precarious position as Sarah Pears at New Harmony and Eliza M'Knight at Franklin: that of an outsider who did not believe in the "system" and who had no power within it because she had joined communal life as an appendage to her husband. But in Eliza Flower's case, she had an additional worry—her husband's devotion to another woman.

Eliza Flower's discontent probably sprang from various reasons, not the least of which was George's attachment to Frances Wright. Wright's fervor, her altruism, her energy were the sparks that ignited George Flower's own willingness to leave his quite comfortable home in Albion and venture into the wilds of Tennessee, with no comforts except intellectual ones. The primitive log cabins and the lack of food were obviously problems to everyone at Nashoba, but all the white adult residents except Eliza Flower had gone there because of their dedication either to Wright or to their belief in her system to end slavery (or both). Only Eliza was present as a "wife." At least one of Wright's friends hints that Wright and George Flower had an affair before she purchased Nashoba: Frances Trollope (who traveled to America without her husband but with a young male artist) reported to Harriet Garnett that Fanny "had had a connection with George Flower . . . before she purchased Nashoba" (December 7, 1828, G-P Collection).[10]

The epistolary evidence suggests that it was Eliza, not George, who wished to leave the community. George Flower's letter to the Wright sisters after having left Nashoba depicts a man who did not leave willingly: "just to hear the sound of yr voices and see the lines of yr countenances. . . . All these things you know are necessary to come to the heart of the matter. To view those remote, or as they are called, the secret springs of action is the real pleasure."[11] Whether they had an affair or not, Fanny and George Flower did have a strong friendship built on common interests and aims. Wright, unlike Eliza Flower, was committed not to children and family but to an idea. Certainly that idea held the interest and respect of George Flower also; thus George's dedication to Wright's community and to her ideas was intrinsically threatening to Eliza's concept of family. Being devoted to husband and children, Eliza could only view Nashoba as a threat to her—it made her give up her own comfortable home and her power within it. George was not her husband solely; he belonged to the community and to Wright as well—emotionally more to Wright than to Eliza.

Having no place in Nashoba, Eliza's only recourse was to persuade her husband to leave the community.

By all accounts Nashoba, at George Flower's leaving in the fall of 1826, was progressing in an orderly way. Visiting the community in December 1826, William Maclure wrote to Fretageot that Nashoba, unlike New Harmony, was running smoothly—the slaves were working hard, and he predicted a good future for the community. But Richesson Whitby, the New Harmony commissary worker Maclure brought to Nashoba as a reinforcement, simply could not take Flower's place. Despite his background in a Shaker community, he had none of Flower's expertise in farming or organizing. George Flower's loss was of vital importance to Nashoba. Wright, despite her enthusiasm, had no experience farming in the American South; though she was willing to suffer deprivation for her experiment, she had to rely on others for the actual supervision of crops and the slaves' work. At Nashoba, then, yet another unhappy married woman helped end a utopian experiment that in no way met her needs.

By the summer of 1828 Wright took what she had learned at Nashoba and entered a new phase of her life. Understanding that she could not convert "the existing generation" to her plan but had to address herself to the "scattered individuals" who wanted reform, Wright's focus changed (*NHG*, January 30, 1828). The new direction of Wright's life as a persuader, writer, and speaker who would carry out her Owenite ideals took shape when she visited New Harmony in the spring of 1828 and found the *New Harmony Gazette* languishing. She agreed to become its coeditor because her friend Robert Dale Owen was overwhelmed with the affairs of New Harmony in the wake of his father's departure. Though Wright had written before, she had written primarily fiction, drama, or "letters" from America, intended to amuse as well as to illuminate ideas. At New Harmony as the coeditor of the *New Harmony Gazette*, on her lecture tours around the country, and eventually in New York, Frances Wright spread Owenite thought. Her enthusiastic support of women's rights, her scathing criticism of the appalling customs women were compelled to follow, convinced the impressionable young Robert Dale Owen to devote himself also to writing and lecturing for true equality between the sexes. The working partnership of Wright and Owen, thus begun, was to last for little over two years, but in those two years, the forceful Wright and her increasingly bolder younger companion created a dynamic journal that contained Wright's pleas for women's rights and sexual equality. Their attacks on religion and culturally accepted mores continued to provoke all but the most liberal minded. It was in this partnership, according to Richard Leopold, Robert Dale Owen's biographer, that the "first fruits of Owenism appeared." These "fruits" were not socialism or communism but "a militant free discussion of religion, morals, and sex relations" (62). Similarly, Arthur Bestor writes that Wright and the younger Owen effectively translated Owenite radicalism from the language of communitarian experience into the different language of grad-ualist reform in the late 1820s (*Backwoods,* 226–27).

Wright began her lecturing career in Cincinnati, where she went, at Robert Jennings's urging, to "more fully explain" her views to the public (C. Wright to H. Garnett, November 20, 1828, G-P Collection). Her Cincinnati lectures, along with her writing in the *New Harmony Gazette* and then the *Free Enquirer,* form the core of her feminist thought—thought that ques-tioned the basis of the patriarchy. For the first time she wrote clearly and forcefully on two issues of the most importance to her: the amalgamation of the races and women's wrongly constricted sexuality. Having seen that her community was not going to provide an example of how to free America's slaves, Wright wrote in her "Explanatory Notes on Nashoba," published in the *New Harmony Gazette* of January and February 1828, that the only way for blacks and whites to be truly equal was to obliterate the distinctions between the races through intermarriage. Wright believed that the races should be equal—the "prejudice of color" she found as absurd as the European prejudice of birth. The mixing of the races was to be found "in nature": "if not in nature, it could not happen; and, being in nature, since it does happen, the only question is whether it shall take place in good taste and good feeling and be made at once the means of sealing the tranquility, and perfecting the liberty of the country, and of peopling it with a race more suited to its southern climate than the pure European." Education, she wrote, would make the amalgamation of the races more rapid as well as more creditable. The combining "of the two colors," Wright wrote, would be a prospect "equally desirable for both." Her attempts at Nashoba, she declared, had been to raise the blacks to the level of the whites by "edu-cat[ing] [their] children with white children . . . and thus leav[ing] the affections of future generations, to the dictates of free choice" (*NHG,* February 6, 1828).

At the same time, Wright wrote forcefully on women's sexuality. Always insisting on sexual equality in Nashoba's plans, Wright had, from her very first book on America, attacked social customs that doomed women to inadequate education and a limited focus in life. But by 1828 she wrote of the social customs that shrouded "woman's bodies, wants, desires, senses, affections, and faculties in mystery" and suggested that women were victims of "unnatural restraints." As she saw it, society "condemned [its daughters] to the unnatural repression of feelings and desires inherent in their very organization." Women were "victims—not of pleasure, not of love, nor yet of their own depravity, but of those ignorant laws, ignorant prejudices, ignorant code of morals, which condemn one portion of the female sex to vicious excesses, another to as vicious restraint, and all to defenseless helplessness and slavery, and generally the whole male sex to debasing licentiousness, if not to loathsome brutality" (*NHG,* February 6, 1828). It was her own class of women that Wright believed felt the brunt of what she called the "coercive prejudice" of "unnatural restraints"—the "cultivated, talented, and independent women" who "shrink equally from the servitude of matrimony, and from the opprobrium stamped upon unlegalized connexions." Certainly Wright must have felt the "opprobrium" that was stamped on her "connexion" with General Lafayette during the early 1820s, and perhaps also on her relationships with George Flower and Robert Jennings. Her personal affronts must have increased her passion as she wrote of the cultural barriers to women's physical "connexions." She argued passionately that the source of human happiness was in the moral, intellectual and physical cultivation of both sexes:

> let us not teach that virtue consists in the crucifying of the affections and appetites, but in their judicious government. Let us not attach ideas of purity to monastic chastity, impossible to man or woman without consequences fraught with evil, nor ideas of vice to connections formed under the auspices of kind feelings. Let us enquire, not if a mother be a wife, or a father a husband, but if parents can supply to the creature they have brought into being, all things requisite to render existence a blessing! . . . Let us teach the young mind to reason, and the young heart to feel, and instead of shrouding our bodies, wants, desires, senses, affections and faculties in mystery, let us court enquiry, and show that acquaintance with our own nature can alone guide us to judicious practice, and that in the consequence of human actions, exists the only true test of their virtue or their vice. (*NHG,* February 6, 1828)

In her Cincinnati lectures, Wright continued the thinking she had begun earlier in the year. Convinced that "the melioration of the human condition could be reached only by the just informing of the human mind," Wright distinguished "two main strongholds" of human error to attack: the neglected state of the female mind, and the corruption of the public press (*Course of Popular Lectures,* vii). Her own editorship of the *New Harmony Gazette,* soon to be moved to New York and renamed the *Free Enquirer,* ameliorated the second evil. The first she addressed over and over again, hoping to remove women from "that worst species of quackery, practiced under the name of religion" (*Course,* vii).

Criticizing the "truisms" such as the "vulgar persuasion" that approves of ignorance for women because it insures their "utility," or the belief that "hoodwinked and unawakened" women will make better servants and playthings, Wright throughout her discourse refuted accepted ways of thinking about women. Her argumentative technique, much like that of Robert Owen before her, first questioned accepted customs, ideas, or patterns of belief, then posited what she regarded as more rational thought. Women's ignorance, for example, came as no surprise to Wright, as she noted in her first Cincinnati lecture, "for violent efforts are everywhere made for its countinuance." "A thousand phantoms," she continued, "conjured from the prolific brain of insatiate priestcraft, confound, alarm, and overwhelm her reason!" Priests, those "hired supporters of error," believed that "if the daughters of the present, and mothers of the future generation, were to drink of the living waters of knowledge, their reign would be ended—their occupation gone." Appealing also to "fathers and husbands," Wright convincingly argued that "in the mental bondage of your wives and fair companions, ye are yourself bound" ("Nature of Knowledge," 20–21).

In her next lecture Wright resumed her argument for the eradication of ignorance in women. In order to attain "the highest excellence of which our nature is capable," Wright suggested "engag[ing] collectively . . . as children of one family." But, she continued, no cooperation could be effective "which does not embrace the two sexes on a footing of equality" ("Free Inquiry," 24). In order to achieve this sexual equality, Wright proposed that "male power" and female "fear and obedience" both be eliminated. The only way to limit man's power and eliminate women's fear was through that great equalizer—education. "Without knowledge, could your fathers have conquered liberty?" Wright asked her Cincinnati audience. "And without knowledge can you retain it? Equality! where is it, if not in education? Equal rights! they cannot exist without equality of instruction" ("Free Inquiry," 24).

The critical response to the first woman to speak such words on the American platform was overwhelming. Wright's repeated stress on the importance of equality, especially sexual equality, on subsequent rights for women, and on the importance of amalgamation of the races did little to endear her to middle-of-the-road Americans. Wright's friend Frances Trollope, describing her reaction to Wright's Cincinnati lectures, found "little that could be objected to . . . [except] one passage from which common sense revolted; it was one wherein she quoted that phrase of mischievous sophistry: 'all men are born free and equal.' " Trollope continued with a description of Wright as a brilliant orator who possessed "overpowering eloquence," as well as a "tall and majestic figure. . . . the simple contour of her finely formed head, unadorned, excepting by its own natural ringlets, her garment of plain white muslin which hung about her in folds that recalled the drapery of a Grecian statue, all contributed to produce an effect unlike anything I had ever seen before" (*Domestic Manners*, 98). Few other commentators were so taken with Wright's attractive appearance, though many agreed with Trollope's comment equating "freedom and equality" with "mischievous sophistry."

Wright's frank discussion of the unnatural sexual restraints upon women and the unnatural social limitations upon blacks inspired only fury and scorn throughout the United States. The most resounding and impassioned criticism concerning Wright focused on her sex and what she was saying about women. As Frances Wright traveled around the Midwest in the summer and fall of 1828, such columns as those written by a correspondent of the *Louisville Focus* appeared in every city in which she spoke:

Miss Wright, considered as a lady, agreeable to the conventional pro-
prieties of civilized society, has, with ruthless violence, broken loose from
the restraint of decorum, which draw a circle round the life of woman; and
with a contemptuous disregard for the rule of society, she has leaped over
the boundary of feminine modesty, and laid hold on the avocations of
man, claiming a participation in them for herself and her sex. . . . Miss
Wright stands condemned of a violation of the unalterable laws of nature,
which have erected a barrier between man and woman, over which neither
can pass, without unhinging the beneficent adjustments of society, and
doing wanton injury to the happiness of each other. (Reprinted in the
NHG, December 10, 1828)

Not only was Frances Wright claiming participation in life for herself and
other women, she was also advocating equal intellectual and sexual participation for women. Another critic, incensed that Wright wanted to "amalgamate" the races, called Wright's actions "a dark subject, one which must
cause the virtuous female to blush for the disgrace which has been brought
upon her sex by this hair-brained [*sic*] enthusiast." Her intent, he concluded, was to turn the world into "a universal brothel" (Everett, 32, 34).

This Frances Wright was a different woman from the one who, only three
years earlier, had asked General Lafayette's "permission" to remain in
America to create a monument to his own ideas. This Wright no longer
asked the most important men in America their advice; she no longer
sought approval from "fathers." What she advocated in Cincinnati and
elsewhere was not, by any stretch of the imagination, "proper," and it was a
different kind of impropriety from being a young woman who wanted to
have her play produced on Broadway while following generous advice
from the important literary men in New York. Wright's new kind of impropriety was deeply threatening to the social system (the mainstream
culture or Owen's); she advocated racial and sexual equality on its most
primal level: blacks and whites should have sexual intercourse to produce
mulatto children in order to erase racial differences, and women should
enjoy sexual intercourse as easily and as often as men.

Everyone criticized her. Wright's old New York friends avoided her; her
beloved general could barely disguise his criticism of her one-track passion
for realizing equality: as he wrote to a friend in July of 1829, "all [her essays]
turn on the same subject. . . . I grieve to think there is no intercourse
between them and their New York old friends" (July 11, 1928, G-P Collection). Even Robert Owen and her relatives condemned her. James Mylne
wrote in the late summer of 1827 that he had just talked to Owen about
Wright, whom Owen believed to have gone to "much more extravagant
lengths" than he himself did (though Mylne added that Owen knew very
little limit to his own extravagance) and that her folly "cannot fail to
obstruct the very objects of a philanthropical kind she has in view, to bring
ruin upon her project and disgrace upon herself" (to J. Garnett, August 12,
1827, G-P Collection).

Frances Wright had indeed overstepped her sphere. Though Wright's male colleagues, including Robert Dale Owen, Robert Jennings, Josiah Warren, and even Robert Owen, were saying many of the same things she did, they were never the target for such hatred and malicious gossip that she was, in part because her thought was more radical than theirs, but also because Wright was a female. Wright's colleagues were male, and it was their "proper sphere of action" to attempt to sway *men's* minds; Wright was a woman who by her very public speaking "leaped over the boundary of feminine modesty." Her tone, her subject, her passion placed her outside the proper sphere of women writers. As long as she had been writing "travel books" and esoteric literature about ancient Greece, her intelligence was tolerated, her mind respected. But when she stepped into men's sphere by setting up her own utopian community and then lecturing in public and writing scathing articles with the intention of changing the world, she became "a woman in the shape of a monster," or "a madwoman."[12]

In January of 1829 Wright decided that she could influence more people if she were closer to the journalistic center of the United States—New York City—and she decided to issue the *Free Enquirer* from New York, "the head seat at once of popular energy . . . wealth and power, and financial and political corruption" (*Biography,* 43). Robert Dale Owen continued to print the New Harmony version of the paper for only a short time in Indiana; then he, too, moved to New York. Camilla Wright's advanced pregnancy delayed her move to New York until the spring of 1829, when she and her infant son could travel. Other New Harmony reformers such as William Jennings, Josiah Warren, and William Phiquepal and some of his students joined Wright in New York, the new center for extended Owenite thought.

In New York, Wright and Robert Dale Owen became the Free Enquirers, self-appointed crusaders who set about to lobby for the individual rights that were the basis of the American Revolution. Influenced by the elder Owen, of course, but surpassing his reform thinking, the Free Enquirers argued passionately for those very abstractions that the American Declaration of Independence had propounded fifty years earlier. As Wright wrote in 1828: "Liberty without equality, what is it but a chimera?" (*NHG,* January 30, 1828).

The Free Enquirers' task was to attack errors in thinking. On one level, the young Owen and Wright continued the work of the front pages of the *New Harmony Gazette* by criticizing and holding up to ridicule the accepted customs or beliefs that most people held about women. Wright and Owen concomitantly argued for the necessity of releasing women from cultural pressures that restricted their behavior and thought. One such pressure was obvious every time that Frances Wright spoke publicly and was criticized for "demeaning her sex." Furious at a criticism of Wright for "overstepping her barrier" when she appeared in public to lecture, Robert Dale Owen lambasted the customs and history that relegated women to "obedience." He castigated St. Paul for leaving woman "a privileged slave, subject to her lord because of her weakness." Angry also at "the charms of poetry" that aided "the dictates of religion," Owen cited Shakespeare's "duties of a wife"—to give "love, fair looks, and true obedience"—as his final example of how "this arrogant assumption of privilege by the powerful" had uniformly permeated all of history (*NHG*, December 10, 1828).

Because most cultures value, above all, this "obedience" and meekness in women, and because rational opinions were considered too "masculine" for women to espouse, both Wright and Owen wrote forcefully to combat this idea.[13] It was their hope that women who thought rationally would not believe that they had only one passion in life, that of living for a man. In Robert Dale Owen's most powerful tract, "Situations," he impelled his audience to do away with society's pressures that limited a woman to one "occupation" in life:

> Why must woman, any more than man, be a being of one occupation, one passion, one interest only? . . . A time is coming when the indefeasible rights of mankind will be recognized and . . . women will not be restricted to one virtue, one passion and one occupation. Mothers will not tell their daughters that the object of life is to gain a husband and an establishment. . . . Men and women will be equally judged . . . by their real virtue; by their adherence to honour and justice; by the sweetness of their tempers; by the qualities of their hearts. Men and women will equally be encouraged to explore the fields of science, and to aid in the great work of human improvement. (14–15)

Owen here attacked the basic tenet underlying the Cult of True Womanhood and posited a future era where sexual equality could become a reality—all based on the fact that women can and should have a passion beyond entrapping a supporter for life.

Needless to say, the techniques of "entrapping" a man and the "fashionable" clothes used in laying the trap also came under the Free Enquirers' attack. Horror stories appeared often in the *Free Enquirer*, telling of women who had died internally deformed because of wearing "fashionable" corsets.[14] Frances Wright wrote disdainfully of training women in "mental error and bodily helplessness" so that they looked more like "the wasp in shape" than young creatures reared in reason and liberty (*FE*, August 26, 1829). Owen made fun of "cagemaking," that pursuit young women were supposed to dedicate themselves to wholeheartedly in order to "entrap" a husband. To Wright and Owen, such "matrimonial manoeuvers" were inconsistent with women's happiness and dignity (*FE*, July 19, 1829).

The custom though that came under Wright's most brutal attack was that of keeping women ignorant. As she said in her first public lectures in Cincinnati, and then wrote of again and again, the meshes of custom are laid to enslave the female of every age and only knowledge can render the meshes useless. The importance of education, of equal education for boys and girls, and men and women, was thus Wright's favorite leitmotif. As she said in her Fourth of July speech in Philadelphia in 1829, "the right of equal instruction should have been enumerated among those human rights which preface your constitutional codes," because if the Founding Fathers declared Americans to be equal at birth, only education could prepare "the next generation to be equal in life." Neither liberty nor equality would be possible, concluded Wright, until the "people shall legislate for the equal instruction, the rational education, and the national protection of youth."[15]

Thus, for Frances Wright, as for Robert Owen before her, education would be the great equalizer; however, Wright addressed herself more specifically to women's problems than the elder Owen ever did. Both Wright and the young Owen had accepted the Owenite premise of the mental equality of the sexes and the concomitant notion that "each man and woman . . . be afforded an equal share in every . . . advantage," but Wright expanded these working premises into a detailed plan for national education, which she lectured on and wrote of several times.[16] Her plan for free, public schools was a simple one, similar to Robert Owen's plans at New Lanark, William Maclure's plans at New Harmony, and her own plans for her school in Nashoba. Wright, interested in reforming education for all people, suggested that "state legislatures be directed . . . to organize, at suitable distances . . . establishments for the general reception of all the children resident within the said school district" ("Evils," 114). Her proposed schools were to be divided according to children's ages: ages two to six, six to twelve, and twelve to sixteen were to be grouped together. The similarity between Wright's hypothetical public schooling and twentieth-century public eduction stops with her mandatory resident requirement. In Wright's plans, all children from two years on were to board at the schools, and the parents, "who would necessarily be resident in their close neighbourhood, could visit the chidren at suitable hours, but, in no case, interfere with or interrupt the rules of the institution" ("Evils," 114). To pay for these schools, Wright offered a twofold tax system—a parental tax, a "moderate tax per head for every child, to be laid upon its parents conjointly, or divided between them, due attention always being paid . . . to the undue depreciation which now rests upon female labour" (115), and a property tax, levied in increasing percentage with the wealth of every individual residing in the school district. Thus Wright again foreshadowed modern public education, this time by funding her schools with a graduated property tax proposal, but she also remembered that in her other tax, on parents, women's unequal income might cause a mother problems if she were to pay "conjointly" with her husband a tax for her child's education. Although Wright understood, theoretically, how important it was for parents to pay for their children's expenses together, she comprehended that women, living in a society which does not value female labor, could not be "equal." In her schools, though, all this was to change.

Because Wright believed this race of free and equal women and men was still a generation removed, she believed the present world needed more than a restructured educational system to increase women's rights. Like Robert Owen, she was deeply concerned with the ill effects of society's foremost institution, marriage. But where Owen was concerned only abstractly with "marriages of the priesthood," and more specifically with the importance of divorce reform, Wright, being a woman in a patriarchal world, was more interested in the effects of marriage on women and advocated increased rights for women within marriage. By the late 1820s, only Massachusetts had passed a married woman's property bill, which provided a woman with her own property in the case of a divorce. Railing against the necessity to pass such an obvious law, Wright wrote that it was "truly inconceivable and truly monstrous that the mass of absurdity, injustice, and cruelty, styled the common law of England, should still be the law of revolutionized America" (*FE*, April 29, 1829). That a woman at her marriage swore away "at one and the same moment her person and her property, and as it but too often is, her peace, her honor, and her life," that a married woman had no protection under the law, horrified Wright, who wanted to "impeach all written law, even as I have impeached all written creeds" (*FE*, March 4, 1829). Mixing strong emotional appeals with her logic straight out of the Declaration of Independence, Wright pleaded with "every father not absolutely dead to all human feeling" not to allow his daughters "blindly to immolate all their rights, liberties, and property by the simple utterance of a word, and thus place themselves, in their tender, ignorant, and unsuspecting youth, as completely at the disposal and mercy of an individual, as in the negro slave when bought for gold in the market of Kingston or New Orleans." She asked readers to imagine

> a young creature, untaught to reason . . . pledging her troth to one who, some moons, or, it may be, years after, turns gambler, or drunkard, or speculator, staking at one throw, or wasting over nightly potations, not *his* property only, but hers also. . . . See her, moreover, compelled to endure the company of her destroyer, experience its vitiating example, and entail its evils on a yearly multiplying progeny! Look at this, ye that praise existing institutions, and *dare* to call them moral, rational, or just! (*FE*, April 29, 1829)

Despite the prolific hate columns appearing in numerous New York papers decrying Wright's "ban on marriage," Wright herself wrote little on the institution of marriage per se for the *Free Enquirer* and lectured on the subject only once when pressed by an audience. Her friend and first biographer, Amos Gilbert, quoted Wright as saying: "I desire not the repeal of the marriage law, nor any other, so long as the necessity for it exists; when the people become better than the law requires, it will be repealed or become a dead issue" (51). Her choice of articles and tales on marriage that the *Free Enquirer* reprinted from other journals reflected her particular interests; stories such as "Intoxication and Matrimonial Tyranny" described in great emotional detail the wretched life of a woman married to a drunk, while essays like "The Law of Marriage" castigated the loss of woman's rights at her marriage.[17]

Because women had so few rights in marriage, Wright and Owen urged women to "make fortunes for themselves." The Free Enquirers believed that women could not be "securely happy" unless they earned an honest living by "their own exertions." "Money," conceded Owen, "unfortunately is the passport to power, to influence, even to independence of body and mind." Concomitantly, a woman rendered economically dependent upon her husband could discover, after marriage, that her pecuniary dependence lessened his respect and his affection. Admitting that men had monopolized almost all lucrative employment, Owen passionately urged young women, before marrying, not to throw away the little security remaining to them: *"If you have property, settle it on yourselves"* (*FE*, February 4, 1829).

Because most women in the 1820s were prisoners of their reproductive systems as well as of the existing economic and legal systems, the Free Enquirers urged one last "right" for women—the proprietorship of their own bodies. Since this right was based on the correct knowledge of physiology, Wright and Owen often urged their readers "of each sex" to attend public lectures on anatomy and physiology.[18] In the *New Harmony Gazette* of January and February 1828 Wright had advocated the acceptance of women's "natural" sexual needs, whereby women would not have to crucify their "affections and appetites" but could be free from "unnatural restraints." Likewise, Robert Dale Owen wrote one of the first birth-control tracts published in America. A strong, assertive work, as was all of Owen's writing in the late 1820s, *Moral Physiology* spoke to the moral and practical questions of birth control. In the brief latter part of the book, Owen described the three methods of birth control: withdrawal, the sponge, and the "baudruche," the latter two—an internal sponge for women and an outer covering for men—being of "doubtful efficacy." Though Owen's preferred method of withdrawal placed "the power chiefly in the hands of the man, and not, where it ought to be, in those of woman," Owen suggested that women must "refuse connexion with any man void of honor," so that they would not be victims of his carelessness or selfishness (66–67). Owen's advocacy of woman's control over the number of children she would bear, and thus over her life, was an almost unimaginable idea, especially in the age of True Womanhood. That Robert Dale Owen questioned the notion that "the whole life" of a woman should be spent bearing and raising children reflected his acceptance of the most radical of the Free Enquirer's goals. As Richard Leopold has suggested, *Moral Physiology* represented Owen's most militant free thought (84).

Frances Wright's year and a half in New York, from the winter of 1828 until June of 1830, when Frances and Camilla left for France, was the most utopian time of her life. Finally, she lived with a community of friends, in a way that she had probably imagined she would at Nashoba. Together in New York were the Wright sisters, Camilla with her baby (her husband remained at Nashoba as the overseer), Robert Dale Owen, Phiquepal and several students from New Harmony, and sometimes Robert Jennings and David Dale Owen, Robert Dale's brother. Wright and her sister and the rest of their extended "family" lived in a large house in the country, some five miles from New York City, where they could have both privacy and communal life on a small scale. They raised vegetables, got their milk from their cows, and seldom ate meat. Camilla wrote to the Garnett sisters that she believed her sister capable of effecting "a great moral revolution throughout this country" (August 1, 1829, G-P Collection). Writing, editing, and often lecturing in the hall she hired in New York City, Wright was a woman obsessed with her ideas, full of enthusiasm for her task at hand. She was at the height of her power.

Meanwhile, as Wright and the rest of the household were actively engaged in changing the world, Camilla had become the group's "wife." As in all the Owenite communities, the one left "at home" to do the domestic work found the utopia not so utopian. Camilla, the self-described housekeeper for the entire group, suffered during the summer of 1829, first from the unexpected death of her seven-month-old son. Her misery at her child's death was exacerbated by her sister's absence during much of the fall and winter of 1829. Her depression lingered as all the other members of the house had more active roles to play than she did. For the first time ever, she contemplated life without her sister. She wrote to Julia Garnett on November 1, telling her of her present "situation" as the group's housekeeper and her wish to leave the East River house and travel to Germany to be with Julia:

> Fanny had established her residence in the country, a beautiful situation on the east river 5 miles distant from the city—the house is large and commodious sufficiently so to comprise the printing office for the Enquirer—as you must imagine the household arrangements of such an establishment require an assiduous and careful superintendence, and in as far as the state of my mind and health permit I have endeavored to discharge the office, but shd Fanny be successful in engaging a valuable person with whom we are acquainted, and who has lately left her situation . . . I shall be released from my present responsible situation as housekeeper and consequently at liberty to consult my own feelings as to my future destination—write to me dear Julia, nor hesitate to give me your free and candid opinion as to the possibility of my taking passage from hence to Hambourg.

Less than a year earlier, Camilla had written Julia Garnett saying that "no circumstances" could ever separate her from her sister, but as an unknown, unimportant woman in utopia, she suffered an estrangement from Fanny.

She wrote to Harriet in February of 1830, telling her "the painful truth": "the sister—the friend with whom I have suffered much & with whom I have sympathized still more is no longer the sharer of my thoughts & feelings & only ceased to be so from my discovery that *I shared not hers.*"

During the months that Camilla was her most miserable, Fanny was the opposite. As Cam wrote in the same letter:

> strange as it may seem I have never at any period of my life seen her so apparently happy & contented with her situation and prospects than at present—her time fully occupied, her thoughts engaged by pursuits which are certainly congenial to her tastes & which seem admirably qualified to exhibit & usefully to employ her extraordinary talents. It is not surprising that all minor objects of interests—which once sufficed to fill her heart should now be lessened if not altogether lost in the midst of the wide sea whereon she is now embarked. (Quoted in Heineman, 83–84)

Cam's letter reflected her jealousy. She admitted that her "regret" was "purely selfish" and that she was trying to be satisfied seeing her sister "engaged in a cause worthy of her talents," but her feelings lingered, nonetheless. Camilla's situation had turned her into a quite typical woman in utopia—a married woman whose only place was to serve those who were actively trying to change the world.

In the midst of Camilla's misery, Wright decided to end her responsibility to her slaves in Nashoba by removing them to Haiti, where they could be free. Certainly the low agricultural output at Nashoba had never provided the necessities for anyone at Nashoba, let alone stored up a surplus for the slaves' emancipation, and the slaves' upkeep continued to be a source of financial loss and anxiety for Wright. The freeing of the slaves entailed Wright's meeting them in New Orleans and sailing with them to Haiti. Leaving New York in late October 1829 with William Phiquepal, who lived in the East River house with the Free Enquirers and was familiar with the West Indies, Wright first worked in a lecture circuit, speaking in Albany, towns in western New York, Philadelphia, Cincinnati, and finally New Orleans. This lecture series, ending a year of extensive effort since she had first appeared on the podium in Cincinnati the year before, left her exhausted, with no free time, but enthusiastic about her cause.

While taking her slaves to their emancipation in the winter of 1829 and spring of 1830, Frances Wright became pregnant, and the direction of her life changed against her will, as had been the experience of so many thousands of women before her. Her subsequent flight to France on July 1, 1830 (on the pretext of Cam's continuing depression), and her virtual disappearance from public life for the next six months assured her privacy at the expense of her successful public lecturing and writing. William Phiquepal, presumably the father of the baby, left the West Indies in late March 1830 to return to New York; then he, too, sailed to France. By the spring of 1831 Fanny was openly living with him in Paris with their daughter, christened Sylva after one of Phiquepal's family names. Only James Fenimore Cooper left a record of seeing Wright pregnant in Paris. He wrote to her one-time friend Charles Wilkes in New York in April of 1831:

> As for Miss Wright. . . . I saw her once, about three months ago, at one of Lafayettes [*sic*] receptions. She looked haggard and much changed for the worse. . . . She excited much attention on account of her appearance, and the women avoided her. I should have spoken to her, had I known her previously, but I did not like to see an introduction, under the circumstances, as it would have been disrespectful to Mrs. Cooper, who was present. I do not think she repeated her visit.[19]

During her secretive months in France, shortly after her baby was born, Wright suffered yet another blow—her sister died in early February 1831. As she wrote to Robert Owen on March 16, 1831: "a few words and those painful I know . . . will suffice to explain my silence. Camilla died in my arms on the 8th of last month, February, of a sudden attack of hemmorage, after having flattered me with perfect recovery from the weak state of health and spirits which had decided me on a voyage to Europe. M. Phiquepal and GenL Lafayette have rendered me all the care and sympathy which circumstances have demanded" (RO Papers, #407).

The birth of her baby and her sister's death combined effectively to exclude Frances Wright from public life for a number of years. Before Cam's death, Wright had planned on returning to New York and the *Free Enquirer* as soon as her period of confinement was over; Robert Dale Owen wrote to his father in February 1831, before he had heard of Camilla's death, that "Frances leaves France for this country about the 10th of March next. I have been very lonely throughout the winter fighting the battle single-handed. [It will be] a relief when she returns" (RO Papers, #396). Robert Dale also added that Camilla "talks of staying the summer in Paris," having been "restored to that health and cheerfulness which she lost at the death of her boy, and which, I was beginning to fear, she would never recover." Even after Cam's death Wright told the younger Owen that she might return to the States after being some weeks in seclusion, but that for the time being, Phiquepal would sail to New York, having delayed his return for some time "to render me assistance under the afflicting circumstances which have surrounded me" (RO Papers, #407).

Despite all her plans and her former writing and lecturing, Wright married Phiquepal on July 22, 1831, when their daughter Sylva was over six months old, without any type of marriage agreement. Asking him to resume his family name of D'Arusmont, Wright assumed it as well.[20] As a wife and mother, though, her vision was inexorably changed. Gone was her freedom to do exactly as she pleased, and gone, too, were her energy and enthusiasm.

Visitors to Wright's Parisian home during the winter of 1831 tell a bleak story of her life. Harriet Garnett wrote in November of 1831 that she had just seen Fanny, "now Phiquepal d'Arusmont, for her husband is the Dr. Phiquepal whose name you must have heard. I found her with a child a twelvemonth old, a little girl, like her, and naked. . . . I own I felt very unhappy. I have not had the courage to return and shall probably seldom see her . . ." (to J. Garnett, November 25, 1831, G-P Collection). Though Harriet did continue to see Fanny sporadically, she found her much changed, and indirectly blamed her for Cam's death; for example, she wrote to Julia on March 20, 1831, from Geneva, "bitterly do I lament her [Camilla's] death, altho' little happiness as life seemed to await her. . . . She had . . . hired an apartment by herself not with Frances who remains with Mr. Phiquepal, and the fourth day after her arrival [in Paris] she expired." Similarly, Marie Fretageot unexpectedly found Fanny in what she had assumed was Phiquepal's apartment in December 1831, with a naked child she (wrongly) believed to be "about six months old." Her description of Fanny's new life makes it sound bleak indeed:

> in my astonishment I [saw] Frances with a little girl of about six months old that she was undressing to put to bed. The baby was nearly to fall if I had not put my hands in the way. . . . She asked me who gave me her address. I did not answer but said, "I thought you would see me with some pleasure." "I receive no visits," was her answer. "Then I suppose you write much?" "I do not. I am totally occupied with my family." (Marie Fretageot to William Maclure, December 25, 1831)

At the time Harriet and Marie Fretageot visited her, Fanny was pregnant again; her second daughter was born in April 1832. Harriet wrote that after the birth of her second child Fanny was ill and had no female with her. Phiquepal was "in charge" of the older girl, though, much to Harriet's disapprobation, the baby, like Sylva before her, was naked (to Julia, May 27, 1832, G-P Collection). Between Harriet's visit in May and the middle of June, Fanny's infant died. Lafayette wrote to Harriet on June 14 that he "had a visit from dear Fanny before I left town. She no doubt has informed you of the loss of her child. Poor Fanny!" Mrs. Garnett had also written on June 29 to her daughter that "Miss Wright . . . has lost her little girl. Harriet has written to her but has not received an answer. Perhaps she is in the country with her eldest child" (June 29, 1832, G-P Collection). Perhaps to save her older child embarrassment when she grew older, Wright gave Sylva the younger child's birthdate, though at least fifteen months separated the children's ages. Sylva had been born at least six months before Wright and Phiquepal had married, but the dead infant had been born a more respectable nine months after their wedding.

Less than three months after the death of Wright's infant, Robert Dale Owen and his new bride, Mary Jane, came to Paris to visit Fanny and Phiquepal. Unlike Wright, Owen had married with great hesitation and elaborate planning. His April 1832 wedding was performed in accordance with the Free Enquirers' ideas on marriage and religion: no clergyman was present and no prayers or promises were given. Owen's "marriage statement," reprinted in the June 2, 1832, *Free Enquirer,* reflected his Owenite attitudes toward marriage:

> We contract a legal marriage, not because we deem the ceremony necessary to us, or useful . . . to society; but because, if we became companions without a legal ceremony, we should either be compelled to a series of dissimulations which we both dislike, or be perpetually exposed to annoyances. . . .
>
> Of the unjust rights which, in virtue of this ceremony, an iniquitous law tacitly gives me over the person and property of another, I cannot legally, but I can morally divest myself.

The contrast between how Robert Owen and Frances Wright arranged their marriages or between their reasons for marrying could not have been greater.

Mary Jane and Robert Dale left an epistolary record of their time apart while Mary Jane stayed with Fanny and Phiquepal when Robert Dale went to England to see his father. Robert Dale's letters reveal a nervous young husband who apologized for his sexual "blunders." Mary Jane, isolated and alone and probably not as concerned with her new sexual relationship as her husband was, recorded a subdued Fanny, now a "wife," with different demands on her time than in her former, spirited life as a young single woman. It was a time of few visitors; only Lafayette came to call. Nothing, not even the visit from Mary Jane, broke Fanny's isolation.

Isolation enveloped Fanny from her first pregnancy and virtual disappearance from public life in the fall of 1830 until the mid-1830s. Returning to the United States in 1835, Wright attempted to regain her position as a public lecturer. She gave two lectures in Cincinnati in May of 1836, and in November of that year she joined an old friend, former Free Enquirer Abner Kneeland, in Boston, where he was editing his freethinking *Boston Weekly Investigator.* For a brief six months in 1837 she published a journal, the *Manual of American Principles* from Philadelphia, that she hoped would reteach the principles of the American Revolution. Crossing and recrossing the Atlantic Ocean, Wright tried to recreate her former life but found she could not. She was often separated from Phiquepal and Sylva, spending much of her time traveling between Europe and the United States. Her marriage disintegrated rapidly in the 1840s as Wright found herself in constant battles to retain the property she brought into the marriage.

During the last years of her life Wright confronted patriarchal power on a personal level, as she battled Phiquepal for her property and for Sylva, who, living primarily with her father, sided with him. Meanwhile, she continued to write—her autobiography and a book on England. These works contained many of the same ideas as her writing of the late 1820s but also included a real knowledge of having lived through the problems she had only thought about in 1829. For example, in a letter to the *Workingmen's*

Advocate in March 1845, she wrote that she regarded marriage "as utterly worthless as the rest of our legal system," and reiterated that the key to sexual equality was throwing the door "wide open to both [sexes] and each individual among both to earn his and her own; and to hold his and her own." Yet her experience told her of the near impossibility of equal individual rights for women, and she added: "But until women are rendered fit for something in mind and body than kept mistresses . . . men should be forced to keep them . . . under male government they should be fed, clothed and protected" (*WA*, March 8, 1845).

By the 1840s, Wright fully comprehended the vast power of the patriarchy, and in her last book, *England the Civilizer,* she wrote:

> Up until the present time, society has ever submitted to male government under one or other of its forms, variously styled the patriarchal, monarchal, oligarchal, aristocratic, democratic [and has] submitted . . . to the . . . selfish principle. And this by forcibly circumscribing all the holy influences and lofty aspirations of woman within the narrowest precincts of the individual family circle. There indeed she reigns the providence and guardian angel of beings dependent upon her care. Yet sustains this character only by forcibly closing her eyes upon the claims of the great human family without that circle. . . . Man, on the other hand, feels, calculates, aspires, dares, grasps, conquers, conducts, destroys, for self alone, and keeps all things in a state of standing warfare, litigation, and confusion. Here, for the two sexes, is the rule; departure from it, the rare exception. (12–13)

Wright herself had felt, calculated, aspired, dared, grasped, and conquered until she was confined by the marginality of her existence as a wife and mother. Unlike any male reformer, Wright experienced the perspective of both a "male" reformer and a "female" wife when she was "forcibly circumscrib[ed] . . . within the narrowest precincts of the individual family circle." Her efforts to break out of this constricted space won her only more hatred. Her zeal had alienated most of her former friends. When she tried to resume her lecturing career in America, her former friends openly condemned her: "Her best friends regret her course," wrote Lucy Sistaire Say in an 1837 letter; "[she] is more obnoxious now than ever" (to Maclure, November 7, 1837).

Even her fellow Free Enquirer Robert Dale Owen regretted his acquaintance with her. In his old age, he recalled his life with Frances Wright, a woman who had a "strong, logical mind which had not been submitted to early discipline," as he wrote in his autobiography, *Threading My Way.* Her enthusiasm, he added, was "easy but fitful, [and] lacked the guiding check of sound judgment" (297). Looking back on the "masculine" traits of his former coeditor, Owen believed that he should have associated with a more "genial, gentle, sympathetic, thoughtful . . . and above all, womanly" woman during his formative years (322). This woman's influence "would have been much more salutary. I required to be restrained, not urged; needed not the spur, but the guiding rein" (323). As for the "social and religious" reforms the *Free Enquirer* proposed, Robert Dale Owen summed up his activities during the late 1820s in two words: "immature and extravagant." Though he did become an Indiana state legislator in the 1830s, adding one more cause—"habitual drunkenness for two years"—to Indiana's already liberal divorce law and inquiring into the expediency of adopting Louisiana's civil code on women's rights in marriage, Robert Dale Owen never again pursued any of the reforms he and his "impulsive" influence Frances Wright had proposed in the late 1820s. He dismissed in old age his involvement in utopian schemes to liberate women from biased laws and cultural pressures as merely a "sowing of wild oats" (*Threading*, 296).

Frances Wright was so "obnoxious" because she never renounced her belief in Owenite reform, never stopped writing and speaking for women's equality, and never ceased criticizing the patriarchal society that created and perpetuated secondary citizenship for women. Whereas Robert Dale Owen "grew up" and denounced his former attitudes, and Robert Owen's egalitarian rhetoric was too abstract to pinpoint, Frances Wright became and continued to be a target of hatred because of her clarity; she "overstepped her bounds" and never repented. Wright died at age fifty-seven, alone and crippled from a fall that broke her hip, a fitting end, most believed, for the first women's rights activist in the United States. A final irony, which stamped an exclamation point on Wright's life, came some twenty-two years after her death, when her beloved daughter, Sylva, testified before the House Committee on the Judiciary in "opposition to the enfranchisement of women in the District of Columbia and elsewhere." Sylva's reasons for opposing voting rights for women were simple: the ballot in the hands of women would "demoralize society, undermine the state, and tend to detract from the finer qualities of the sex, and consequently destroy her usefulness as a mother, wife, and citizen."[21]

Though her own life from the moment she accidentally got pregnant in 1830 was steeped in loss and disappointment, Frances Wright made the Owenites' finest hour possible. She was unable to retract, to forget, to tone down and "grow up," to accept her proper place in the world as a wife and mother. For most women in utopia, such as Wright's sister Camilla, being a woman in utopia meant daily sacrificing, endless "women's work" so that the makers and doers of utopia could get on with their attempts to change the world. As one of the world's makers and doers, though, Wright discovered an even more horrifying lesson for herself: women who try to alter the way the world is organized end up ostracized without a family or a public. Wright is, finally, an example of what happens to a woman seeking equality for women within a patriarchal state.

CHAPTER

5

THE END OF EQUALITY
The Owenite Communal Tradition
in America

Few are prepared to sacrifice their present
comforts for the establishment of a principle.

—A. J. Macdonald Manuscript, 362

By the end of the 1820s the Owenite communities had all disbanded, and most American newspapers did not even mention Robert Owen's return to England in the summer of 1829. Former members of the communities left Owen's new moral world with different levels of satisfaction. The Pears family joined their relatives in Pittsburgh, relieved that New Harmony was behind them. Paul Brown continued his search for a community that would live up to his expectations but was to be disappointed everywhere he lived. The M'Knights of Franklin returned to New York, pleased to be finished with the economic experiment that had failed miserably in their eyes. Many residents of New Harmony simply remained in the growing town—some out of preference, some because they had no money to return to their former homes. At Blue Spring and Kendal many of the residents continued living on the same land, doing what they had always done, only not to the end of creating a new social system. Although a few of the Franklin and Yellow Springs members remained in the area of their Owenite communities, most returned to Cincinnati or New York, respectively. The slaves at Nashoba became free men and women in Haiti.

Despite the lack of functioning Owenite communities in the 1830s, the American Owenite movement was far from dead. Like Frances Wright, many of the reformers who had created or had joined one of the communities in the mid-1820s continued to promulgate Owenite ideas. These reformers expressed Owenite theories in different shapes during the 1830s, picking what they found to be most meaningful from Owen's conglomeration of beliefs. Marie Fretageot, one of the teachers at the New Harmony

142

school; Abner Kneeland, a New York City preacher; and Samuel Underhill, the doctor at Forestville and then Kendal, illustrate the directions American Owenite reformers took in the years after the original communities dissolved. By the mid-1840s another Owenite communal movement was under way, fueled by the reformers who had remained active in the 1830s, by emigrating groups, and by people influenced by Robert Owen.

For Marie Fretageot, continuing to teach in and administer the New Harmony schools was the path to changing the world quietly and slowly. Even without Robert Owen, the New Harmony schools continued to provide the Midwest with outstanding experimental, learner-oriented education from kindergarten on. Like others associated with the New Harmony School of Education, Marie Fretageot remained at New Harmony, running the schools, long after the communal experiment was over.[1] After Owen left New Harmony, not much changed at Fretageot's schools except for the absence of arguments concerning which community children should have to pay fees. Her mission was not simply Owen's; it was, instead, her continuation of Owenite reform, tempered by her dedication to her own and Maclure's ideas on education. To Fretageot, and to William Maclure, whose money made the continuation of the schools possible, the best schools followed Pestalozzian principles by which students learned from life, from observation and experimentation, not from rote memorization. The best teachers, according to Maclure and Fretageot, were scholar-teachers who were themselves busy with their own experiments, writing, and thinking—an integration of scholarship and pedagogy that would be, by the late nineteenth century, a model for universities.

A variety of soon-to-be famous men remained in New Harmony and continued their research and teaching throughout the 1820s and thirties. Maclure, though he spent almost no time in New Harmony during the late 1820s and 1830s because of his health, nonetheless stayed in touch with its schools and scientific accomplishments through his correspondence with Fretageot. In 1838, just before his death, Maclure established the Workingmen's Institute at New Harmony, thus making concrete his dream, grounded in the Scottish Enlightenment, that "useful" education should be available to working-class people. Thomas Say, after marrying Lucy Sistaire, one of the young women Fretageot brought to New Harmony, also remained, and by 1830 his *American Conchology* began to be issued from the New Harmony School Press. William Maclure's essays in the *New Harmony Gazette* and the *Disseminator* (the New Harmony journal after *The New Harmony Gazette* moved to New York City in 1828) were collected and published by the School Press as well.

But it was Marie Fretageot who took charge of the experiment after Robert Owen left New Harmony. The town that remained was her monument as much as it was Robert Owen's or William Maclure's, astutely writes Arthur Bestor (*Education and Reform*, 406). It was Fretageot who convinced Maclure and his scientific friends to come to New Harmony in the first place; it was Fretageot who acted as a go-between for Robert Owen and William Maclure, each too absorbed in his own notions of reform to tolerate the other's. Finally, it was Fretageot who continued on at New Harmony helping the scientists gather information and publish their works. Because of her efforts, New Harmony's reputation grew as America's most important scientific and educational center in the second quarter of the nineteenth century.

Abner Kneeland also spread Owenite thought throughout the 1830s. A preacher in the Universalist church, like Robert Jennings, the Franklin Community president, Kneeland arrived in New York City in 1825 and there heard of Robert Owen and his new social system. Preaching the glories of Owenism from his New York pulpit, Kneeland urged people to join the Franklin Community in Haverstraw, New York. He publicly gave up religion in 1829 and moved to Boston the next year. In 1831 he began publishing a weekly radical newspaper, the *Boston Investigator*, which advocated his Owenite ideas of "rational" marriage and the rights of women. Kneeland believed the subordination of women was a projection of male self-interest and thus advocated equal wages for equal work, separate names for husband and wife, and marriage contracts for women entering into marriage.[2]

Kneeland's main claim to fame, though, was not his Owenite newspaper; rather it was the fact that he was the last person in Massachusetts to be jailed for blasphemy. Convicted of reprinting an article from the *Free Enquirer* that ridiculed prayer and of printing his own essay that differentiated the Universalists' beliefs from his own, Kneeland went to jail in June 1838 for two months. Upon his release he decided to move himself and his family to Iowa to establish the utopian community Salubria. There he continued to send back news to the *Investigator* of his activities, including planting melons and pumpkins, talking to people who were not "too" susceptible to prejudice, and lecturing on the Owenite subjects dearest to his heart—free inquiry into religion, manners, and morals. Kneeland died in 1844.

Samuel Underhill, who had been a founding member of Forestville and the primary letter writer in Kendal, left communal life but never deserted his Owenite ideals.[3] After he, his brother Nathaniel, and the rest of the Forestville members left Kendal to move one half mile away to Massillion, they established a school and built up a thriving village. By 1831 the town had four to five hundred residents. Underhill continued his Owenite reform by lecturing to interested groups on such topics as "Mysterious Religious Emotions" and "Thomas Paine." In the early 1830s he moved to Cleveland from Massillion in order to take a position as professor of chemistry at the Willoughby University of Lake Erie, though he was soon dismissed from his professorship, probably for his lack of religious beliefs.

Underhill, like Frances Wright, turned his Owenite energies to lecturing and editing several journals, the most noteworthy being his weekly, *The*

Cleveland Liberalist, published from September 10, 1836, until he ran out of money in October 1838. Always the "liberal" journalist, always true to his Owenite principles—which included his belief that all knowledge was gained through the senses and that human nature was not morally depraved until corrupted by vicious teaching—Underhill wrote in the first issue of his journal that, although he had considered devoting part of his time to his medical practice, he decided to be a full-time editor of the *Liberalist* because no weekly liberal paper existed west of Rochester, and the "friends of Liberty of Thought and Equality of Rights and Privileges" needed a journal of their own (*CL,* September 10, 1836).

Underhill's *Liberalist* reported on the activities in the late 1830s of Owenite reformers such as Robert Dale Owen and Frances Wright, whom Underhill had not met but wanted to. He wrote of the death of William Thompson and Abram Combe; he published letters from New Harmony on Robert Owen's socialist/rationalist ideas. He informed his readers of the liberal conventions being held in the eastern part of the country and of new societies forming for the "Diffusion of Knowledge."[4] Of two issues growing in popularity among Owenites in the late 1830s—abolition and temperance—Underhill wrote that he was against slavery, but that his paper aimed at breaking the chains of *mental* slavery. Enough other papers, he believed, were devoted exclusively to abolishing negro slavery. Speaking at a temperance meeting, Underhill lectured that temperance ought to be separate from religion and churches, an unpopular sentiment that kept him from being invited back to temperance meetings.[5]

The important Owenite issues of education for all, and especially education for women, played an important role in Underhill's weekly journal. Underhill had written Robert Owen in May of 1828, while he was still at Kendal, telling Owen of the "woman problem" at Kendal, as quoted in chapter 4. The "sore evil" that was the women's opposition to communal living, Underhill then attributed to women being "cruelly kept on the background of intelligence" (RO Papers, #126). Ten years later, Underhill still believed in the powers of a good education. For children, he advocated a school "without any superstition" (*CL,* October 1, 1836). For women, he urged "raising the standard of female education" (*CL,* October 29, 1836). Women needed to be educated, Underhill lectured to the Massillion Lyceum in 1838, partly because their "influence" was all important but also because education increased women's opportunities (*CL,* September 8, 1838). At the same time, Underhill reprinted an essay on the "Rights and Property of Married Women" that illustrated how married women were slaves, entirely divested of their right and title to personal property (*CL,* January 7, 1837).

Despite (or perhaps because of) Underhill's understanding of the legal discrimination against married women and of the necessity for a good education to increase their options in life, the *Cleveland Liberalist,* just like the *New Harmony Gazette,* published numerous editorial essays aimed at advising women, especially married women. Essays such as "The Young Wife" (January 31, 1827) and "Advice to a Young Lady after her Marriage" (December 31, 1836) sound similar to articles in popular ladies' magazines of the time. Always, Underhill depicted the "scolding wife" as the scourge of a happily married man. His tone was patronizing as he simplistically addressed women readers, but as a reformer deeply believing in the powers of education, Underhill could not help but lecture. As an advocate of women's education, Underhill sometimes expressed frustration in his paper or his speeches that it was women, particularly married women, who were so threatened by his ideas that they refused to read or discuss them. Hearing that many married women would not allow his weekly paper in their homes, he urged the "Ladies of Cleveland" to welcome the *Liberalist* into their homes, telling them that they should read every piece of information given to them, that they should not forbid or censure (November 19, 1836). Underhill's lecturing and writing continued the flow of Owenite information throughout the 1830s. Even after his paper folded, he continued to write and speak for Owenite reforms.[6]

While reformers in America spread Owenite thought through education, persuasive journalism, and lecturing in the 1830s, Robert Owen himself continued to plan his new moral world by focusing on specific reforms rather than on building communities. In England, Owen became actively involved in the burgeoning Owenite cooperative movement that his disciples George Mudie, A. J. Hamilton, and Abram Combe had begun in the early 1820s. According to Owen's biographer, Frank Podmore, by 1830 the English landscape was populated with over three hundred cooperative societies. Two years earlier the *Cooperative Magazine,* the organ of the London Cooperative Society, the "parent organization" of the wildly growing cooperative movement, had listed only four cooperative societies (Podmore, 388). Within two years' time, thousands of people, primarily from the working class, were converted to Owenite cooperation, if not by living in intentional communities then by working with each other to buy and sell goods and to educate their children in common.

The Owenite thrust in Great Britain in the late 1820s and early 1830s modified Robert Owen's plans because it downplayed what had been central to Owen in the 1820s—building intentional communities. The semiannual Cooperative Congresses, begun in Manchester in 1831, brought together hundreds of people interested in cooperation. Though a few people, such as Robert Owen, believed these cooperative societies should be the first steps toward an intentional community, others were interested in cooperative societies as ends unto themselves. Owen also helped to promulgate other working-class reforms, such as trade unions and labor exchanges, whereby workers could "exchange" their goods for the product's worth, based on the cost of raw materials plus the worker's time.

By 1834, with the labor exchanges failed and many of the cooperative societies broken up, Owen turned to journalism for the same reasons that Kneeland and Underhill did in America. Editing and writing for his weekly, *The New Moral World*, Owen could keep his ideas alive while educating the reading public about his plans for changing the world. Although for Owen, writing always took second place to speaking, the *New Moral World* allowed him to encourage the building of communities. Owen had never been overly enthusiastic about the joint stock cooperative societies that focused on retail trading. Although he spoke positively about setting up labor exchanges, they were, to him, always a first step toward changing the world.

In Britain, as in America, several cooperating societies had tried to establish communities in the 1820s, but all of the communities failed either to materialize or to last more than two or three years. A. J. Hamilton and Abram Combe had begun Orbiston, Great Britain's first Owenite community, in 1825. Economic hardship and the death of Combe in 1827 doomed this experiment to a two-year existence. After Orbiston's failure in 1827, a few other Owenite experiments began in Great Britain, but most of the attempts never became more than ambitious plans. One such example was the London Cooperative Society, whose leaders searched for land so that they could incorporate their radical sexually egalitarian ideas but never actually began communal life.

The communities that did get off the ground were for the most part small-scale attempts. In 1826, for example, a Mr. Vesey began the Exeter Community with a few families and with grand plans for four hundred families. After "domestic circumstances" led to Vesey's departure later that year, the group took another farm nearby and then disappeared from the pages of the *Cooperative Magazine.* In Ireland, young landowner John Vandeleur had been impressed with Owen's speeches in Dublin in 1823, and in 1830 turned his estate into a modified Owenite experiment. This experiment in County Clare, Ireland, closer in concept to Owen's New Lanark than to an egalitarian community, allowed the peasants living on Vandeleur's land to pay him a fixed rent and, in turn, work the land cooperatively. The manager of this experiment, Thomas Craig, was a Manchester Owenite imported for the purpose of educating the peasants in the Owenite system. Though it is not clear that any of the residents except Craig and Vandeleur were enamored of Owenite theory, the community lasted three years, until Vandeleur gambled away his estate.

The most ambitious of the British experiments, and the only one sanctioned by the Owenite movement, was the community of Harmony Hall.[7] The *New Moral World* reported that the community began on October 1, 1839, when the estate of Queenwood, consisting of 533 acres of land, was purchased at East Tytherly, Hampshire (*NMW*, May 16, 1840). Owen refused the position of the community's first "governor" because he believed the project to be unprepared "either with funds or experience."[8] The rapid succession of governors (three in the first six months) and the dissension among members reduced the number of residents from fifty-seven to only nineteen in the fall of 1840 (*NMW,* July 11, 1840). When the community needed funds in 1842 to continue operating, Owen and the Home Colonizing Society poured money into Queenwood, building Harmony Hall, a lavish building with piped water to all the bedrooms, a library, lecture rooms, classrooms, and a communal dining room and well-equipped kitchen. But Harmony Hall was to take up a disproportionate share of the society's funds, and in May of 1844, a revolution of members voted Owen expelled from the community, where he stayed as a paying guest in the best accommodations. These attempts to save the community were too little and too late, and Queenwood's demise in 1845 signaled the end of the Owenite communitarian movement in England.

By 1844, seeking a new vista, Owen once again turned to America. Just as he had left Britain twenty years earlier because too many British reformers were muddying the water of his clearly thought-out reforms, in 1844 he left the *New Moral World* and the failing Harmony Hall to travel in America until June 1845. In America, visiting his children and participating in a variety of "Infidel" conventions, Owen spent his time doing what he did best, lecturing, and his lectures sound similar to those he delivered in the mid-1820s. He spoke to "The People of the United States" in September of 1844 in his typical evangelical style: "Americans! I have come to you a missionary from the other side of the Atlantic, to endeavor to effect, in peace, for the permanent advantage of all, in every country, the greatest revolution ever yet made in human society" (*New York Daily Tribune,* September 24, 1844). Owen's speeches, even though they may have begun with the same glowing rhetoric as his first speech to the new members of New Harmony, reflected a somewhat changed man from the person who addressed Congress twice on his "system." By 1844 Owen talked not always about his views but about the people he once knew. He dropped names shamelessly, often bringing up Thomas Jefferson, James Madison, John and James Adams, General Jackson, and Henry Clay all in the same speech. At the same time he bemoaned how "misunderstood" he was, especially concerning his views of marriage.

As for women, Owen, long separated from the egalitarian rhetoric of William Thompson (who had died in 1833), continued to talk about "women's work" in terms of relieving women from the drudgery of housework without modern conveniences, and about marriage and divorce reform in terms of the "happiness" of the parties, not the liberation of one of the sexes. Because, Owen said to the "American Public," the "object of human society is to increase the happiness of each individual," all "human laws of marriage needed to be based upon these divine or natural laws" (*Tribune,* September 24, 1844). Nowhere in Owen's 1840s lectures do we find his socialist critique of marriage from 1826, when he linked the rise of private property with "ownership" of women and thus perceived a need for a socialist state in order for women to be equal to men. The term "equality" was conspicuously absent from Owen's rhetoric in the 1840s; his references to liberation for women came exclusively in terms of reformed marriage and divorce laws, reforms that were aimed at protecting *men* from having to spend their adult lives tied to a woman whom they no longer loved. Although Owen was eloquent in many of his speeches and essays of the 1840s about marriage, his aim was not equality but rather reform of existing laws, primarily for men's benefit.

If Owen's advocacy of equality had grown less forceful in his years away from Thompson's influence, this idea had not diminished for groups of young Owenites in various American locations. With Owen's egalitarian ideas being kept alive through the writing and speaking of such Owenite reformers as Frances Wright (in Cincinnati and Philadelphia), Robert Dale Owen (in New York City), Samuel Underhill (in Cleveland and throughout Ohio), and Abner Kneeland (in Boston and Illinois), a whole new generation of Owenites was ready for action by the early 1840s.

By 1845 Owenite communalism was once again dotting the American landscape. Owenite societies and intentional communities both in the East and in the Midwest tried once more to find equality in communal living. The economic depression of the late 1830s, coupled with the growing interest in America's new darling of the intellectuals, Charles Fourier, and his brand of "Association," added to the general fervor that stimulated people to become interested in communalism again in the 1840s. By the mid-1840s, Owenite societies proliferated along the eastern seaboard, and these societies successfully began several Owenite communities and assisted others. In England and France numerous Emigrating Societies formed to establish communities in the midwestern United States.

Though the fascination with Charles Fourier developed almost twenty years after Owen's brand of communalism had first taken hold in America, Fourier had been born less than one year after Owen. Many of the Owenites had read Fourier's writings or had listened to Marie Fretageot read Fourier to them as they traveled in the Boatload of Knowledge to New Harmony in the winter of 1825–26, but they had responded to his ideas with only mild interest because Fourier's plans did not call for the most important aspect of Owenite communalism: egalitarianism gained through community of property. As soon as Charles Brisbane translated part of Fourier's writings into English in 1840, however, Fourier's notion of forming "associations" swept through Boston and other cities where people met to talk of his ideas. Brisbane had carefully, in the words of T. D. Seymour Bassett, "pruned Fourier's imaginative vagaries," removing bothersome suggestions of irregularity in marriage and morals, while at the same time simplifying Fourier's complicated reasoning (176). Numerous Fourieristic "phalanxes" sprang up in the early 1840s, particularly in the East and Midwest. Brook Farm, the communal experiment in Roxbury, Massachusetts, begun in 1841 as an extension of transcendentalism where the head and the heart would work together, became a Fourieristic phalanx in 1844 after George and Sophia Ripley became converts to Fourier's ideas.

Followers of Robert Owen, labeled Socialists, Social Reformers, or Rationalists in the 1840s, were greatly outnumbered by Associationists or National Reformers, who espoused Fourier's beliefs. Like Robert Owen, Fourier wanted to change the social organization of the world, calling his utopia a "new social world," a term not much different from Owen's "new moral world." Like Owen, Fourier was a critic of a world that allowed, even encouraged, great poverty to coexist alongside the great wealth of a small minority. In individual households, Fourier saw great waste of food and labor. Like Owen, Fourier believed that group living based on scientific and rational production and distribution would be much more efficient for human beings. Also like Owen, Fourier wanted to put his theory into practice, but, not having a fortune at his disposal, he searched in vain for his entire lifetime for wealthy benefactors and a parcel of land.[9]

Fourier's new social world centered not on Owen's socialism but on psychology: all social organization had to provide an outlet for every human passion, Fourier believed. There were, he wrote, twelve radical passions, and each had to be expressed if humans were to be happy. Fourier was convinced that monogamous marriage overstressed family passion to the detriment of other, equally important passions such as the passion for variety and change and the passion for friendship. From his twelve passions Fourier constructed a classification system for individual personality types. Believing that most people were ruled by one passion, Fourier hypothesized that a random sampling of 1,620 men and women would produce the perfect range of passions. Thus each community—which he called a phalanx—should consist of 1,620 people, who would provide the correct personality type for every possible function the community needed.

Also like Owen, Fourier wanted to reorganize society in order to alter the "unnatural subservience of Woman" (*Reg*, January 8, 1844). Fourier's theory, however, provided for a "natural" subservience of women. Women in the Fourieristic phalanxes were to be grouped, with the most beautiful young women being the Vestals, the young virgins who would be pursued by many suitors. Another group of young women, the Bacchantes, would provide sexual satisfaction for the rejected suitors of the Vestals or for any of the men who needed or wanted sex.

Though both the Associationists and the Socialists had as their main goal the reorganization of society, neither group could say much that was positive about the other, and radical newspapers leave a lively record of their snipes at each other. Robert Owen did counsel his admirers in the January 11, 1845, *New Moral World* that "the Fourierite system . . is advocated and supported by good and talented men and women," who were "doing good by exposing the utter worthlessness of the present system of society," but then added that Fourier's system was "deficient in a knowledge of society or human nature."[10]

The resurgence of Owenite communalism in America, which began in the 1840s and lasted throughout the nineteenth century, manifested itself in three forms: (1) the short-lived "pure" Owenite communities, (2) the short-lived communities founded by people intent on changing the world in ways similar to the Owenites, and (3) the longer-lasting communal attempts of Owen's disciple Etienne Cabet. All three groups tried to establish communal property. All of them advocated completely unfettered religious practices or no religion at all. All intended to establish schools where the community children would learn the "new" principles. All of them promised women equality with men in their community constitutions. The experiences of these communities, though, in many ways recreated the circumstances of the 1820s communities—all suffered from economic hardship and from an ideology of gender that relegated women to be the servers of men and that doomed egalitarian rhetoric because reformers were saying one thing and doing the opposite. From the communities that were able to overcome their initial economic problems and last for more than two or three years, we learn something else: The mere act of joining property communally does nothing to create sexual equality. A socialist state like the Icarian Community in no way solved the problem of women's subordination. In fact, in some ways the attempts to create "equality" within the group had the opposite effect: they exacerbated the inequality of the female members of the group. In an intentional community where all must cooperate with their labor, where all must sacrifice themselves for the good of the group if they are to survive, who better than the women of the community—believed to be the people with "natural" submissiveness and self-sacrifice—to do most of the sacrificing?

THE PURE OWENITE COMMUNITIES

The first of the pure Owenite communities originated in early 1843 when a group of New York socialists who met regularly at the Social Hall at Broadway and Grand formed a "Social Reform Association of One Mentians," meaning a society of "one mind," and effectively reopened the Owenite search for communal egalitarianism. By summer, the group had formed One Mentian Societies in numerous eastern cities and had purchased 750 acres of land in Monroe County, Pennsylvania, on which to form the Promisewell Community.[11] Unlike the Associationists everywhere around them, the founders of the One Mentian Society believed that "private property is the prime cause of all evils that have hitherto afflicted the human race," and that the science of society, as propounded by Robert

Owen, was "the only science that can be beneficially adapted to relieve the world of those evils" (*Reg,* February 5, 1844). A visitor to the One Mentian Society in May 1844—Paul Brown, the misanthrope from New Harmony—told the group that they were too "hidebound and circumscribed" to ever found a real republican community, but the 1840s Owenites ignored the 1820s Owenite (*Reg,* June 1, 1844).

Despite the fact that the members of the One Mentian Society were a generation removed from Robert Owen (and Paul Brown) and from his impassioned call for communitarianism, the 1840s Owenites sounded remarkably like Owen had in the 1820s. By February of 1844, members of the One Mentian Association in New York were writing persuasive letters to radical newspapers urging people to join their venture. At Promisewell, the community begun by the One Mentians, J. R. Smith wrote that there would be no landlords, no poverty, no unhealthy shops, no masters and servants, no competition. Instead, he promised that all would be alike in wealth, food, clothing, education, and labor (*Reg,* February 5, 1844). Benjamin Warden, the newly elected president of the One Mentian Society, also promised to build a home for the entire human race, where all could enter without money and "where equality will reign triumphant" (*Reg,* April 15, 1844). John Hooper went even further in linking this Owenite venture with Robert Owen's 1820s rhetoric by spelling out the importance of equality and women's rights in the community: at Promisewell, he eloquently wrote, "the rich and the poor will meet in equality. . . . Here man and woman will balance the scale of justice and equity." In their Owenite community, woman, once the "domestic slave" of man, would finally "stand erect, his equal and his companion." Here also "marriage shall be in fact a communion of souls, not, as now, a vile article of merchandise . . . for here, her home will be as freely and fully hers as his. Her right as his right" (*Reg,* February 12, 1844).

As branches of the One Mentian Society spread to at least seven cities in New York, New Jersey, and Rhode Island, John Hudson, the treasurer of the New York Reform Organization, led a group of people to the Promisewell Community in May of 1844 to join the other members and their families who were already there. During their trip, the group took time out to celebrate Robert Owen's birthday on May 14, because, Hudson wrote, his "writing and actions have done more towards unity . . . than whole hosts of priests from the earliest history of man" (*Reg,* June 1, 1844). Though the Promisewell Hudson described was a primitive one with few comforts, his enthusiasm was infectious. At his arrival, Promisewell had paid only for acreage, stock, and farm buildings. Adequate housing for the members, as well as a sawmill, was only in the planning stage. The planned dwellings, which comprised separate apartments for each family, including a sitting room measuring twelve feet by twelve feet and a bedroom twelve feet by eight feet; a public dining room; and dormitories and schools for children, followed Owen's 1820s plans almost exactly.

Hudson's Owenite enthusiasm for his venture spilled over into his Owenite rhetoric about women and their place in the new system. "Woman," gushed Hudson, "may her virtuous perseverance and intelligence speedily realize her independence" (*Reg,* June 1, 1844). He was pleased that, upon his arrival, *all* people, "male and female" told him what they thought and all worked hard. Though Hudson couldn't help labeling women "virtuous," he also recognized their intelligence and wished independence for them.

By October of 1844 the sawmill was operating, the land had been cleared and partially cultivated, and progress was, according to John Hooper writing to the *New Moral World,* "steady and satisfactory." Though there were only thirty persons at Promisewell, Hooper still believed that they could create the quintessential Owenite utopia that would "show the world how the poorest, who have industry, knowledge, and virtue, can redeem themselves" (October 12, 1944).

Despite their plans, the proposed dwellings for the members, who were living in "straitened conditions" without warm enough clothing (*Comm,* January 15, 1845), had still not been constructed as late as March 1, 1845. The underfed and poorly clothed members, living in an ill-equipped log cabin, sacrificing comforts and pleasures, reputedly began to disagree with one another, just as members in similar conditions had in the Owenite experiments in the 1820s (Mac Ms, 335). Though some members were still asking for recruits to come to Promisewell as late as early 1845 and others continued to plan such utopian visions as obtaining five hundred singing birds for an aviary, most wondered why they had left their former homes.[12] After members of both the Philadelphia One Mentian Society and the New York One Mentian Society reported unfavorably on the community's conditions to their respective home groups, John Hudson and a few others left Promisewell and moved to nearby Goose Pond, the abandoned property of the Fourieristic Social Reform Unity, where they briefly attempted another Owenite experiment, but it too soon ended. Extreme hardship did as much to squelch utopian optimism and put an end to equality-seeking in the mid-1840s as it did in the 1820s.

Though the renewed interest in Associationism and Socialism was located primarily in the East, "pure" Owenite experiments also sprang up in the West in the 1840s. This western movement originated not so much from the eastern fascination with Fourier and Associationism but from the same source that brought Robert Owen to New Harmony in the first place—emigration. From the early 1820s on, various men, upon hearing of Robert Owen's "plan," met with Owen and were thus inspired to begin Owenite communities, often in America. Many (probably most) of the resulting communities remain unknown today for a number of reasons, including the obscurity of the leader, the lack of letter-writing members, and the inability of many of the planned communities to keep going. Those that were formed were often buried in an obscure part of unsettled America, and their people, eventually, assimilated into the land.[13] Although we know few of the details of many of these communities, their very existence illustrates Owen's continued influence. The one emigrating community from which we do have extensive letters, the Equality Community in Wisconsin, provides us with yet another look at the effects of both hardship and stark living on an Owenite community. The emigrants who came to Wisconsin give us one specific illustration from the 1840s of why Owenite communities did not last and of how an ideology of gender fit into that picture.

At least three different emigrating groups came to Wisconsin from England to establish an Owenite community, but only one group actually undertook communal living. This group, led by Thomas Hunt, called the community "Equality," a fitting name for the last pure Owenite community in the United States.[14] Thomas Hunt had been a member of the Owenite "Rational Society" in London. Like Robert Owen himself, Hunt had been displeased with the management of the British Owenite experiments and believed that America's "liberal institutions" and available fertile land with no taxation presented "to the industrious man of small capital the means of securing a permanent existence immediately" (*Report to a Meeting*, 3). Like a good Owenite, Hunt wrote extensively of how a society of emigrants should be prepared and how a plan like his could (and would) work. The first society, he wrote, should consist of twenty to twenty-five families who would purchase an "improved" farm of two hundred acres. In June of 1843, he planned that twenty people should sail to Wisconsin and purchase the land necessary for the experiment, taking with them twelve months' supplies and food. These first twenty people, the scouting party, would consist of a general superintendent, a person qualified to direct farming operations, a person to direct building operations, and other workers who could farm and construct the buildings required by the community. The first winter in Wisconsin, Hunt wrote, the party would build a public building measuring sixty feet by twenty feet and detached cottages, arranged in a crescent, consisting of four rooms each, one room to each single person twenty-one or older and two rooms to a married couple. Included in Hunt's plan was an elaborate three-year calculation of the profit the group would make on their produce: they would grow wheat, barley, oats, Indian corn, and potatoes the first year and in subsequent years add sheep, poultry, cows, and a mill (*Report to a Meeting*, 11).

In keeping with Owenite theory, Hunt proposed that no person reside in a community unless that person adopted Owen's principle that "the character of man is formed for him, not by him." Also like Owen, Hunt promised an arcadian paradise for his communitarians: "permit me to say that the imagination never conceived—the poet never yet described—nay, that noble of nature, the benevolent OWEN himself, whose entire heart is one intense feeling of desire for the happiness of his species, never yet presented to the world a picture of human felicity more congenial with human nature than is this modest, unpretending, noiseless effort capable of attaining . . ." (*Report*, 21).

The emigrants, some twenty-one of them as according to plan, left London in the summer of 1843 to journey to Equality. They had been selected, according to Thomas Hunt, "with as much care as our means of knowing each other would enable us" (*NMW*, August 2, 1845). Hunt made sure that the members' trades were varied and useful: Thomas Steel was the group's physician, who would also bring in money from seeing patients around the Wisconsin countryside; Mr. Coyle was the group's architect, and Mr. Johnson, though he had been a butcher in London, was the group's farmer, because he believed he had discovered an important theory respecting "the whole phenomenon of the universe," and he was coming, in fact, to Equality in order to carry his views into practice. After landing in New York and meeting with members from the Promisewell Community about to commence in northeastern Pennsylvania, Hunt and his followers journeyed to Milwaukee, where two families, the Buckingyoungs and the Freemans, not part of the twenty-one people who composed the "first draught" and thus not compelled to go further into the Wisconsin countryside at that time, obtained houses.

Instead of following his plan and purchasing an estate with 50 acres of land already cultivated, Hunt and his group purchased 160 acres of land with only 3 acres planted at the time of their purchase with turnips, potatoes, French beans, and melons, and in "a wretched state."[15] The property came with a twelve-by-seventeen-foot log house that had none of the amenities the English emigrants were used to. In Milwaukee, Hunt decided that only eight people, six men and two women, would journey to Mukwonago, the site of their land and small log cabin, to prepare the land and build housing for the rest of the party of twenty-one. Like Owen before him, Thomas Hunt was absent during his community's first months; he, for unknown reasons, decided to remain with many of the women and children in Milwaukee while the others were building the necessary housing and preparing the soil for farming.

Living in such close conditions without their leader for inspiration soon "dampened the beauty of our principles," wrote the physician, Thomas Steel (September 13, 1843, TS Papers). The group had little to eat but bread and butter and cold meat. Adding to the problems was the group's inexperience with agriculture and building. At one point their horses broke tether and escaped; another time the great oak trees they had cut down were too heavy to be "raised"; yet another time the pulleys they fetched from Milwaukee sank in the mud when their horses refused to pull a "waggon" across a creek. Their cattle, as soon as they were "liberated" in an unfenced area, immediately strayed away, and community members spent much of their time chasing the errant cows.[16]

To make matters worse for the first eight settlers, Thomas Hunt and the women and children lost their patience waiting in Milwaukee for crops to be planted and the new dwelling to be finished and journeyed to Muk-wonago in mid-October, less than two months after the first eight people had left. In Mukwonago all twenty-one people wound up living in a small log cabin the size, as Steel complained, of a London parlor. Needless to say, such close living quarters created additional problems. Soon after the arrival of Hunt and the women, Thomas Steel related that "our party are not altogether so harmonious as would be necessary for bodily comforts—particularly amongst the women and children. . . . I am afraid that the jump they have taken from the old state of society to this is more than any are fitted for" (October 23, 1843, TS Papers).

Thomas Steel, the letter-writing physician who was quick to criticize others in his group for not making the jump from the old state of society to the new, himself illustrates why Owenite communities failed and how the "woman problem" fit into the picture. Steel began his voyage to Equality optimistically and commented that his fellow communitarians were well behaved and of a "superior class." Yet even on the voyage to America, Steel wrote that he had a bed to himself, a "luxury enjoyed by few." Thus from its beginning, "Equality" was as abstract a concept as it had been at New Harmony, not a premise that people lived.

By the time the group arrived in Milwaukee, Steel had begun criticizing many of the people in the group, especially the women. He had nothing good to say of Mr. Johnson, the butcher-turned-farmer, who was "our farmer—a cool, calculating man . . . thoughroughly [sic] selfish," or of his wife, with her "high idea of her husbands [sic] ability," or of their six badly brought-up children. Though he conceded that Mrs. Turner might be a well-meaning woman, he wrote that she was "a regular scold" who was unfit for "the new society." On his "good list," however, was the Freeman family, who, not belonging to the "first draught" of twenty-one settlers, had obtained a house in Milwaukee. Steel was particularly taken with the "nice" eldest Freeman daughter, Catherine (September 1, 1843, TS Papers).

Steel's complaints, particularly about the women, and his discomforts continued throughout the fall of 1843. He complained of the want of comfortable accommodations, of being forced to write his letters "upon my knee—surrounded by a dozen people" in a cold, drafty house. He cited his sunrise-until-sunset workday, with little time for "mental recreation." The mental recreation he did write of—a local Society's discussion on the topic "Should women be educated equal to men"—reflected his intellectually liberal ideologies: he was disappointed that "the question was carried in the negative." But Steel's biggest complaint about the women in Equality illustrated his ideology of gender with its discrepancy between Owenite rhetoric and his own deep-seated beliefs about women's roles. Irritated that he had to go out to work and that upon his return no one coddled him, Steel wrote, with great pique, that not one woman in the house "attended to my wants." When dealing with real, live women in his community, Steel placed their equality second to his own comfort.

In contrast to the stark equality in Equality were Steel's frequent trips to the Freeman house in Milwaukee. He was always reluctant to leave "an affectionate and kind family to join a scene of wrangling discontent, and everything disagreeable." At the Freeman house his dirty shirts and stockings were washed by the agreeable young Miss Freeman, and his socks mended, "an attention to which I have been quite unaccustomed of late" (November 13, 1843, TS Papers).

Steel used his complaints to justify his leaving the struggling community in November of 1843, less than three months after arriving. As he wrote:

> I had to travel everyday and on my return, cold, wet and hungry—I met with no kind fare to welcome and assist me to a dry pair of stockings or offer me a seat by the fire—and in many cases was obliged to content myself with what scraps I could pick up—or bones I could scrape—never was a stocking mended (except by Miss Freeman . . . in Milwaukee) nor my trousers mended—nor a button sewed on my shirts nor anything else (December 2, 1843, TS Papers).

Leaving the community, Steel went to live with the Smiths, a "liberal" family from New York. Miss Smith, related a much happier Thomas Steel, "does everything to make me comfortable without making any fuss" (December 2, 1843, TS Papers). Miss Smith's virtues included always having a hot dinner ready upon Steel's return from work and looking after "all my little wants without thinking that I know anything about it" (February 10, 1844, TS Papers). While staying with the Smiths, Steel began building his own home on land he had purchased, after being in Equality less than a week, "to retire to" in case the "tempers and old habits of the greater part of our body" broke up the communal attempt.[17] Soon Steel wrote of his finished house and upcoming marriage to the agreeable Freeman daughter, Catherine, an "amiable" person, "not what the world would call a beauty," but, nevertheless, a darner of socks, a sewer-on of buttons, a woman who would be there with a warm supper fixed when he returned from work.

Though the members of Equality attributed different causes to its eventual demise in 1846—everything from Steel's criticism of Hunt as lacking leadership qualities to Hunt's lament that they bought uncultivated land and could never get adequate crops in or out of the ground—Thomas Steel's experience is illustrative. It is easy to argue verbally for women's equal educational opportunities with men, yet the realization of such theory might result in just the kind of situation prevalent at Equality, with no one person or class of persons tending to the needs and wants of others. How easy for a man like Thomas Steel to retreat from the harshness of communal equality to individual houses and wives. An "informant" related to A.J. Macdonald that the Equality Community failed because the "circumstances" at Equality were not superior to those the members left. As the informant said, "few are prepared to sacrifice their present comforts for the establishment of a principle" (Mac Ms, 362). For Thomas Steel, the principles were overlooked for a sewn-on button.

Equality, then, broke apart for reasons quite similar to the reasons the other Owenite communities of the 1820s and 1840s lasted such a short time. At Equality, as at Promisewell, a group of people unschooled in farming tried to create a life out of the land. Their mistakes, especially at Equality, provide amusing anecdotes but illustrate at the same time their unsuitability for their venture. Their incompetence resulted in the same dismal conditions prevalent at most of the other Owenite communities: they suffered from what Steel called "a complete want of every physical comfort" (November 13, 1843, TS Papers). Leadership at Equality, as at New Harmony during most of its first, formative year, was nonexistent. Thomas Hunt, the careful planner and ostensible leader, did not follow his carefully thought-out plan to purchase a certain amount of good, cultivated soil; thus all the members' time was spent cultivating the land rather than building the planned Owenite housing that would allow the members to live in physical comfort. Rather than join his group, Hunt remained behind in much more comfortable circumstances than the eight people who tried to forge a community out of the Wisconsin backwoods. When he did arrive at Mukwonago with the rest of the group, he, too, was unable to cope with the conditions and the quarreling of community members. Steel wrote that Mr. Hunt, shortly after arriving in the desolate community, "never opens his mouth and appears to be in the sulks" (November 13, 1843, TS Papers).

Finally, at Equality as at Promisewell, the community did not last long enough to get beyond the struggle for survival that consumed most of everyone's daily time. No one had the time or inclination to begin to implement schools, cultural events, or even to build adequate, comfortable housing. The conditions, particularly in Wisconsin, were too primitive, too isolated to support a group of untrained communards, however idealistic. Given the abundant, inexpensive land surrounding them, the members of Equality simply blended into the countryside, as did Thomas Steel, or returned to Milwaukee, as did Thomas Hunt, retreating to the comforts of individual homes furnished with private wives.[18]

The notion of Woman, as in the 1820s communities, created an ideology in members' minds that made it difficult to deal with real-life women unless they were behaving in "acceptable" ways. Whereas the 1820s communities broke up, at least in part, because of the "woman problems" married women caused, Equality failed, from Thomas Steel's perspective at least, because of a lack of "wives."

THE OWENITE COMMUNAL TRADITION

The Owenite communities of Promisewell and Equality were not the only experiments furthering the cause of Owenite communitarianism. Other reformers created communities, though not self-consciously labeled "Owenite," that also advocated much of Owen's ideology. The many

"World Conferences" held throughout the early 1840s helped to bring these reformers together. Visibly present at several of these indoor revival meetings for intellectuals was Robert Owen, in addition to well-known American reformers such as George Ripley, Frederick Douglass, John Collins, and "westerners" such as John O. Wattles.

Abolitionist-turned-reformer John Collins provides us with an example of one such community builder from the East. His Skaneateles Community, founded on January 1, 1844, in upper New York state, looked so much like Owen's New Harmony that both Collins's contemporaries and twentieth-century scholars label the community as "Owenite."[19] Whereas Promisewell and Equality were specifically founded as Owenite communities, John Collins claimed to have discovered and promulgated Owen's main tenets without ever reading Owen. He wrote on September 4, 1844, that until "recently," he knew "little of Mr. Owen's principles" *(Communitist).*

In all aspects, John Collins sounded like an 1840s version of Robert Owen, and his community duplicated with flawless fidelity the same problems that beset New Harmony. The community at Skaneateles was dedicated to being a "community of social equality" *(Comm,* September 18, 1844), just as was New Harmony almost twenty years earlier. As at New Harmony, the Skaneateles Community boasted a "liberal" school, a radical weekly newspaper, and a few crops. Collins had purchased a farm in upstate New York of 300 acres, with over 200 acres tilled, even though he had earlier spoken of the necessity to begin with 1,500 to 3,000 acres *(Bird's Eye View,* 21).

The seventy-five to ninety people who populated Skaneateles during its first year were all "usefully" employed. The women were relegated to household affairs (despite Collins's promises in a printed pamphlet that it should be men doing the household work), though their labor in the kitchen was noted by at least one visitor to the community to be "light" *(WA,* July 21, 1844). All appeared at first, at least to the editor of a local paper, to be "satisfied and content" *(WA,* July 20, 1844), working on a number of "useful" occupations: he noted some men laying an aqueduct to bring pure water to the main house, some in the corn field, some chopping trees in the woods, and yet others in the mill. A visitor of two weeks, Marenda B. Randell wrote in March of 1844 of the beautiful location for the seventy-five people, who all worked hard, abstained from meat, alcohol, tobacco, butter, cheese, and rich pastry for their purely vegetable diet, a diet similar to the popular Grahamite diet *(Reg,* April 1, 1844). Robert Owen, himself, was extraordinarily pleased with Skaneateles during his four-day visit in May of 1845. He told members there that he would find "great pleasure" ending his days at Skaneateles *(Comm,* May 21, 1845).

As in New Harmony, conflicts soon erupted in Skaneateles. Collins, apparently to avoid the suspiciousness of ownership, let the community's other important leader, Q. A. Johnson, a Syracuse lawyer, sign the deed to the land. As at New Harmony when Owen and Maclure disagreed about the direction the community should take, so Collins and Johnson found almost no common ground, and their disagreements divided the community. The dispute between two powerful men, in addition to the primitive conditions and lack of realized equality, only served to further the discontent in Skaneateles. Only seven months after writing her first letter full of all the glories of her newfound "Humanity's home," Marenda Randell revealed that "Communists at Skaneateles have been preaching one thing and trying to practice something else" (*WA*, November 31, 1844). Later, having left Skaneateles, Randell wrote from Vermont that the community had "failed" because the "great and beautiful ideas" that attracted people to Skaneateles could not be realized (*Reg*, December 1, 1845).

Also attending several of the eastern conventions was John O. Wattles, a western reformer, who was fascinated with building communities and with marriage in communities, where reproduction would not necessarily be part of a sexual relationship.[20] When he returned to Ohio after attending an 1843 World Conference, Wattles helped organize the Prairie Home Community, established in early 1844 to provide a home for primarily "western" people and former Quakers. It was a place where the fashionable Grahamite diet predominated and where laws were forbidden. Located in Logan County, Ohio, the anarchical Prairie Home consisted of around 500 acres, where 130 members lived together for scarcely a year (Mac Ms, 271). A. J. Macdonald, visiting in the summer of 1844, noticed a typical pattern of work: "the young women were most industrious attending to the supper table and the provisions in a very steady, businesslike manner; but the young men were mostly lounging about, doing nothing" (278).

Attracted to the Prairie Home Community was another reformer with Owenite sympathies, the outspoken newspaper writer and editor Orson Murray.[21] The community intrigued the anarchist Murray because of its lack of government. Believing in "no creeds" and "no constitutions," he lambasted both Bibles and constitutions: "both are the conjured instruments of priests and politicians" (*The Struggle*, 5).

Murray's weekly newspaper, the *Regenerator*, became a unifying force for social reformers in the mid-1840s. Although Murray professed to have no creed, he was sympathetic to the Owenite communitarians, and his paper recorded the activities of the "western" communities, such as Prairie Home, as well as the eastern Owenite communal movement. He moved his press to Ohio at the end of 1844, a few months after the Prairie Home community disbanded. He reported in August 1845 that although Prairie Home failed, Grand Prairie Home Community was being established in Warren County, Indiana, on 350 acres of land complete with a fine orchard and two buildings. At present, a communicant told Murray, there were about twenty people who were building a common house on Owen's parallelogram model. They were quite concerned with making "the female portion comfortable" and with inviting unmarried persons who were "fully prepared and convinced of the principles of universal brotherhood and unanimity of interest" (*Reg*, August 4, 1845). Though they were not prepared to receive any more families, suitably prepared single people were most welcome. The school that they intended to set up, the Grand Prairie Harmonial Institute, proposed to educate boys and girls similarly, "so that if it should turn out that the 'faculties' of the minds of man and woman are the same, there can be no distinction of sex in the schools, and both shall have equal advantage" (Mac Ms, 300).

The Owenite communal tradition was also carried on through reformers who, having met Robert Owen, decided to take some of his ideas and mix them with their own to establish their own distinct communities. In the 1820s several men who heard Owen speak, such as Joseph Davis or William Hall, tried to synthesize the economic benefits of communal living through their own versions of a modified Owenite community. Josiah Warren, who had been a resident of New Harmony, left Indiana determined to create his own brand of community living and formed, throughout the 1830s, 1840s, and 1850s, a series of communities with property held individually, instead of in common, which existed as handmaidens to what Warren labeled "individual sovereignty."[22] But it is Etienne Cabet's Icarian communities that provide us with a look at Owen's ideas realized over several decades. In many ways a discussion of the Icarian communities is a fitting end to a study of the Owenite communal tradition. Icaria, in several permutations, lasted longer than any Owenite community and incorporated a community of property. Thus, we can study over a period of several decades communities that promised equality to women.

ETIENNE CABET

Perhaps the most significant reformer to continue the Owenite tradition after meeting Owen was Etienne Cabet, a Frenchman whose long-standing American communities owed at least part of their theoretical underpinnings to Robert Owen. Cabet's ideas, A. J. Macdonald wrote, "reminded one much of Mr. Owen's as he looked rather disdainfully upon the experiments of the Fourierites and other associationists in the country" (142–43). To Cabet, in the change from individualism to communism, "brotherhood must come first, then equality—and liberty would follow" (143).

Born of working-class parents in 1788, Etienne Cabet was exiled from his French homeland in 1834 for writing an article on the "crimes of the kings against humanity" and thus metamorphosed from a lawyer/organizer to a visionary communist. Exiled in England during the early 1830s Cabet met Owen and read Sir Thomas More's *Utopia*, two events that radically changed his life.[23]

In England, under Owen's influence, Cabet wrote a utopian novel, *Le*

Voyage en Icarie, in 1838. Framed like Sir Thomas More's *Utopia,* with a narrator/author meeting a utopian traveler at General Lafayette's home, *Le Voyage en Icarie* depicts Cabet's ideas of an ideal communist state, founded on Robert Owen's most basic principle: equality. All people, Cabet insisted, are equal, because such is the natural condition of humankind. Bemoaning the fact that Robert Owen, that "rich friend of humanity who sacrificed 1,200,000 francs and all his life to happiness," had too much confidence in the bounty of aristocrats and too little capital for the needs of a model community, Cabet created in fiction a community much like the one Owen tried to create in reality (*Voyage,* 519).

The fictional Icarians, according to Cabet, were a society founded on the basis of the most perfect equality. All citizens were equal in rights and in work, though no one worked too hard. In each family the women and children did the domestic work from 5:00 or 6:00 A.M. until 8:30 A.M.; then the children went to school and the women went to their professional workshops from 9:00 A.M. until 1:00 P.M. But in Icaria the women were not expected to do the domestic work on top of everything else. While they did domestic work, the men were working too; from 6:00 A.M. until 1:00 P.M. they labored at their professions in the workshops, all of which were, of course, large, airy, and comfortable. The Icarians arose at 5:00 A.M., went to work at 6:00 A.M., and could then meet with their families at 1:00 P.M. to begin the day's leisures: dining from 2:00 to 3:00, miscellaneous activities such as work in gardens, walking along the streets, or going to the theater from 3:00 to 9:00 P.M. All retired at 10:00 P.M. No one worked longer than seven hours a day in the summer and six hours a day in the winter. Likewise, no children worked in the workshops: boys chose a profession at the age of eighteen; girls at the age of seventeen (*Voyage,* 98–107).

Until choosing professions at seventeen or eighteen, the young people of the community received excellent, rational educations because Cabet considered education to be the foundation of society, just as Robert Owen did. A child's first education, said Cabet, came from its mother during its first five years. At five, the child began its communal learning, culminating at the age of sixteen or seventeen with an introduction to comparative religions, taught to the children by a professor of philosophy, not a priest. Up until that time, the children of the community had no exposure to religion because influencing children about religion before the age of reason was forbidden in Icaria (170).

Cabet's ideas on marriage also echoed Owen's: after completing their educations, young people in Icaria were encouraged to find a suitable spouse, though no one was allowed to marry before age eighteen (for women) or twenty (for men) or unless the parties had known each other at least six months (139). Should the marriage be unhappy, Cabet proposed, as Owen had before him, that the parties be allowed to divorce in order to find a new, happier conjugal association (141). Since marriage and conjugal fidelity were the basis of family order in the Icarian nation, and since each citizen had had an excellent education and had the facilities both to marry and to divorce, the Republic branded the voluntary celibate as an ingrate and declared that concubinage and adultery were crimes without excuse (141).

After his return to France in 1839 and the publication of *Voyage* in 1840, the dismal economic conditions in his country helped turn Cabet from a writer into a social reformer. Throughout the turbulent decade of the 1840s the Icarian movement grew, especially among the working class in small French towns, reaching the height of its power in 1845–46. This movement was, according to Christopher Johnson, the beginning of a communist movement in France (144–45). In 1847 Cabet gave up on political action in France and returned again to England to visit Owen before he decided upon a location for his "Icarian" community. Attempting to "mirror Owenism in his own Icarian communities," Cabet met Owen and discussed establishing his utopian community in Texas.[24] Owen himself had briefly considered establishing another community in Mexican territory after New Harmony failed, but in 1847—with Texas having just joined the union the previous year and offering large inducements to settlers—the southwest United States looked to be an even more favorable place in which to build a community.[25]

The community of Icaria, though, was not established on Texas soil. A vanguard of seventy men, labeled the "soldiers of humanity," did indeed leave France for Texas in February of 1848. Cabet himself and the other "companies," groups of people ready to emigrate to America, had remained in France because of the uprisings in late February 1848. The men who ventured to Texas found themselves in much the same circumstances as did the vanguard of the Equality Community in Wisconsin: neither had a leader with them and both discovered unplanned physical problems such as rain and snow in Wisconsin and swampland in Texas. Neither group knew how to clear land, start crops, or build dwellings. The conditions that induced Thomas Steel to abandon his egalitarian principles also forced the Icarians to abandon Texas. Retreating from Texas, the vanguard met Cabet and 500 hopeful Icarians in New Orleans. Faced with the impossibility of returning to Texas, Cabet purchased an abandoned Mormon community in Nauvoo, Illinois, where the remaining faithful 142 men, 74 women, and 64 children could live in Icarian harmony.[26]

In March of 1849, the Icarians established themselves temporarily in the American "West," isolated by their foreign language much the same way German emigrants a hundred years earlier in Pennsylvania had been isolated. Their foreign culture also protected them from the notoriety that Owen experienced with New Harmony. The community that they erected on a former Mormon dwelling was a monument to their industriousness and dedication. They built in a short time what Owen had only hoped to build—a large building, 120 feet long and 40 feet wide, which created the nucleus of the community. The first floor was divided into a workshop for the women, a theater, and a huge dining hall, where a buffet on wheels moved from the kitchen to the hall, loaded with food, plates, and silverware. The dining hall could seat 1,200 people, at tables of 10 each (I. G. Miller, 104). The second story was divided into rooms, with each family having one room and bachelors sharing a room, complete with baths and running hot and cold water. As Owen had wanted, all meals were taken in common, and all children lived in dormitories in their schoolhouses because "too much intercourse with their parents would have a contaminating effect" (Vallet, 30).

Also as in Owenite communities, schools were immediately established, one for boys and another for girls. Though girls were primarily taught by women and boys by men, in the higher classes both sexes learned about sciences and geometry (I. G. Miller, 104). Both French and English were taught, and, according to one former resident, the schools were so good that "outsiders"—twenty of them—sent their children to the Icarian schools for schooling (I. G. Miller, 105) Children had plenty of time for "amusement," being provided with a large playground.

As in New Harmony and Franklin, Sunday was the day for both social and intellectual recreation. The dining hall was given over to scientific discussions or to concerts. Sunday evenings, particularly in the winter, saw weekly theater productions as well as dances. Most of the members of Icaria were freethinkers, though joining a church was not forbidden.

Philosophically, Icaria was based on Owen's socialistic tenets. Cabet, like Owen, wanted to create a "useful" community. Whereas Owen created "sensible signs" for children's learning, Cabet had planned to make the Texas desert "useful," while creating a community "capable of insuring happiness to the human race"—the very thing Owen wanted to do at New Harmony. Though Cabet said that his community did "not resemble any other," he added that the very reason his community was unique was because it had as its object "not only the interest and happiness of its members, but the interest and happiness of entire HUMANITY" (Mac Ms, 147). Owen, of course, had said the same thing about New Harmony. Cabet also, like Owen, emphasized the importance of women's education in the community. He believed that "a young lady [must] receive the same education as a young man" (Mac Ms, 153). Like Owen, Cabet promised and then (unlike Owen) actually built a common kitchen and dining room, because, as Cabet said, "Equality reigns in the repasts as in other things" (Mac Ms, 149). Though each family might have individual lodgings, Cabet believed that in Icaria, "the property, in place of being individual or personal, is social, undivided, and common. Happiness is found in fraternal association and in equality" (Mac Ms, 153).

During the first few years that the community was establishing itself, the familiar "utopian" conflicts ensued that undermined community harmony. Though Cabet's published information about the community's first six years looks remarkably positive, members left a record of growing discontent. In 1855 the community had 500 members, working farms, a flour mill, a distillery, a band, and numerous workshops. Then, according to William Hinds, a visitor to the community in the 1870s, "a war broke out" (66). The ensuing battle between Cabet, who apparently regretted giving up so much control of "his" community, and other community members, who were appalled at the dictatorship of their leader, resulted in Cabet's being expelled from the community in 1856. Summarily dismissed, Cabet led a remaining minority of Icarians who still valued his leadership to a new site in St. Louis, the Cheltenham Community. After only four weeks in St. Louis, Cabet died of apoplexy (not from "freezing to death because his faithful few had deserted him," as one apocryphal story goes).

Cabet's leadership problems resemble Owen's at New Harmony and Collins's at Skaneateles. All three men were successful at something other than leading communities before founding their utopias. Both Cabet and Owen found European soil too constricting for their earth-shaking plans; both planned communities that they believed would save the world. All three men gave up much control of their community once they came to America (or once they were in their community), because their main tenet was, after all, the equality and brotherhood of all. They all regretted their actions once they understood that all their disciples did not envision utopia the same way they did. In Owen's case, he could do no right—one faction, represented by Paul Brown, castigated him for not giving up all his property to be held in common; others, like William Maclure, believed New Harmony to be too centered on community of property. Similarly, Collins disagreed with the religiously bent people in his community and was unable, or unwilling, to compromise with them. Likewise, Cabet was an opinionated man who knew "the truth" and who appeared tactless and ruthless to those who opposed him. He was, according to one critic, a "poorer leader if possible than Robert Owen—full of words and theories" (*Am Soc*, September 28, 1876).

After Cabet died, the Cheltenham Community members continued living communally for eight more years but eventually broke up for both economic and philosophical reasons: making ends meet in a new environment was difficult, especially when many members had to go into St. Louis to find work. At the same time members quarreled about what kind of political system to have and could not reach a compromise. Several members wanted to have all control vested in one person, having seen what happened at Nauvoo; others wanted to retain a democracy.

Meanwhile, communal life at Nauvoo continued without Cabet. Though the community was reduced in size and suffered from money problems, the remaining Nauvoo Icarians had by 1859 moved to Iowa, where they created a new community, abetted by rising land values during the Civil War. In Iowa for the next four decades, the Icarians built, just as Robert Owen had wanted to, a dozen small white cottages arranged on the sides of a parallelogram and a large, central building containing a kitchen and a dining hall, where all members ate in common, which was also used for community amusements. They constructed a bakery, a laundry, a dairy house, barns, and several log cabins. Over the entrance door to the central building was the word "Equality," reminding them always of their central goal.

Icaria in Iowa looked like an Owenite community in everything but its longevity. People who visited Icaria quickly noted its similarities to an Owenite venture. Albert Shaw, who visited in 1883, wrote that the Icarian movement was "most akin to . . . Owenism," with Icaria being "an attempt to realize the rational, democratic communism of the utopian philosophers" (viii).

One of the most striking similarities between the Icarian and the pure Owenite experiments was the ideology of gender that made the attainment of equality impossible for women. The Icarian Constitution that Cabet wrote in 1850 and then revised in 1851, like the constitution at New Harmony and other Owenite communities, laid some groundwork for equality between the sexes but at the same time revealed that women were secondary citizens. One of its first premises was that women have the same social rights as men, while the Icarians' "first interest and first duty [is] to ensure happiness to the women" (Mac Ms, 13). It stipulated that husband and wife are equal and the duty of fidelity in marriage is equally the same for both parties (Mac Ms, 181–82). It also stipulated that women, married or unmarried, must fulfill "all the foregoing conditions as for men," adding that when a woman is not imbued with the spirit of Icarianism, "she can draw her husband away and bring to the community more trouble and disorder." Such was the case in 1849, Cabet wrote, when "vain, ignorant, egotistical women" caused their "feeble and blind" husbands to desert the community (Mac Ms, 172). As in Cabet's fictionalized account, the Icarian Constitution provided for no servitude, no wages, no salaries, no taxes, free choice for marriage partners, fidelity as duty for both, and divorce (Mac Ms, 178–181). Yet, juxtaposed with all these constitutional promises of equality, Article 2 of the first section of the constitution reads that "this society is made up of all Icarians who have been definitively admitted, with their wives and their children" (Prudhommeaux, *Histoire*, Appendix [my translation]). In the constitutional discourse women are not Icarians; rather they are appendages to the real Icarians, the men, their husbands.

Though Cabet, like Owen, promised equality "in all things" between the sexes (Mac Ms, 154), he suffered from the same ideology of gender. While the Owenite communities qualified the concept of equality only covertly, the Icarian constitution states flatly: "this equality is not absolute but relative" (Mac Ms, 154). For women in the community this relativity meant the lack of certain privileges—particularly voting privileges. According to the Icarian Constitution written in 1851, women were only "allowed" to "assist in the deliberations without the privilege of voting" (Mac Ms, 155). The same law governed provisional members and young men from the ages of fifteen to twenty. Any of these three groups that lacked full adult status were to be heard only concerning community matters that related to their special interests.

Daily life in the community even after Cabet was expelled reflected the constitution of Icaria in many ways, with women taking a secondary position to men. For example, Jules Prudhommeaux wrote that at lunch, men had soup, vegetables, or meat, while women generally took only "café au lait." One former member of the community remembered that the kitchen was presided over by "one male cook with a detail of four women." Likewise in the bakery, one man was in charge of the work, but "his helpers were women." That domestic help was the realm of women was never in question. The same resident remembered that "although there were many families, there were, at one time 106 bachelors. Think what the mending must have been for this number. Of course the women attended to this" (I. G. Miller, 104). Had Thomas Steel lived in Icaria, he might have remained in "equality" a bit longer.

The promise for equality and the reality of women's limited enfranchisement had both a predictable and an unpredictable outcome. As in New Harmony and other Owenite communities, this discrepancy caused tensions that hastened the community's end. By the 1870s, the young men and women who had grown up in a community promising equality between the sexes decided it was time they did something about the lack of women's equality; thus they formed a "youthful party," with the complete enfranchisement of women as its main tenet. In October of 1877 this party wrote a justification of the division in Icaria; the young people reiterated that it was equality that was the fundamental principle in communism, and its consequences were brotherhood and liberty. "Is there brotherhood, liberty, in a community where one part (the men) can impose their laws and will upon another part (the women)? No, there is inequality, with neither brotherhood, nor liberty" (Prudhommeaux, *Histoire,* 321 [my translation]). What they wanted, they wrote, was for all individuals, men and women alike, to be equal in rights and in work. These young people then broke away from their elders and established a new constitution in October 1879, which reaffirmed the spirit of the original 1850 Icarian Constitution in its proclamation of communism as the first tenet but differed drastically in its references to women. In its Article 2, for example, where the constitution of 1850 referred to Icarians and "the women and children," the dissenters' constitution read that "this society encompassed all the Icarians who are full members, with their children (Prudhommeaux, *Histoire,* 444 [my translation]). Even more obvious, the young Icarians clearly stated just who should vote in the General Assembly, where women had always been only "advisors": "The General Assembly is composed of all Icarians of both sexes having admitted to signing the articles, which incorporated the community, being at least 20" (Prudhommeaux, *Histoire,* 447 [my translation]). This young party consisted of the majority of Icarians in 1879—forty-two adults and forty children, with most of the adults being between twenty and forty-five, thus having grown up in the community.

The older Icarians, known as the "New" Icaria Party, in turn, relocated one mile away, where they continued to espouse only limited voting rights for women and lived together communally until 1898. A visitor to this new community made up of the community elders reaffirmed that "on most current questions [women] do not vote." The constitution the New Icarian Community wrote in 1879 affirmed their dedication to a "complete" community of property as well.[27] By 1881 several members of the young party, encouraged by the glowing letters they were receiving from a member who had relocated in northern California, moved to the Sonoma Valley, where they formed the Icaria-Speranza Community and lived together communally until 1886. In California the Icarians made sure that their General Assembly consisted of all full members "of both sexes."[28] The new sex-neutral California constitution maintained community property and communal meals but also allowed for a division of extra profit among members and permitted some private ownership of clothes, furniture, and bedding. By 1886, communal life broke up, but as one former member, Marie Leroux Dehay, wrote in 1934, the year she died: "though [we] failed . . . the principle stays, and in time will be perfected" (quoted in Hine, 77).

The Icarian communities, finally, reinforce many of the lessons learned from the Owenite communities, but they also provide us with a perspective over time, as the experiments lasted long enough for the children to wrest power from the first-generation Icarians. The experience of the Icarians tells us, first of all, of the utter importance of the kind of people who join together to create a more perfect life. The Icarian communities' longevity was due, at least in part, to their population. Made up of foreigners who could not speak English, Icaria fostered interdependence among its members, much the same kind of interdependence engendered by the religious foreign-language communities that formed in America in the seventeenth and eighteenth centuries. Unlike the British emigrators at Equality, the Icarians' language barrier kept them from blending into the countryside, purchasing individual parcels of land. This language barrier coupled with their physical isolation created a microcosm similar to the Puritans' Massachusetts Bay Colony, where communal values, by necessity, had to take precedence over individual liberty. Only when the young women and men of the community demanded "equality" for the women did the importance of individual liberty surface and inevitably help lead to the demise of the community.

A final lesson the Icarian experiments illustrate is that a socialist state does not, in and of itself, liberate women. Instead, when bounded by patriarchal thought, the liberation of women acts as friction against the smoothly running gears of communal life. The gender equality that had formed the basis of community rhetoric at Icaria was, in practice, inimical to an efficient community. The communal structure of the Icarians was strong as long as the women accepted, without question, their subservience to men. As foreshadowed at Yellow Springs, where the "young maidens" caused problems when they arrived at the community expecting the equality they were promised, the daughters of Icaria sundered the "communal spirit" when they and the young men demanded the equality promised as the basis of community life. The ensuing split separated the community both physically and psychically. But by questioning the price of their community's efficiency, the young women and men of Icaria exposed the patriarchal ideology that undermined their egalitarian principles every step of the way. Like Frances Wright, who spent her life battling for an equality she could only imagine, the young Icarians show us how the search for equality was (and is) more difficult than they and the Owenites could ever have imagined.

CONCLUSION
Voices from the Past

> The past is a great darkness. . . . Voices may
> reach us from it . . . and we cannot always
> decipher them precisely in the clearer light
> of our own day.
>
> —The concluding sentence from Margaret
> Atwood's *The Handmaid's Tale*

When we listen to women's voices from the past—women such as Frances Wright, Camilla Wright, Sarah Pears, Eliza M'Knight, and countless other now-nameless women—we must learn to decipher their words very carefully. We do not wish to imitate Margaret Atwood's scholars in *The Handmaid's Tale*, who believe they are listening to a woman's tale in the "clearer light of [their] own day," but who are, in effect, still so enmeshed in their own ideology of gender that they cannot comprehend the clear voice they hear.

We hear the voices of the women from the nineteenth century only as they come filtered through our own ideology of gender, an ideology that has altered remarkably little from the time of the cult of True Womanhood. Our current ideology posits that women can indeed have it all—marriage, children, meaningful work—if they are willing to remain subservient to the dominant patriarchal culture. Translated into action, that subservience means that women are still the gender responsible for children, for domestic work, for soothing their husbands' worried brows, and for working twice as hard in the workplace as their bosses, the men. Our ideology is, in fact, not far removed from the Owenites' version. Just as the women in New Harmony found themselves caught in a "double day," so "super-women" of the late twentieth century find that they, too, work full-time jobs while remaining responsible for their families' domestic needs. We have added to the Owenites' ideology of gender only an illusion of women's power in the workplace. Statistics telling us of "women's worth" in the marketplace as compared to men's—their lower pay for comparable work, their segregated pink-collar occupations, and the feminization of poverty—belie our assertions of progress.

For many years I was unable to escape our contemporary ideology of gender. Anxious to discover at least one Owenite utopia where women's needs were met, I wanted to believe that Frances Wright had found such a utopia during the last years of the 1820s when she lived in New York City. Wright had it all—meaningful work, power, a loving "family" group, and a modified community of kindred spirits. Then, I reread Camilla Wright's letters written at the time of her sister's greatest happiness. Cam, the person at home, was miserable. Her voice rang out through the century and a half since she had tried to compose her thoughts. Its anguish was palpable.

Indeed, while Frances Wright's living arrangement met *her* needs quite nicely, the woman left "at home" was in the same position that Sarah Pears or Eliza M'Knight or Eliza Flower had found herself in: watching the great experiment take place and having no place within it other than that of a server. Camilla had no meaningful work to do other than acting as a housekeeper for the Free Enquirers. She functioned, in all practical ways, as the group's "wife." Whether the community was a large intentional one, "far from humanity's home," or a small group house in New York City, the result was the same: the frustration of those women whose job was defined as serving others was due, in time, either to fester and then explode or to subside into a deadening depression.

It finally became clear to me, as I listened to Camilla and then to the other women, that they were not simply troublemakers who did not know a good thing when they saw it. For many years I, like their husbands or the Owenite reformers, had been exasperated with them for toppling the utopian ventures, for ruining good Owenite experiments simply because they could not understand what utopian living was all about. Poor husbands, I commiserated, to be stuck with such insufferable complainers. I had absorbed, without thinking, the patriarchal view of complaining women. Oblivious to their pain, ignoring the voices I heard, unable to understand their silences, I placed their misery within the only framework I knew: if they did not like the communities, something was wrong with the women themselves. It took me many years to learn to trust my own ears, to hear that these women's misery was real and justifiable, and to realize that the "something wrong" was with the communities, not with the women.

In community life, being a "wife" meant serving everyone, not just one's individual family. For married women such as the elder Icarians, who chose to join the community and who believed in the community's tenets, such service was given freely and with good will. In fact, the gender inequality there acted as a glue that held the community together. But for most of the married women who went to an Owenite community because of their husbands' wishes, such expected service supported an idea they did not believe in. What happened, I propose, was that the ideology of gender hardened into a cultural practice that few of the married women could escape. As in the mainstream culture, married women were expected to live out their roles as helpmates, to practice self-sacrifice. Whether they liked it or not, the married women in the communities were considered to be the servers of everyone, to "belong" to the community. Believing in the community's tenets was beside the point for married women who were expected to *be* the community's wives.

The case of Brook Farm will provide us with one final group of women in utopia to study as a counterpoint to the women's experiences in the Owenite communities. Brook Farm, a Transcendental community begun in 1841 by George and Sophia Ripley and transformed into a Fourieristic phalanx in 1844 for its remaining two years, had many of the same egalitarian principles as the Owenite communities. Just like the Owenite experiments before it, Brook Farm promised through its constitution that "all rights, privileges, guarantees, and obligations of members expressed or implied . . . shall be understood to belong equally to both sexes" (Article 7, Section 6, Constitution of the Brook Farm Community). At Brook Farm, however, as in the Owenite communities, an ideology of gender reared its ugly head almost from the first. Nathaniel Hawthorne grumbled only briefly about having to milk cows; shortly after he complained, he was "relieved" of all his work assignments so that he could spend more time on "important" activities.[1] Yet no woman was excused from her menial labor. If a woman did not work appropriately long, arduous hours, she could quickly be dismissed from the community. Young Sophia Eastman wrote only one letter back home complaining of the inordinate amount of work women in the community were expected to perform before George Ripley notified her father that his daughter was being sent home because "she is not the kind of person contemplated in our plan," i.e., "skilled in all sorts of domestic labor and capable of taking the lead in the most fatiguing duties."[2]

Although all of the women writing letters from Brook Farm commented on their long work days and domestic services, the Brook Farm women, with few exceptions, viewed their busy workdays from an entirely different perspective than did most of the Owenite women. The Brook Farm women were single (Charles Lane wrote in the *Dial* of 1844 that there were only four married couples out of the seventy people living in the community at that time); they had chosen their lives; they were in control and could leave whenever they wished. These women, most of whom were between sixteen and twenty-two, wrote of their happy life at Brook Farm as a college-like experience, replete with a popular vegetarian diet, clubs, weekend trips to nearby Boston, and regular lectures by such people as Margaret Fuller and Ralph Waldo Emerson.

The difference between the unhappy married women in the Owenite communities and the happy Brook Farm women stems not from the communities' intentions (which were the same), but from the fact that at Brook Farm the ideology of gender did not become encased into an institution—marriage—from whose demands and roles the women could not escape. Because most of the Brook Farm women were single, they had a high status in the community. As Alexis de Tocqueville observed in the mid-1830s, single women in America were afforded considerable freedom while married women were "confined within the narrow circle of domestic life and their situation is in some respects one of extreme dependence" (2:255). John Codman, a resident of Brook Farm, reminisced about this issue: "it has been asserted that Associations [are advantageous] for men, but that women can never get along with them. The experience of Brook Farm testifies against the assertion." The only unhappy women, he wrote, were those who were married to men whose whole energies were devoted to their work. Sophia Ripley, the one married woman living at Brook Farm during its entire existence, escaped the oppressive roles and "innate" self-sacrificing nature assigned to married women by being a "sisterly rather than a wifely woman" (Kirby, 172–73). Though several Brook Farm residents complained that Sophia Ripley had no "motherliness" to her and that "nature had not endowed her with deep human sympathy," such a "lack" in her makeup allowed her to escape her predestined roles as a married woman (Kirby, 173). Women did "get along" in Brook Farm because there were few married women whose only stake in the community's future came through their husbands. The single women were perceived without innate obligations, without preconceived roles.

Because the single status of the Brook Farm young women allowed them to escape automatic gender stereotyping, they could also escape the notion that all the "drudgery" fell to them. The young people wrote letters illustrating how often work in Brook Farm crossed sex-role barriers. Though women probably did perform more of the domestic work than did the men, the young men of the community remembered to "help." Frederick Pratt wrote that he helped in the washing room; George William Curtis also wrote how he aided the women in the laundry and hung out the clothes, while several men often volunteered to assist with the dishes. Arthur Sumner remembered learning how to iron towels at Brook Farm. George Bradford wrote in 1892 that he too served in the washroom, pounding the clothes in a hogshead with a wooden pestle and then wringing them and hanging them out; his rationale (couched in good Victorian rhetoric) was that "it was a part of our chivalry in order to save labor and expense to the women for the men to take on themselves the more exposing portions of the work." Men working in the "washing department" often changed their former attitudes about female beauty. Fred Cabot, assigned to do the washing, gave an impromptu lecture on the absurdity of "ladies wearing 'little fixings,' some hundred of which he had been compelled to hang out to dry." "Little fixings" turned out to be women's nightcaps edged with lace.[3]

The single women's behavior also crossed the mid-nineteenth century's strict demarcations of "proper" employment. John Van Der Zee Sears wrote that he and a young woman, Annie Page, took the same work whenever they could, often feeding the rabbits together or cultivating the herb garden, where they raised mint, anise, cumin, sage, marjoram, and saffron for the Boston market (68). Amelia Russell remembered that she once passed the laundry room and went in to help (helping out with others' work was a commonplace occurrence at Brook Farm), but all declared her "inefficient," and she left laughing (Russell, 464).

As well as working at various tasks with other agreeable young people, the Brook Farm women had time to play. All left records of the evenings when the community gathered to play instruments, sing, dance, participate in theater, or tell stories. At least one Brook Farm resident claimed that Hawthorne's *Wonder Book* was plagiarized from the stories of Brook Farm orator Charles Hosmer. Other times the group listened to various members (or people from Concord or Boston) discuss pressing issues of the day. Former member John Sears recalled when "a young lady" came to deliver "what was doubtless an eloquent discourse on Woman's Rights, and was much put out, after orating a while to note that her flowing periods were falling on dull ears. Our women-folk had all the rights of our men-folk. They had an equal voice in our public affairs, voted for our officers, filled responsible positions, and stood on exactly the same footing as their brethren" (89).

If women did not wish to participate in the community's activities, there was no social pressure to do so. Elizabeth Hoxie wrote of her busy days filled with sewing, mending, darning, and long conversations with "mighty pleasant" people. Never was she in such a hurry that she did not take time to "see all the flowers and hear the birds sing, which makes a very pleasant little morning pilgrimage." But in the evenings, she was content to read alone or go skating and often missed the formal readings, musical entertainment, and talks by such men as Robert Owen, or, as she said, discussion on "tedious" theological subjects. Her favorite evening activity was to talk to other young people in a casual way.[4]

Descriptions of casual enjoyments permeate all the letters written by the young people of the community. Whether they were sledding, picking blueberries, or working together in the gardens or in the washing room, the young women and men of Brook Farm enjoyed a few years of the kind of good times now associated with college. Besides the work they performed, there were balls and theater. A group of the young people formed an R.L.S.G. (or Rejected Lovers Sympathising Group). Marianne Dwight wrote of the club's beginning: "well, you can't think how amusing it was, a day or two ago, to hear Charles Dana announce gravely at table, a meeting of the R.L.S.G. to be held at half past ten that evening, in the nursery, a punctual attendance required from all the members and from all those candidates for admission who were expected ere long to become members, and no one to be admitted without the usual badges—and measures were to be taken for the admission of honorary members. All this was said very solemnly and created not a little fun and enquiry" (March 2, 1845). Finally, of course, it comes as no surprise that four couples were married while at

Brook Farm, and thirteen more marriages can be traced to friendships beginning there (Haraszti, 20).

The happiness of the Brook Farm women, though, came not from these marriages but from the freedom they found at the community—freedom, of course, to meet interesting men, but also freedom from being the community's "wives." While the married women in the Owenite communities were free in almost no respect, for they could leave the communities only if they convinced their husbands to do so, and their only possible escapes while in the community were dissimulation and disobeying the "rules," the women at Brook Farm enjoyed the best advantages that American culture had to offer its single women. Their enthusiasm for their lives (and work) is best illustrated in Marianne Dwight's letter to her friend Anna, written August 30, 1844:

> And now I must interest you in our fancy group, for which and from which I hope great things.—nothing less than the elevation of woman to independence, and an acknowledged equality with man. Many thoughts on this subject have been struggling in my mind ever since I have come to Brook Farm, and now, I think I see how it will all be accomplished. Women must become producers of marketable articles; women must make money and earn their support independently of man. So we, with a little borrowed capital (say twenty-five or thirty dollars; by we, I mean a large part of the women here), have purchased materials, and make up in one week about forty-five dollars worth of elegant and tasteful caps, capes, collars, undersleeves, etc., etc.,—which we sent in to Hutchinson and Holmes, who have agreed to take all we can make. If they find a ready sale, we shall be greatly encouraged,—and be able to go on extending our business. . . . By and by, when funds accumulate (!) we may start other branches of business, so that all our proceeds must be applied to the elevation of woman forever. (Quoted in Sams, 122)

But Marianne Dwight did not go on to elevate Woman forever. Her future was more traditional: Marianne married John Orvis, a fellow Brook Farm resident, in the winter of 1846–47, because "he wanted the settled home feeling that marriage will give," and left Brook Farm (October 17, 1846). By the 1850s she was in the same position that the women in New Harmony had been in—she had something to lose by living in a "utopian" community, namely, the only power that the culture afforded a wife—power within the realm of her autonomous family. The freedom to direct her life was left behind to her young single womanhood; her desire to produce marketable articles remained just a pipe dream, laid aside once she put on the mantle of a wife.

The issue that remains with us today is how one can be a "wife" and be free and equal at the same time. For the Owenites, the solution to being free and equal was simple. They believed that socialism would correct the cause of inequality and that one effect of economic socialism would necessarily be gender equality. Yet, as we have repeatedly seen, within the framework of a patriarchal world, socialism does not liberate women any more or any less than any other kind of economic system. Socialism, by itself, cannot alter the pervasiveness of gender ideology and cannot keep such an ideology from turning real-life women into "wives" whose practice is to serve those around them.

Although this book began with a patriarch, Robert Owen, it must end with a different subject, the women speaking to us from the communities. If we will take the time to listen to the women's voices, we will learn a quite different history. In a patriarchal world, it is difficult to take women seriously; it is easy to dismiss their complaints, to ignore their problems, to relegate them to certain roles and duties that are to be enacted without thought. Within the framework of a patriarchy, women—particularly married women—are objects and must remain objects to fit into the jigsaw puzzle of cultural practices that get the work done efficiently and without question. An egalitarian world, though, as envisioned if not enacted by Owen and his followers, has the power to transform objects into subjects. And in this transformation lies utopia for women.

Abbreviations

Am Soc: American Socialist, 1876–79
BI: Boston Investigator, 1837–39
BS Const: The Blue Spring Constitution, Lilly Library, Indiana University
CLG: Cincinnati Literary Gazette, 1825–26
CL: Cleveland Liberalist, 1837–39
Comm: Communitist, 1844–46
Coop Mag: The Cooperative Magazine and Monthly Herald, 1825–26
DDMac: "The Diaries of Donald Macdonald," edited by Caroline Dale Snedeker
DWOwen: "The Diary of William Owen," edited by Joel Hiatt
Econ: The Economist, 1821–22
FE: The Free Enquirer, 1829–33
G-P Collection: Garnett-Pertz Collection, Houghton Library, Harvard University
Genius: The Genius of Universal Emancipation, 1825–28
K Const: The Kendal Constitution and letters, Massillion Museum, Stark County, Ohio
Mac Ms: A. J. Macdonald Manuscript, "Materials from a history of ideal communities in the United States," Beinecke Rare Book and Manuscript Library, Yale University
M/F: The Correspondence of William Maclure and Marie Fretageot, in *Education and Reform at New Harmony*, edited by A. Bestor
NHG: The New Harmony Gazette, 1825–28
NMW: The New Moral World, 1834–45
NWR: Niles Weekly Register, 1820s
Pears: The Pears family letters in *Adventures in Happiness*, edited by Thomas Pears
Pelham: William Pelham's letters in *New Harmony as Seen by Participants and Travelers*
Reg: Regenerator, 1844–46
RDO-TJ: Robert Dale Owen's Travel Journal, 1825–26 and 1827, edited by Josephine M. Elliott
RO Papers: The Robert Owen Papers, The Cooperative Union, Ltd, Manchester, England
TS Papers: Thomas Steel Papers, The State Historical Society of Wisconsin, Madison
WA: Workingman's Advocate, 1844–46

Notes

INTRODUCTION

1. Read, for example, in Keith Melville's *Communes in the Counter Culture*, about a commune in Taos, New Mexico: "Hanging over the counter next to the stove was a sign-up list for kitchen chores and laundry, with the names of several girls listed opposite the jobs. 'We don't believe in laying down too heavy a structure here,' explained Allen. 'So there is just this one list. Somehow everything else seems to get done sooner or later. . . . the women do what most women were happy doing until dishwashers, laundromats, and day care centers made housewives obsolete." See also Robert Houriet's book *Getting Back Together* and the collection of essays, poems, and excerpts edited by Ruby Rohrlich and Elaine Hoffman Baruch, *Women in Search of Utopia*, to find the same point repeated throughout history.

2. For a discussion of the concept of "patriarchy," see Adrienne Rich, *Of Woman Born*; Zillah R. Eisenstein, *The Radical Future of Liberal Feminism*; Michele Barrett, *Women's Oppression Today*; Rosalind Coward, *Patriarchal Precedent, Sexuality and Social Relations*; Christine Delphy, *Close to Home: A Materialist Analysis of Women's Oppression*; and Gerda Lerner, *The Creation of Patriarchy*. As are many people, I am uncomfortable with the term "patriarchy" because its use can mean both a historical description of family life and an entire orientation to the world. At the same time, to use the term makes history sound vaguely conspiratorial, as if most (all?) men were consciously trying to keep women barefoot and pregnant. However, we have to be able to use some term to describe the usually unconscious form of social organization that transcends all societal institutions, that turns women as a class into secondary citizens through laws, customs, habits, language. And, like it or not, the term "patriarchy" is the best we have.

3. See, for example, Kathryn Kish Sklar's book *Catharine Beecher: A Study in American Domesticity*, xiii–iv. See also Philippe Aries, *Centuries of Childhood*, which notes other reasons besides economic ones for the changing attitudes toward children in the nineteenth century.

4. Some critics blame this demarcation for exacerbating women's inequality— see, for example, Delphy, *Close to Home*.

5. See the second chapter of *Birth Control in America*. See also Janet James, "Changing Ideas about Women in the United States, 1776–1825," 282. This ideal woman was, of course, not a representative woman. She was white and middle or upper class, though lower-class women absorbed and believed what they heard and read about Woman. For a discussion of how the Lowell factory women accepted this ideal, see my "Women and Work."

6. See Barbara Welter's ground-breaking essay, "The Cult of True Womanhood," as well as her "Anti-Intellectualism and the American Woman," 71, and "The Feminization of Religion," 102, all included in her collection *Dimity Convictions*. Many scholars in addition to Welter have devoted book-length works to understanding the True Woman in her cult of domesticity. See, for example, Barbara Berg, *The Remembered Gate: Origins of American Feminism*; Ann Douglas, *The Feminization of American Culture*; Nancy Cott, *The Bonds of Womanhood: "Woman's Sphere" in New England, 1780–1835*; Susan Conrad, *Perish the Thought: Intellectual Women in Romantic America, 1830–1860*; Mary P. Ryan, *Womanhood in America*; and Glenda Gates Riley, "From Chattel to Challenger: The Changing Image of the American Woman, 1828–1848."

7. See Welter's "The Feminization of Religion," and Conrad's *Perish the Thought*,

for a discussion of how the ideology of True Womanhood co-opted romanticism's revision of the Enlightenment and turned it to its own uses.

8. See Keith Melder, "The Beginnings of the Women's Rights Movement in the United States, 1800–1840."

9. A number of scholars have written about medical attitudes toward women in nineteenth-century America. See Carroll Smith-Rosenberg and Charles Rosenberg, "The Female Animal: Medical and Biological Views of Women in Nineteenth-Century America"; Carroll Smith-Rosenberg, "Puberty to Menopause: The Cycle of Femininity in Nineteenth-Century America"; Ann Douglas Wood, " 'The Fashionable Diseases': Women's Complaints and their Treatment in Nineteenth-Century America"; Barbara Welter, "Female Complaints: Medical Views of American Women"; and G. J. Barker-Benfield, *The Horrors of the Half-Known Life*.

10. There is less written on clergymen's advice to women than on medical attitudes toward women in nineteenth-century America. See Ann Douglas's excellent book, *The Feminization of American Culture*. See also sample advice manuals from clergymen such as the Reverend John S. C. Abbott, who loved to give women advice: see his *Letters to Young Women* or his *The Mother at Home*.

11. See the Reverend H. P. Powers, "Female Education": Rev. Powers brings both his religion and his position as an educator to his advice to women.

12. For a discussion of these writers, see Ann Douglas Wood, "The Scribbling Women and Fanny Fern: Why Women Wrote," as well as her "Mrs. Sigourney and the Sensibility of Inner Space"; Kirk Jeffery, "Marriage, Career and Feminine Ideology in Nineteenth-Century America: Reconstructing the Marital Experience of Lydia Maria Child"; Milton Meltzer, *Tongue of Flame: The Life of Lydia Maria Child*; and Ruth Finley, *The Lady of Godey's, Sarah Josepha Hale*.

13. See various "ladies' " magazines for these sentiments, repeated in each issue. Specifically see *The Mother's Assistant* 9 (1846) and *The Ladies Magazine* 3 (1830).

14. The quotes come from Minnigerode, 78, quoting Hale in *Godey's*, and Furness, 216–17, quoting M.A.B. in *The Female Companion*.

15. Robert Owen's most forceful lambasting of what he called the "trinity of three evils" comes from a speech he gave on July 4, 1826, to his New Harmony Community. The entire speech is reprinted in *NHG*, July 12, 1826.

16. The wording in this and the following two sentences comes from Robert Owen's *Lectures on the Marriages of the Priesthood of the Old Immoral World* (20; 45–46).

17. The publisher is quoted in H. N. Brailsford, *Shelley, Godwin, and Their Circle*, 53–54.

18. Certainly Arthur Bestor, in his brilliant book *Backwoods Utopias*, singlehandedly restored Robert Owen and New Harmony to American history, though Bestor's concern is integrating Owen's form of communalism into an American communal tradition. He is not much concerned with women's proposed and actual position in the communities. J. F. C. Harrison's *Quest for the New Moral World* is an excellent social history of the Owenites in America, but like Bestor, Harrison is not interested in women per se. Raymond Muncy's book *Sex and Marriage in Utopian Communities*, which does focus on women, contains one chapter on New Harmony, but Muncy's book is a general introduction to several of the most important nineteenth-century utopian experiments. His reliance upon "official" community documents—which sometimes results in errors of fact—combined with his lack of a feminist perspective lead him to make such statements as: "both Margaret [Fuller] and Fanny [Wright] were pathetic creatures in search of fulfillment in life and eventually bowed to the urge to marry and bear children, thereby contradicting by their actions their earlier tirades against marriage" (216). See also Jeanette C. Lauer and Robert H. Lauer, "Sex Roles in Nineteenth-Century American Communal Societies," and Jon Wagner's excellent analysis of the current work being done on gender in utopian communities, "Sexuality and Gender Roles in Utopian Communities: A Critical Survey of Scholarly Work."

19. See my essays of 1980 and 1981, which illustrate how important the Owenites were in the history of women's liberation in America. For a more recent work on the same point, see Barbara Taylor's *Eve and the New Jerusalem*. For a typical response to Owen's role in economic or social history, see Eric Roll, *A History of Economic Thought*, which does not discuss Owen because "his influence" has not "been very great" (234). Recently, Owen's and the Owenites' importance in the history of social and economic thought has been reassessed. See, for example, Anne Taylor's *Visions of Harmony*, which focuses on the Owenites' millenarianistic thought; Gregory Claeys's *Machinery, Money, and the Millennium*, which illustrates Owen's distinctive economic thought; John C. Spurlock's *Free Love, Marriage and Middle Class Radicalism in America, 1825–1860*, which documents how important Owenite theory was to the Free Love movement; and Edward K. Spann's *Brotherly Tomorrows, Movements for a Cooperative Society in America, 1820–1920*, which begins with a conceptual discussion of Owen and his experiments at New Lanark and New Harmony.

20. See *Marx and Engels, Basic Writings on Politics and Philosophy*, ed. Lewis Feuer, 78, 80. See also Hilda Schott's *Does Socialism Liberate Women?* where she writes that it was John Stuart Mill who supplied the philosophical basis for the women's rights movement, but that it was Engels who introduced a new way of looking at the family. Nowhere does she mention Owen. See also Jean Kelly-Gadol, "The Social Relations of the Sexes," where she writes that Engels' analysis of the subordination of women in terms of the emergence of private property is basic to much of feminist scholarship. See Evelyn Reed and Charnie Guettel for the same point. Today, though, some critics fault this link between the rise of private property and the cause of women's subordination as too simplistic. See, for example, Gerda Lerner's persuasively argued book *The Creation of Patriarchy* and Linda Nicholson's *Gender and History*. In part, this book will provide examples that illustrate that socialism alone does not eliminate the roots of sexual inequality. Sexual inequality goes far deeper than economic issues or class struggles.

1. THE BRITISH BACKGROUND AND THE AMERICAN LANDSCAPE

1. Numerous people, including Robert Owen himself, have told the story of the life of Robert Owen. See Robert Owen, *The Life of Robert Owen, by Himself*; Frank Podmore, *Robert Owen*; G. D. H. Cole, *The Life of Robert Owen*; Margaret Cole, *Robert Owen of New Lanark*; Rowland H. Harvey, *Robert Owen, Social Idealist*; and William Sargant, *Robert Owen and his Social Philosophy*.

2. This Enlightenment "rights of men" ideology, so say many political scientists, automatically included women as well as men, because the term "man" is generic, yet I tend to agree with Susan Okin when she writes in *Women in Western Political Thought* that the "great tradition of political philosophy consists, generally speaking, of writings by men, for men, and about men" (5). Okin persuasively argues that "human nature," as defined by such thinkers as Aristotle, Locke, and Rousseau, is intended to refer only to male human nature. Our political heritage, from the ancient Greeks to the present, she posits, is built upon the assumption of the inequality of the sexes, which comes, in turn, from a prescriptive view of woman's nature and "proper mode of life" based on her role in a patriarchal family structure (10–11). Enlightenment figures were indeed calling for equality and freedom, but the call was for male ears.

3. Perhaps this tendency to use other people's ideas is the reason one of Owen's biographers, G. D. H. Cole, labeled him "a man with no original ideas." See *A New View of Society*, ed. Cole, xvii.

4. Edmund Wilson, writing in *To the Finland Station* that Owen did give the highest wages in the county, is simply wrong.

5. See the four essays on character formation included in *A New View,* ed. Cole.

6. See "An Address to the Inhabitants of New Lanark," included in *A New View,* ed. Cole, 95.

7. See Owen's *Life,* 140, 135; see also Robert Dale Owen, "An Outline of the System of Education at New Lanark," 32, 57; and *Robert Owen at New Lanark,* 8.

8. See Bellers's essay, included in Robert Owen's 1818 version of *A New View of Society.*

9. See the "Report to the Committee for the Relief of the Manufacturing Poor," in *A New View,* ed. Cole, 156–69.

10. Though Owen never cited Godwin as his "master," the two men knew each other well. See the recent biography of Godwin by Peter Marshall, *William Godwin.*

11. Marshall, *William Godwin,* 310. The next time they met, though, Owen believed he had been "too precipitate." It took Owen close to seven years from this first revelation until he accepted Godwin's premise on the evil of private property.

12. Just as he did not credit Godwin with the inspiration for some of his ideas, neither did Owen credit Mary Wollstonecraft. Wollstonecraft's daughter Fanny Imlay repeats a conversation she had with Robert Owen: "He told me the other day that he wished our mother were living, as he had never before met with a person who thought so exactly as he did, or who would have so warmly and zealously entered into his plans." See Ford K. Brown, *The Life of William Godwin,* 310.

13. The *New Harmony Gazette* of February 14, 1827, explains in a footnote that "The Social System," just then being published for the first time, was written in 1821. Owen writes that in the six years since he wrote the essay he had obtained "most extensive confirmat[ion]" for his theories. See Robert Owen's "Social System," published in the *NHG* of November 22, 1826; January 3, 1827; January 10, 1827; January 24, 1827; and February 14, 1827.

14. George Mudie has been called by R. G. Garnett "the first Owenite," 41, but the first Owenite was actually A. J. Hamilton. Though Mudie says that Hamilton had only known Owen a short time when he offered Owen land to begin a community in 1820—see Mudie's *The Economist* for December 8, 1821—in actuality, Hamilton and Owen became friends in 1816; see Hamilton's autobiographical manuscript, "The Soldier and Citizen of the World," at the Motherwell Library, Motherwell, Scotland.

15. See R. G. Garnett, *Co-operation and the Owenite Socialist Communities in Britain, 1825–45,* 70. Also see *Motherwell and Orbiston,* 52. Hamilton limited the primarily agricultural community to five hundred people, specifying that children above two years of age should live in dormitories and be given the best physical and intellectual education available. He, like Owen earlier, promised that in Motherwell, "all members were to be equal in rights and privileges." Women, following Owen's dictates, would prepare food and clothing, take care of the dwelling houses and public buildings, manage the washing and drying houses, and help educate the children. But the rules of Motherwell added a new rationale for the benefits of communal life for women: in a community, wrote Hamilton, a woman could work more efficiently than she could outside of communal life. Thus the wife of a working man with a family, instead of being "a drudge and slave," would be engaged only in healthy and cleanly employments and thus acquire better manners and have sufficient leisure for mental improvement and rational enjoyment.

16. See *The Economist,* or the "Proceedings of the First General Meeting of the British and Foreign Philanthropic Society," June 1, 1822; reprinted in *Motherwell and Orbiston;* also see "List of Donations," in *Motherwell and Orbiston,* 17–20.

17. For background information on Donald Macdonald, see his Diaries, and the letter he wrote to the people of New Harmony, published in the *NHG,* February 16, 1826.

18. *Economist,* January 27, 1821; also see entire "Report of the Communities," in *Owenism and the Working Class.*

19. John Gray to Robert Owen, August 5, 1823, RO Papers, #24; see also Gray's "Lecture on Human Happiness. . . ," published in London in 1825.

20. See "The Sphere for Joint-Stock Companies: or, The Way to Increase the Value of Land, Capital, and Labour, with an Account of the Establishment at Orbiston," by Abram Combe, including "Articles of Agreement," and "Proceedings at Orbiston," in *Motherwell and Orbiston;* also see Garnett, *Co-operation,* chap. 3, "Orbiston," 65–99, and Combe, *The Life and Dying Testimony of Abram Combe.*

21. For information on Anna Wheeler, see Pankhurst, "Anna Wheeler," and B. Taylor, 59–65. Wheeler's daughter believed she was "poisoned" by feminism. See Taylor, 60.

22. See *An Inquiry into the Principles of the Distribution of Wealth,* 556. Also see Thompson's *Appeal of One Half of the Human Race, Women, Against the Pretensions of the Other Half, Men . . . ,* published in London in 1825, 192–96.

23. These articles are printed at the end of the London publication of John Gray's "Lecture on Human Happiness . . . ," 4.

24. Thompson was not the first to suggest that certain kinds of unpleasant work be given to the youth of the community. He might have gotten this idea from Charles Fourier's grandiose utopian plans, which had assigned the most unpleasant work in a community to the children, though Fourier did not include housework in this category. The Owenites were familiar with Fourier's writings. See Robert Dale Owen's *Travel Journal* (1826) for the days of December 16 and 17, 1825, for references to their evening readings of Fourier.

25. Robert Owen to Rev. Rapp; see Appendix to George Flower, *The History of the English Settlement,* 372–73.

26. See Bestor, *Backwoods,* especially his checklist on the dates and places of all sectarian and secular utopian experiments in America, 277–85. Also see Holloway, *Heavens on Earth,* Arndt on the Rappites, and Kern, *An Ordered Love.*

27. See Lockwood, *The New Harmony Movement,* 12. But this celibacy was not always enforced. See William Owen's Diary for December 4, 1824, his first visit to the Rappites' Economy in Pennsylvania. He writes: "men and women who are married sleep together; yet Rapp's power is so great as to conquer nature. One man had contrary to agreement got a son by his wife. He expected to be turned out, but Rapp said 'he might have done much worse.' "

28. See Rosina Rapp to Gertrud [*sic*] Rapp, September 12, 1824; reprinted in *Harmony on the Wabash in Transition,* ed. Karl Arndt.

29. See the *Manafest* [*sic*] *of the Fundamental Principles of the Church of God,* from the Coal Creek Community and Church of God Record Book, Article 13.

30. See the gossip about George Flower's leaving his English wife and children in Camilla Wright's letter of January 10, 1826, to the Garnett sisters (G-P Collection).

31. *Letters from the Illinois,* 22; see also George Flower, *The History of the English Settlement.*

32. See William Owen's Diary, ed. Joel Hiatt, 14–15.

33. See "Mr. Owen's Address to the City of the United States, at sea," reprinted in *NWR,* October 29, 1825.

2. THE PROMISE OF EQUALITY

1. Owen quoted in Frank E. and Fritzie P. Manuel, *Utopian Thought in the Western World,* 76.

2. See Bestor, *Backwoods,* 78, for Fourier quote; Harrison, *Quest,* 76; and Manuel, 690.

3. See Donald Macdonald's Diaries, 159. Much of the firsthand information we have about Robert Owen's first trip to the United States comes from Macdonald's diary and William Owen's diary.

4. See Mac Ms,, 175–84; for a more detailed description of the New Yorkers that Owen met, see Arthur Bestor's review of *The Diaries of Donald Macdonald*, in *New York History*, 80–86. Bestor corrects Macdonald's spelling and gives brief biographical information about the people Macdonald mentions.

5. See his review of Macdonald, 84. Also see descriptions of several evenings in New York when Owen visited noted dignitaries and enthusiastically talked about his plan in Macdonald, 178–84, and in William Owen, 26.

6. See Abishai Way to Frederick Rapp, December 4, 1824; reprinted in *Harmony on the Wabash in Transition*, 313–14.

7. A copy of agreement, signed January 3, 1825, is reproduced in *Harmony on the Wabash in Transition*, 377–78.

8. See DDMac, 256–261, and DWOwen, 85–92.

9. See the *NHG*, April 18, 1827; both Owen's February 25 and March 7 lectures were published in the *NHG* over a year after he gave the addresses. The February 25 lecture appears in the *Gazette* of April 18, April 25, and May 2, 1827; the March 7 lecture was printed in the *Gazette* of May 9, 16, and 23, 1827.

10. For a more complete description of the community when Owen purchased it, see *NHG*, October 1, 1825.

11. Robert Owen to William Allen (April 21, 1825), reprinted in *Harmony on the Wabash in Transition*, 533.

12. This first speech is reprinted in the *NHG* of October 1, 1825. The *Gazette* gives its date as April 27, 1825, but both Macdonald's diary and William Owen's diary reveal that Owen's first big speech took place on April 20, not April 27.

13. All wording comes from the Preliminary Society Constitution, printed in the *NHG*, October 1, 1825.

14. One exception was "persons of color," who, according to the preliminary constitution, could not become members of the Preliminary Society. "Persons of color" could only be "helpers" in the community, which would "prepare and enable them to become associates in Communities in Africa; or in some other country, or in some other part of the country."

15. Pears, 13. See also the Bakewell Family Book at the Historical Society of Western Pennsylvania for the ages of the Pears children and parents.

16. One of the members of the Price family had taught in Owen's New Lanark school, for example, in 1824. The constitution of the Preliminary Society was particularly conducive to attracting wealthy people as it allowed people with money who did not wish to be employed to partake of the benefits of community living by paying an annual sum.

17. Pelham writes about the ages of the people at New Harmony. On December 29, 1825, he says that he is the second oldest person in the community; most are much younger—e.g., Robert Jennings is around thirty, Judge Wattles is thirty, William Owen is probably twenty-five, Mr. Schnee, perhaps thirty-five.

18. Jennings's passage to New Harmony was paid for by the Owenites; likewise, he received $1,158.74 in cash in Cincinnati to bring to New Harmony when he came to the community in the spring of 1825. See the items charged to the Owenites' account in a letter from Frederick Rapp to William Owen, June 21, 1825; reprinted in *Harmony on the Wabash in Transition*, 572.

19. See descriptions in Pears, 52; and in William Owen's letters to his father dated October 14, 1825, and December 16, 1825 (RO Papers, #78 and #54).

20. The October 1 beginning date for the *NHG* was planned deliberately to coincide with the anniversary of Robert Owen's departure for America the previous year. See Pelham, September 20, 1825.

21. The wording is Bestor's, *Backwoods*, 296.

22. The constitution of the Friendly Association at Valley Forge is printed as an appendix to the Philadelphia printing of John Gray's "A Lecture on Human Hap-

piness." For other sources on the Valley Forge Community, see the *NWR*, December 17 and December 31, 1825; see also the M/F correspondence for July 31 and September 19, 1826; and the *NHG*, February 8 and March 29, 1826. Also see DDMac, 308, 312, and Harry E. Wildes's inaccurate *Valley Forge*.

23. For life on the boat, see RDO-TJ and DDMac. The boatload did not all travel together, though. Macdonald visited Thomas Jefferson and did not join the rest of the party until January 8, the day before the boat left "Safe Harbor," the place it was stuck for four weeks. Robert Owen, busy lecturing in Pittsburgh and then visiting a new Owenite community at Yellow Springs in central Ohio, never did return to the stayed boat, reaching New Harmony by foot some twelve days before the boatload arrived. Marie Fretageot and William Maclure left the boat during its iced-in state to await its departure in more comfortable surroundings in a nearby town. Robert Dale Owen, though, remained with the boat, enthusiastic about the trip and the hardships, pleased that he was being toughened up for life in New Harmony.

24. This rationale is contained in Owen's essay "Retrospect," published in the *NHG*, May 10, 1826.

25. See Pears, 57, for a list of the New Harmony residents voted to serve on the committee and the number of votes each received.

26. See the *NHG*, February 15, 1826, for a reprinting of the constitution. This constitution does not refer to the status of "persons of color," who were relegated to being "helpers" in the Preliminary Society's constitution. Letters from New Harmony members reveal that blacks were not allowed to become members.

27. See Owen's May 28, 1826, "Address," printed in the *NHG*, June 7, 1826.

28. See Owen's speech of July 4, 1826, to the residents of New Harmony, reprinted in the *NHG* of July 12, 1826.

29. See Pelham, September 7, 1825, for a description of the many activities at New Harmony and for the wording of quotations in this paragraph, unless otherwise noted.

30. See Pelham, September 7, 1825, and October 10, 1825.

31. See Pears Papers, November 11, 1825, and October 5, 1825.

32. See the description of the New Harmony "uniform" given by the visiting Duke Bernhard and the description given by Sarah Pears, April 8, 1826.

33. See Pelham, September 7, 1825, and Duke Bernhard, April 15, 1826.

34. See Pears, 33; for other descriptions of the New Harmony schools, particularly from students attending the schools, see Minor K. Kellogg, "Recollections of New Harmony," and Lockwood's *The New Harmony Movement*, 246, where he quotes Sarah Cox Thrall's experience in the New Harmony boarding school.

35. Maclure's letter is printed in the November 1826 *Cooperative Magazine*.

36. Maclure to Silliman, March 16, 1826, reprinted in the *Cooperative Magazine*, November 1826.

37. There were probably many of these attempts; Owen influenced people even when he was not trying. But unless some member of the community was a letter writer or later became famous, most of these communities are lost to history.

38. See Janet Hermann, *Pursuit of a Dream*, for her account of Davis Bend. She notes that Joseph Davis made no attempt to collectivize the economy but then erroneously adds that collectivized economy "had never been the aim of Robert Owen," 242. Perhaps it is this lack of a radical reorganization of society that allowed Davis's experiment to be so long-standing, so "successful." For a community to be successful in terms of the number of years it lasts, the fewer radical ideas the better (and the less these ideas threaten the patriarchy the better). For reformers who dream of intentional communities that will change the world, not just make more money or make life more comfortable, success has to be measured in different terms.

39. See William Hall's journal, "From England to Illinois in 1821," published in the *Journal of the Illinois Historical Society.*

40. See Hall's journal, 238; see also DDMac, 255.

41. See the Wanborough Constitution in the *NHG*, May 17, 1826; also see Walter B. Hendrickson's essay on Wanborough, "An Owenite Society in Illinois."

42. Early twentieth-century scholars had problems dealing with these communities. George Lockwood, the author of the first book on New Harmony, lists Macdonald's nine communities in his chapter "The Ten Lost Tribes of Communism" yet adds that "the total number of communities was nineteen," though he does not name them, describe them, or cite his sources. Frank Podmore, Owen's biographer, mentions seven communities—Franklin, Kendal, Forrestville (in Indiana), Coxsackie, Haverstraw, Blue Spring, and Yellow Springs (333). The more recent work of Arthur Bestor and J. F. C. Harrison clears up this confusion. See A. J. Macdonald's "Materials from a history of ideal communities" (Mac Ms) at the Beinecke Rare Book Manuscript Library at Yale University, one of the most important sources for nineteenth-century American communities. Despite its errors in labeling Owenite communities, the voluminous manuscript contains a wealth of printed materials including constitutions, clippings about the communities from local newspapers, letters from community members, as well as many firsthand accounts of the 1840s communities that Macdonald actually visited.

43. For the beginnings of the community, see the *NHG*, November 23, 1825; the *CLG*, March 12, May 14, and May 21; the *PP*, May 24, 1826; and the Mac Ms, 304. Also see William Galloway, "The History of Glen Helen," and the Galloway Collection at the Greene County Library in Xenia, Ohio.

44. For information about Blue Spring, see the *NHG*, January 31, 1827, and Richard Simons's essay "A Utopian Failure." See also the manuscript collection at the Lilly Library containing the community's constitution and unpublished essays by Rodney Smith, the grandson of a Blue Spring schoolteacher, and by Judge Henry Clay Duncan, who wrote down the oral history of the community.

45. One member of the Franklin Community, James M'Knight, says Jennings was sent to Franklin "at the request of Mr. Peterson and others" (12).

46. See the *NHG*, May 31, 1826, for a clipping on Rev. Kneeland talking about Franklin from his New York pulpit; this same article says the Franklin Constitution is published in the twenty-first number of the *NHG*, but the only constitution printed there is New Harmony's constitution.

47. For information about the Franklin Community, see the *NHG*, May 31, 1826, as well as resident James M'Knight's essay "A Discourse," concerning his experiences at Franklin.

48. The *NHG* for November 7, 1827, says four families formed a community on December 10, 1825. For other sources of the Forrestville Community, see the *NHG*, December 5, 1827, and *A History of Greene County.*

49. For information on Underhill, see his May 4, 1828, letter to Robert Owen (RO Papers, #126), his various publications on free thought, and, primarily, his weekly newspaper, *The Cleveland Liberalist*, published from 1836 until 1838. For the above quote, see his "Lecture on Mysterious Religious Emotions," delivered in Bethlehem, Ohio, in 1829.

50. For the beginnings of the Kendal Community, see the *NHG*, July 26 and December 18, 1826, December 5, 1827, and February 13, 1828. Also see Wendall Fox, "The Kendal Community," and William Perrin, *The History of Stark County.* See also the manuscripts in the Massillion Museum, including the Kendal Community Letters, the Kendal Census, the Minutes of the Friendly Association Meetings, and the Rotch Papers. Joining the local community members in the late fall of 1827 were Samuel Underhill and twenty-seven people from the Forrestville Community, in-

cluding the Underhill family, James Bayliss, Edward Dunn, the Macy family, and the Fosdick family. A vivid description of these people's journey from Coxsackie to Kendal is given by one of the Fosdick children, Eliza, in the April 18, 1910, *Massachusetts Independent*.

51. The Kendal Constitution promises that communal life will increase happiness, but its first principle is not equality; rather it is "Love to the Great first cause and Creator of all things," a sentiment reflecting the religious background of the original members of the Kendal Community. See Kendal Constitution in manuscript in the Massillion Museum. Although the Franklin Constitution is lost, a member of the community wrote extensively about it, quoting passages from it; see M'Knight. The constitutions of the Yellow Springs Community and Coxsackie are also lost.

52. For this information, see the Mac Ms, 304–305; also see the Galloway Collection at the Greene County Library in Xenia, Ohio.

3. THE COLLAPSE OF THE COMMUNITIES

1. Economic problems plagued New Harmony from its founding in January of 1825. Preparing the machinery for production and the land for crops proved to be exceedingly difficult for young William Owen, left to run the community in most of its first year. Few of the arriving community members knew any more about operating the industries than young Owen did. By the time the first edition of the *New Harmony Gazette* appeared, on October 1, 1825, William Owen was calling for skilled workers: "Since the middle of June," Owen wrote in the paper, "our manufacturies have been at work. With the machinery now in hand, our operations in the wool business should turn out one hundred and sixty pounds of yarn a day, but the want of spinners reduces the business." He added that the "frilling and dressing departments" also lacked superintendents and workers, while the cotton-spinning establishment, equal to producing between three and four hundred pounds of yarn per week, was producing nothing because "skilful and ready hands are much wanting." By December young William wrote his father with a tone of desperation, telling him that New Harmony had no superintendent of farming and that it needed workers of all kinds but had no place for them to sleep.

2. See William Owen's letter to his father, October 14, 1825, RO Papers, #78. Information about all the different divisions and "reorganizations" of New Harmony can be found in Bestor's *Backwoods Uotpias*, 172–201; for members' views of the multitude of reorganizations, see Paul Brown's *Twelve Months in New Harmony*, as Brown arrived at New Harmony during the spring of the "reorganizations," and the letters of Thomas and Sarah Pears, who lived in New Harmony before and during the divisions.

3. For a comment on Macdonald's character, see Wright, *Biography*, 38; for Macdonald's leaving, see Pears, 59.

4. See Maclure's letter of July 31, 1826, to Fretageot, where he writes that the members of the Friendly Association "don't seem to follow any part of the cooperative system but the money making part, the division of profits puts all into the individual scramble. I fear their [sic] is not a sufficient number of adults in the continent who comprehend the system to form one community"; quoted in John Reed, "Vision at Valley Forge," 29. Also see Harry E. Wildes's account of the community for the story about the fanatical local preacher. Wildes's story is suspect because he claims, erroneously, that both Robert Owen and William Maclure lived at the Valley Forge community. Though records reveal Blue Spring's demise, none show exactly when it ended. The last published piece of information about it was a *New Harmony Gazette* insert in January of 1827 that related that the community was

prospering and had been for fifteen months. For further information concerning the breaking up of the communities, see the Mac Ms, 411; the *NWR*, October 29, 1825; M/F, 339; and the *NHG*, February 13, 1828.

5. See Owen's "Address to the Citizens of New Harmony," May 6, 1827, printed in the *NHG*, May 9, 1827.

6. See Neef's "Letter to Robert Owen Concerning his Valedictory Address," printed in Brown's *Twelve Months*, 107.

7. The woman who found the society to be "too low" at New Harmony was Mrs. Fisher, the widow of a Price family man. Mrs. Fisher became a special friend to Robert Owen on the trip to New Harmony on the Boatload of Knowledge. In fact they left the boat and traveled together by foot to the Yellow Springs Community to visit it on their way to New Harmony. How much Mrs. Fisher's complaints are simply those of a woman once taken under Owen's wing and then discarded, we will never know.

8. See the Appendix to the 1825 London publication of John Gray's *A Lecture on Human Happiness*, which contains the constitution of the London Cooperative Society. See the 1826 Philadelphia publication of the same essay for the constitution of the Friendly Association at Valley Forge.

9. See the "Reports of Meetings" of the Kendal Community for the community members' repeated "resolution" to establish a school based on Robert Owen's principles, first in August 1826 and again on May 19, 1827. The Charity Rotch School, incorporated in January of 1826, only began operating in 1829. See *Repository*, December 14, 1826, and the Kendal "Reports of Meetings" for August 19, 1826, and May 19, 1827, attached to the Kendal Constitution in the Massillion Museum.

10. The Pears family relates that at one point, shortly after forming the Community of Equality, Owen tried to institute his educational plans: Sarah Pears writes that "all of our elder children, those whom we expected to be comfort and consolation and support in our old age, are to be taken away from us, at an age, too, when they so peculiarly require the guardian care of their parents; and are to be placed in large boarding houses. The single males and females above the age of fourteen are to live together in one house" (72). See also William Owen's desperate letter to his father on December 16, 1825, when he writes of the dismal condition of New Harmony schools before the arrival of Maclure and the "Boatload," with "no teachers, except probably D. Price, who understands how to teach atall, according to the New Principles" (RO Papers, #54).

11. See *NHG*, December 7, 1825, May 3, 1826, and November 8, 1826. All these "feminine" virtues lead women to their most important quality: self-sacrifice.

12. See Carroll Smith-Rosenberg's essays, including "Puberty to Menopause: the Cycle of Femininity in Nineteenth-Century America," "The Hysterical Woman: Sex Roles and Role Conflict in Nineteenth-Century America," and "Beauty, the Beast and the Militant Woman: A Case Study of Sex Roles and Social Stress in Jacksonian America." See also Ann Douglas Wood, "The Fashionable Diseases: Women's Complaints and their Treatment in Nineteenth-Century America."

13. See Pears, 33, 41, 52.

14. See young Owen's *Travel Journal*, 232, 239, 242, 243, and 257. Robert Dale Owen writes most of his journal in English except the sentences where he writes about the women; then he uses German—a clever way of having some private thoughts in a crowded boat.

15. See M/F, November 28, 1826, and the *NHG*, August 30, 1826.

16. See the narratives of Rodney Smith, whose grandfather tells the story of the homespun jeans, and Judge H. D. Duncan, who talked to former members of the Blue Spring Community who told him about the envy among the women. Both men's manuscripts are in the Lilly Library.

4. FRANCES WRIGHT: A WOMAN IN UTOPIA

1. Despite being such an important figure in American history, Frances Wright remains almost completely unknown today, clear evidence of her "offensive" views. Her first biographer was her friend Amos Gilbert. His book, *Memoir of Frances Wright*, published in 1855, was intended, at least in part, to refute negative comments that Sarah J. Hale, editor of *Godey's*, had made about Wright. Other biographies include William Waterman's 1924 *Frances Wright*; A. J. G. Perkins and Theresa Wolfson's *Frances Wright Free Enquirer*, a book marred by a lack of citation of quotes and errors in fact; Virginia Rutherford's "A Study of the Speaking Career of Frances Wright in America," a 1960 dissertation; and the most recent, *Fanny Wright, Rebel in America* by Celia Morris Eckhardt.

Of great interest to Wright scholars is the work of Cecilia Payne-Gaposchkin, the great-granddaughter of Julia Garnett Pertz, a friend of Wright's during the 1820s. Payne-Gaposchkin wrote an unpublished biography of Wright, now housed at the Cincinnati Historical Society, and published many of the letters the Garnett sisters wrote to and received from Wright in the October 1975 *Harvard Library Bulletin*. Excerpts from correspondence of the Garnett women, the Wright sisters, and Frances Trollope constitute Helen Heineman's recent book *Restless Angels: The Friendship of Six Victorian Women*. Anne Taylor also uses the collection in her *Visions of Harmony*, chaps. 12 and 13. The letters are now owned by Katherine Haramundanis, the great-great granddaughter of Julia Garnett Pertz, and are housed in the Houghton Library.

2. It was this similarity in rationale and philosophy as well as their similar reform impulse that convinced many of Owen's and Wright's contemporaries that Frances Wright's community was indeed "Owenite." Certainly A. J. Macdonald, categorizing communities into types in the 1840s, labeled Wright's community Owenite. Critics of Wright's ideas noticed that they were the same ideas as Robert Owen's: the Rev. W. L. M'Calla, for example, wrote that "Miss Wright's System of Knowledge" was the very "soul and body" of "what Mr. Jennings calls the social system." Even Camilla foresaw that her sister would be the perfect speaker on Owenism; as she wrote to Julia in January of 1826: "it would add some years to the life of our amiable friend Mr. Owen could he engage Fanny's talents disseminating his system through the world."

3. See Wright's letter to Julia Garnett of June 8, 1825, G-P Collection, and Wright's letter to Madame de Lasteryrie, as reprinted in Perkins and Wolfson, 135. Also see Camilla's letter to Julia, January 1826, G-P Collection.

4. For information about Nashoba, see particularly Wright's April 11, 1826, letter to Julia Garnett; Wright's December 26 (n.y.) letter to Madame de Lasteryrie, reprinted in Perkins and Wolfson, 141. For secondary sources containing some factual errors, see O. B. Emerson's essay "Frances Wright and her Nashoba Experiment," and Edd Parks's essay "Dreamer's Vision, Frances Wright at Nashoba."

5. See the *NHG*, February 21, 1827 and February 6, 1828.

6. For descriptions of Nashoba, see the *NHG*, March 26, 1828, and Robert Dale Owen's essay "An Earnest Sowing of Wild Oats," 67–78. For a quite negative view of Nashoba in early 1828, see Frances Trollope's letters to the Garnetts on the state of the community when she visited it. Also see Trollope's book *Domestic Manners of Americans*, particularly p. 39.

7. Cam's letter is found rewritten in A. J. Perkins's handwriting in the Theresa Wolfson Papers at Cornell University.

8. This account is suspect because of numerous errors, such as his referring to Camilla as "Sylvia," among other things. See J. M. Keating, *History of the City of Memphis*. The only reason for considering Keating's folklore is that Keating obviously knew Frances Wright's daughter when she lived in Tennessee in the 1880s, at the time he was writing his book.

9. When George Flower stole Eliza Andrews away from Morris Birkbeck on their trip to Illinois and married her, he left behind a wife and children in England. Birkbeck, in his anger, brought a suit against Flower for "bigamy and adultery." Yet, for all his bile, Birkbeck was apparently correct—Flower was a bigamist and adulterer. See Camilla's January 10, 1826, letter to Julia Garnett.

10. Wright's recent biographer, Celia Eckhardt, assumes that Trollope is correct and cites this affair as the reason the Flowers left Nashoba. Eckhardt writes: "George Flower was not a man who could leave a second wife and three small children because he loved another woman. . . . [Thus] Flower had to leave her at Nashoba" (133).

11. George Flower's October 3, 1827, letter to the Wright sisters is found in A. J. Perkins's handwriting in the Theresa Wolfson Papers, Cornell University.

12. Although Wright is not mentioned in Gilbert and Gubar's book *Madwoman in the Attic*, the problems she confronted when she tried to write seriously about issues important to her parallel the problems of the writers of imaginative literature that Gilbert and Gubar concern themselves with in their book. Most of Wright's critics labeled her crazed or a madwoman for her attempts to change the world.

13. See, for example, the *FE*, December 10, 1828, and December 31, 1828.

14. See, for example, the *FE*, August 18, 1829, and July 3, 1830.

15. Wright's July Fourth address is found in her "Course of Popular Lectures," included in her *Life, Letters, and Lectures*. See, specifically, pp. 136, 140. See also Cam's August 1, 1829, letter to the Garnett sisters, in which she tells them that Fanny wishes to "ameliorate the condition of man—to be effected by a system of national instruction."

16. See the *FE*, January 9, 1830, and October 8, 1828, for example.

17. See, for example, the *FE*, January 30, 1830, August 12, 1829, and January 2, 1830.

18. See, for example, the *FE*, May 6, 1829.

19. See *The Letters and Journals of James Fenimore Cooper*, edited by James F. Beard. We can only assume that Fanny's appearance excited so much attention because of an advanced state of pregnancy. It is probable that Cooper misremembers his dates; writing on April 27, 1831, he says that he saw Wright "about three months ago," yet if he saw her pregnant, as the tone of the letter implies, he had to have seen her closer to four months previous, as Phiquepal left the West Indies in late March 1830; thus Wright had to have her baby by late December or early January 1831 at the latest, if its father was indeed Phiquepal.

20. Wright used the name Madame D'Arusmont during the remainder of the 1830s and some of the 1840s, reassuming her birth name during her divorce conflicts with Phiquepal. In the spirit of Wright's legacy, I shall continue to call Wright by her birth name throughout the decade and a half she used her husband's name.

21. See the 1874 newspaper clipping, title missing, in the Library of Congress Manuscript Collection "Frances Wright Papers."

5. THE END OF EQUALITY

1. There is little secondary information about Marie Fretageot. Arthur Bestor gives some background about her in *Backwoods Utopias* as well as in *Education and Reform*, and Josephine Elliott has a recent essay about her in *Communal Studies*. Fretageot was a prolific letter writer, and a collection of her letters to William Maclure, and his to her (over 350 complete letters plus fragments) is housed at the Workingmen's Institute at New Harmony. Fretageot also wrote to Robert Owen; see Robert Owen Papers, #60 and #64.

2. For information about Abner Kneeland, see a variety of personal comments

in Kneeland's *Boston Investigator* from 1837 through the end of 1839. See also Kneeland's "An Appeal to Common Sense," and "A Series of Lectures" in the Boston Public Library, Manuscript Division. Secondary information includes Leonard Levy, *Blasphemy in Massachusetts;* Henry Steele Commager, "The Blasphemy of Abner Kneeland"; and the more recent Roderick French, "Liberation from Man and God in Boston: Abner Kneeland's Free-Thought Campaign."

3. Though few secondary sources on Underhill exist, primary ones do. See Underhill's addresses in the Western Reserve Historical Society, including "Oration," January 29, 1836; "An Address," January 29, 1837; his book, *The Annals of Magnetism;* and the journal he edited, *The Cleveland Liberalist,* published weekly from September 10, 1836, to October 27, 1838. See also Underhill's informative 1828 letter to Robert Owen (RO Papers, #126).

4. See *CL* for October 22, 1836; November 12, 1836; June 2, 1838; February 10, 1838, and October 15, 1836.

5. See *CL,* October 29, 1836, and October 8, 1836.

6. In April of 1852 (?) an "Underhill" wrote Josiah Warren from St. Louis, telling him of the evenings he had spent listening to translations with "an audience of about 50 of the Icarians who have . . . come to that city." See the Autograph File at the Houghton Library for Josiah Warren. The date of this letter is questionable because it is dated "April 17, 25 (52) M. Times." Is the "25" a "Utopian Era" 25? If so then the year Warren wrote the letter is 1846 plus 25 or 1871. But Warren was in Modern Times in 1852, not 1871. Warren refers to Underhill as "our friend Underhill," without a first name. The Underhill he is referring to may be Samuel or another member of his family.

7. For information about Harmony Hall and the other British Owenite experiments, see Garnett's *Co-Operation and the Owenite Socialist Communities in Britain, 1825–45;* Harrison, *Quest,* 168–73; *Owenism and the Working Class,* a collection of pamphlets and broadsides concerning the Owenite movement in Britain from 1821 to 1834; and A. Taylor, chap. 8.

8. See Owen's September 27, 1839, letter reprinted in Podmore, 531.

9. For information on Charles Fourier, see the *Oeuvres Completes de Charles Fourier.* See also the periodical *La Phalange.* For interpretations of Fourier, see Frank Manuel, "Charles Fourier," in *The Prophets of Paris;* Nicholas Riasonovsky, *The Teaching of Charles Fourier;* and the introduction to *The Utopian Vision of Charles Fourier* by Jonathan Beecher and Richard Bienvenu. See also Beecher's biography of Fourier, *Charles Fourier: The Visionary and his World.*

10. See the *New York Tribune* (an Associationist sympathizer) January 19, 1844, and the *Regenerator* (an Owenite sympathizer) of March 25, 1844, for examples of the sniping between groups.

11. For information on the Promisewell Community, see the A. J. Macdonald Manuscript, 332–37, and the *Regenerator,* specifically the issues of February 14, 1844; February 12, 1844; April 14, 1844; April 29, 1844; and May 25, 1844. See also the *Workingman's Advocate* for September 24, 1844; December 7, 1844; and March 1, 1845. See the *Communitist* for November 13, 1844; and January 15, 1845. Also see Thomas Hunt's letter of July 28, 1843, in the *New Moral World.*

12. See *WA,* March 1, 1845, and Mac Ms, 336.

13. One of these communities, the Maxwell Community, named after Robert Owen's house in New Lanark, was established in Canada in the late 1820s. The founder, Henry Jones, had heard Robert Owen speak in the early 1820s, had visited New Lanark, and then decided that he wanted to devote his fortune to establishing an Owenite community in Canada. He visited Canada to find a suitable site on the shores of Lake Huron, returning in 1827 with many families, all dedicated to carrying out "what is called the Owen system of having all things common." The words are from the diary of the Reverend Peter Jones, an Indian Methodist mission-

ary, the only visitor to the community who left a record of it. Jones passed the "new settlement" on August 1, 1829. See Jones's *The Life and Journals of Kah-ke-wa-quo-na-by.* One member of Maxwell did begin keeping a journal in 1831 and thus recorded some specifics of the community. Quoted excerpts from this journal are found in the Reverend John Morrison's "The Toon O'Maxwell—An Owenite Settlement in Lambton County, Ont.," written in 1909 but not published in the *Ontario Historical Society Papers and Records* until 1914. In an interesting case of plagiarism, the same essay was published by Will Dallas in *The Canadian Magazine* in November 1909 (323–28). Whether Dallas or Morrison was the author is a question scholars might never resolve.

During the several years that the community existed, Jones used his funds to build separate apartments for each family, a common kitchen, a school, and a general store. At Maxwell the women worked in common preparing the food, while the men worked in common to clear the land. The community broke up in the early 1830s, reputedly because of the plentiful, cheap land that attracted members of the community who wished to own their own land.

Similarly, Alexander Gardner, a Scotsman who believed in Robert Owen's labor reforms, his ideas on education, and especially his notions of a socialist community, attempted his own version of an emigrating Owenite society in the late 1840s. Gardner came to the United States in 1849 to found his community on the banks of the Mississippi in Iowa. He apparently gathered together interested people to begin communal living and then returned to Great Britain to bring his own family to his utopia. Upon landing with his family in Newfoundland, however, he learned that many of the Iowa community members were stricken by "galloping consumption," so he took his family to New York City instead, where he learned photography under Mathew Brady. He never returned to Iowa and communal life; what happened to the others in Iowa is unknown. The only reference to this community is in Beaumont and Nancy Newhall, *Masters of Photography.* As late as 1876 people who had heard Owen speak in England and America were still trying to build their own Owenite communities. One John Ashton, who had met Owen in 1830 when he helped Owen form a cooperative school in Manchester, advertised in the May 18, 1876, *American Socialist* that he wanted to donate his farm in Rhode Island "to the cause of cooperation."

14. Besides Thomas Hunt's group that formed the Equality Community, known as the First Section of the Co-Operative Emigration Society, a person who had been influenced by Owen years earlier came to Wisconsin to establish a community, and the Second Section of the Co-Operative Emigration Society also arrived in Wisconsin.

A Mr. Tinker, a liberal printer and bookshop owner, met Robert Owen in 1822 and never forgot Owen's influence, even though it was 1841 before Tinker decided to emigrate to the United States with his family to "plant a socialist colony." Always in correspondence with Owen, Tinker decided upon the "Spring Lake" section of Wisconsin and was disappointed to be told that Hunt's Equality Community would be settling there. Undaunted, Tinker chose another nearby site of eighty acres for his community, but before he could settle there he died in Milwaukee in the summer of 1844, unable to begin his Owenite venture. See a letter from Thomas Tinker about his father's activities to Frederick Merk, March 15, 1914, in the Thomas C. Tinker Papers, in the State Historical Society of Wisconsin.

The members of the Second Section of the Co-Operative Emigration Society had put out a Prospectus and "plan of operation" in November of 1843 to clarify their priorities. These priorities, they said, reflected Robert Owen's ideas: a belief in "useful" work and in their plan as a means of providing hope for those large families with small means who desired to better their own condition (Mac Ms, 386–87). Yet the story of the eight men, four women, and children who journeyed from

London to Wisconsin in 1845 reads the same as the stories of Owenite experiments of the 1820s: they disagreed, primarily about "the inequality of the burden of labor" (Mac Ms 386). After one man died of a lightning strike, other members got employment in Milwaukee, abandoning their cooperative venture.

15. Much information about the Equality Community comes from the letters of Thomas Steel, the group's physician, who wrote often to his father and sister back in England. These letters, located at the State Historical Society of Wisconsin in Madison, Wisconsin, provide an excellent firsthand look at the emigrating community. See specifically his letters from August 1843 through January 1844. Steel wrote that his group purchased 160 acres while the Macdonald Manuscript says the purchase was for 263 acres. Thomas Hunt also left his version of the community in his own letters published regularly in the *New Moral World* in 1844 and 1845. See also J. F. C. Harrison, *Quest*, 175, and Mac Ms, 351–62 and 385–87.

16. See Steel, September 9, 1843 and the *NMW*, September 13, 1844.

17. See Steel's September 13, 1843, letter about purchasing land "just in case" Equality did not work out. Leader Thomas Hunt also purchased land nearby at the beginning of the venture.

18. On January 1, 1854, Hunt wrote to Robert Owen that he was still in Waukesha County, Wisconsin, and was now interested in spiritualism. See RO Papers, #2177.

19. The Promisewell Community and Skaneateles had the simultaneous backing of the numerous Social Reform Societies that were the purveyors of Owenism and communalism in America. When the Philadelphia Social Reform Society addressed all the social reformers in the United States, they advised that "the means for truly reforming society" could "only" be found "in the One-Mentian Community, and the Skaneateles Community" (*Reg*, April 15, 1844). By linking the Owenite One Mentian Society and its community at Promisewell with Collins's Skaneateles, the Philadelphia Social Reform Society illustrated just how close the two communities were in underlying philosophies. J. F. C. Harrison also labels Skaneateles as one of the Owenite "lost communities," communities that were either "avowedly Owenite or influenced considerably by Owenite ideas" (163).

Skaneateles, like New Harmony, had its own radical journal, *The Communitist*, published from July 10, 1844, until March 5, 1846. It contains much information on Skaneateles (albeit exclusively positive) as well as articles on such things as "Unpopular Truths" and "Marriage." It gives information about the many conventions and some news of Skaneateles also. For more information about Skaneateles, see the *Regenerator*, April 1, 1844; May 18, 1844; June 22, 1844; and December 5, 1845; the *Workingman's Advocate*; the Mac Ms, 100–15; the *Harbinger*, September 27, 1845, and September 5, 1846; and John Collins's essays, including "A Bird's Eye View." See also the secondary work by Edmund Leslie, *Skaneateles*.

20. John O. Wattles was probably related to Judge James O. Wattles, a member of New Harmony's governing board in 1826. For information on the younger Wattles, see his "History of Communities" in the *Regenerator*, June 18, 1845.

21. For information on Murray, see his *Regenerator* from 1844 through 1846. See also his small book, *The Struggle of the Hour*.

22. Warren was a prolific writer, so there is considerable primary material available by him, including copies of the various journals and papers that he published throughout his life, such as *The Peaceful Revolutionist* and *Equitable Commerce*. See also his *Manifesto* and his letters in the Autograph File at the Houghton Rare Books Library at Harvard, as well as the Mac Ms, 116–40. As for secondary material, William Bailie's 1906 biography, *Josiah Warren*, is sparse. Eunice Schuster places Warren properly in the American anarchist tradition in her "Native American Anarchism," 87–117; Barbara Dubin's 1973 dissertation focuses on Warren's educational theories. See "A Critical Review of the Social and Educational Theories of Josiah Warren."

23. See Christopher H. Johnson, *Utopian Communism in France: Cabet and the Icarians, 1839–1851*, 45, and W. S. Shepperson, *British Emigration to North America*, 101. For information on Cabet, see his tracts *Colonie Icarienne* and *Departure from Nauvoo*. The Mac Ms, 147–85, includes a copy of Cabet's *Colonie Icarienne*, the 1850 constitution, and the May 1851 revised constitution along with Macdonald's own perceptions of Cabet when he interviewed him on July 10, 1852. For firsthand accounts of community life, see Emile Vallet, *An Icarian Communist in Nauvoo*, and Mrs. I. G. Miller, "The Icarian Community of Nauvoo, Illinois." Secondary sources in addition to Johnson and Shepperson include Jules Prudhommeaux, *Histoire de la Communaute Icarienne* and *Etienne Cabet et les origines de Communisme Icarien*; Robert Hine, *California's Utopian Communities*; Sylvester Piotrowski, "Etienne Cabet and the Voyage en Icarie"; William Hinds, *American Communities*, 62–81; Sherman Barnes, "An Icarian in Nauvoo"; Albert Shaw, *Icaria: A Chapter in the History of Communism*; and Lyman Tower Sargent, "The Icarians in Iowa," and his 1965 dissertation, "The Relationship between Political Philosophy and Political Ideology: A Study of Etienne Cabet and his Communitarian Experiments."

24. The words are Sylvester Piotrowski's, in his "Etienne Cabet and the *Voyage en Icarie*."

25. Cabet and Owen corresponded about the Texas venture. In July 1847 W. S. Peters of Cincinnati wrote to Owen, urging him to go to the colony in Texas "immediately" and to take "as many Scotch people as you possibly can this fall and make preparation for a large number to follow in early spring," because, as Peters warned, the gift of rich land "will be positively closed on the 1st of July, 1848." He promised Owen that for every family he took with him, he would give them 16 acres, or "2,400 acres for every 100 families" (RO papers, #1534). Cabet then wrote to Owen in early November 1847, telling him that Charles Sulley would carry out Owen's "commission" in America; but on November 19, 1847, Sulley wrote to Owen that he had acquainted Peters of his (Owen's) wishes—i.e., not to take Scotch families to Texas (RO papers, #1527 and #1542). Peters probably owned the land corporation that defrauded Cabet. See Sargent, "The Icarians in Iowa," and Jane Dupree Begos, " 'Icaria': A Footnote to the Peters Company."

Icarian historian Jules Prudhommeaux admitted that Icarian communism was Owenite communism, only "depouillé," or "skinned." He wrote that, though Cabet was not an Owenite, he sought approval from Owen for his emigration: "Robert Owen, the grand socialist . . . has just arrived from America to London; our friends learn with pleasure that he approves our project of emigration and that he will give it all his influence" (*Histoire* [my translation], 1:6). Cabet also wrote that Owen helped him. He said in a September 14, 1847, letter from London that "we have had a great pleasure of seeing again this venerable patriarch of English communism. . . . Already Robert Owen, in several conferences, has given to us documents, advice, and support which will facilitate us much, and we are convinced that his kindness will win over to him the recognition of the Icarians as his sweet philosophy and his numerous services have conquered him for a long time our esteem and veneration" (in Prudhommeaux, *Histoire* [my translation]).

26. The statistics come from the Mac Ms, 149, from a copy of Cabet's *Colony or Republic of Icaria . . . Its History*.

27. See Shaw, 115–17, who visited the "new" community in 1883; he included a copy of the New Icarian Community "contract," i.e., constitution, as well as a copy of the Articles of Agreement of the Icaria-Speranza Community at the end of his book.

28. See Section 16, Article 57, and Section 17, Article 60, of the Constitution of the Icaria-Speranza Community, reproduced in Shaw.

CONCLUSION: VOICES FROM THE PAST

1. See Hawthorne's passages from *The American Notebooks* for both April 16, 1841, and September 22, 1841.

2. See Sophia Eastman to Mehitable Eastman, July 25, 1843, and George Ripley to Phinehas Eastman, November 24, 1843; the letters are located in the Middlebury College Library.

3. See Frederick Pratt, "Account of Brook Farm," in Joel Myerson, "Two Unpublished Reminiscences of Brook Farm"; G. W. Curtis's letters to John S. Dwight; Arthur Sumner, "A Boy's Recollection of Brook Farm"; George Bradford, "Reminiscences of Brook Farm"; and Marianne Dwight, *Letters from Brook Farm,* for the story of Fred Cabot.

4. See Elizabeth Hoxie's letters to Mary Russell Curson from September 1845 through March 1846, in the Houghton Library.

Manuscript Collections

Abernethy Library of American Literature, Middlebury College (Middlebury, Vermont)
    Brook Farm Letters
Beinecke Rare Book and Manuscript Library, Yale University (New Haven, Connecticut)
    A. J. Macdonald MS
Boston Public Library (Boston, Massachusetts)
    Abner Kneeland Lectures
Cincinnati Historical Society (Cincinnati, Ohio)
    Frances Wright Papers
The Co-operative Union Library (Manchester, England)
    The Robert Owen Papers
Cornell University Library (Ithaca, New York)
    Moses Quinby Diary
    Theresa Wolfson Papers
The Greene County Historical Society (Xenia, Ohio)
    The Galloway Collection
The Historical Society of Pennsylvania (Philadelphia, Pennsylvania)
    Robert Dale Owen Letters
The Historical Society of Western Pennsylvania (Pittsburgh, Pennsylvania)
    The Bakewell Family Book
The Houghton Library, Harvard University (Cambridge, Massachusetts)
    Garnett-Pertz Collection
    Elizabeth Hoxie Letters
    Autograph File, Josiah Warren
Indiana Historical Society (Indianapolis, Indiana)
    Kellogg Papers
    Lockridge Collection
    Twigg Papers
Indiana State Library (Terre Haute, Indiana)
    Coal Creek Community Record Books
Library of Congress (Washington, D.C.)
    Frances Wright Papers
Lilly Library, Indiana University (Bloomington, Indiana)
    Constitution of the Blue Spring Community
    Judge Duncan MS
    Rodney Smith MS
Massachusetts Historical Society (Boston, Massachusetts)
    Constitution of the Brook Farm Community
Massillion Museum (Stark County, Ohio)
    Kendal Community Constitution
    Kendal Community Letters
    Minutes of the Friendly Association Meetings
    Rotch Papers
Motherwell Library (Motherwell, Scotland)
    A. J. Hamilton MSS, including "The Soldier and Citizen of the World"
Purdue University Library (West Lafayette, Indiana)
    Indiana Collection
    Krannert Rare Books Collection

The State Historical Society of Wisconsin (Madison, Wisconsin)
    Thomas Steel Letters
    Thomas Tinker Letters
Workingmen's Institute (New Harmony, Indiana)
    Branigin Collection
    Maclure/Fretageot Correspondence
    Lucy Say Correspondence

Works Cited

Abbott, John S. C. *Letters to Young Women*. New York, 1844.
———. *The Mother at Home*. New York, 1834.
Aries, Philippe. *Centuries of Childhood*. New York: Alfred A. Knopf, 1962.
Armytage, W. H. G. *Heavens Below*. Toronto: University of Toronto Press, 1961.
———. "William Maclure, 1763–1840, a British Interpretation." *Indiana Magazine of History* 47 (1951): 1–20.
Arndt, Karl K. R., ed. *Harmony on the Wabash in Transition*. Worcester: Harmony Society Press, 1982.
Bailie, William. *Josiah Warren*. Boston, 1906.
Banta, Richard. "New Harmony's Golden Years." *Indiana Magazine of History* 44 (1948): 25–36.
Barker-Benfield, G. J. *The Horrors of the Half-Known Life: Male Attitudes Toward Women and Sexuality in Nineteenth-Century America*. New York: Harper and Row, 1976.
Barnes, Sherman B. "An Icarian in Nauvoo." *Journal of the Illinois State Historical Society* 34 (1941): 233–44.
Barrett, Michele. *Women's Oppression Today*. London: Verso, 1980.
Bassett, T. D. Seymour. "The Secular Utopian Socialists." In *Socialism and American Life*, edited by Donald O. Egbert and Stow Persons. Princeton: Princeton University Press, 1952.
Beard, James, ed. *The Letters and Journals of James Fenimore Cooper*. 2d ed. Cambridge: Harvard University Press, 1960.
Beecher, Jonathan. *Charles Fourier: The Visionary and His World*. Berkeley: University of California Press, 1986.
Beecher, Jonathan, and Richard Bienvenu, eds. *The Utopian Vision of Charles Fourier*. Boston: Beacon Press, 1971.
Beer, M. *A History of British Socialism*. London: George Allen and Unwin, 1940.
Begos, Jane Dupree. " 'Icaria': A Footnote to the Peters Colony." *Communal Studies* 6 (1986): 84–92.
Berg, Barbara. *The Remembered Gate: Origins of American Feminism*. New York: Oxford University Press, 1978.
Bernhard, Duke of Saxe-Weimer-Eisenach. From "Travels through North America. . . ." In *New Harmony as Seen by Participants and Travelers*. Philadelphia: Porcupine Press, 1975.
Bestor, Arthur. *Backwoods Utopias: The Sectarian Origins and the Owenite Phase of Communitarian Socialism in America*. Philadelphia: University of Pennsylvania Press, 1970.
———. "The Diaries of Donald Macdonald" (review). *New York History* 24 (1943):80–86.
———. *Education and Reform: Correspondence of William Maclure and Marie Duclos Fretageot, 1820–1833*. Indianapolis: Indiana Historical Society, 1948.
———. "Records of the New Harmony Community." Urbana: Illinois Historical Survey, 1950.
Blatchly, Cornelius. *An Essay on Common Wealths*. New York, 1822.
Bradford, George P. "Reminiscences of Brook Farm." *The Century* (1892): 141–48.
Brailsford, H. N. *Shelley, Godwin, and their Circle*. New York: Henry Holt and Company, n.d.
Brown, Ford K. *The Life of William Godwin*. London: J. M. Dent, 1936.
Brown, Paul. *Twelve Months in New Harmony*. 1827. Philadelphia: Porcupine Press, 1972.

Brown, W. Henry. *A Century of London Co-Operation*. London: The Education Committee of the London Co-Operative Society, 1928.

Cabet, Etienne. *Colonie Icarienne*. Paris, 1856.

———. *Departure from Nauvoo*. Paris, 1856.

———. *Voyage en Icarie*. Paris, 1842.

Carter, Harvey L. "William Maclure." *Indiana Magazine of History* 31 (1935):83–91.

Child, Lydia Maria. *The Mother's Book*. 1830. New York: Arno Press, 1972.

Claeys, Gregory. *Machinery, Money, and the Millennium*. Princeton: Princeton University Press, 1987.

Codman, John. *Brook Farm*. Boston, 1844.

Cole, George D. H. *The Life of Robert Owen*. London: Macmillan and Co., 1960.

———. *Socialist Thought: The Forerunners, 1789–1850*. London: Macmillan and Co., 1955.

———, ed. *A New View of Society and Other Writings*. London: T. M. Dent, 1927.

Cole, Margaret. *Robert Owen of New Lanark*. New York: Oxford University Press, 1953.

Collins, John. *Bird's Eye View*. Boston, 1844.

Combe, Abram. *The Life and Dying Testimony of Abram Combe*. London, 1844.

Combs, Sue Lingo. "The Dialect of Inequality: Constraints and Alternatives in Two Utopian Communities." Ph.D. diss., University of Missouri at Columbia, 1975.

Commager, Henry Steele. "The Blasphemy of Abner Kneeland." *The New England Quarterly* 8 (1935): 29–41.

———. *The Era of Reform*. Princeton: Van Nostrand Press, 1960.

Conrad, Susan. *Perish the Thought: Intellectual Women in Romantic America, 1830–1860*. New York: Oxford University Press, 1976.

Cooperative Communities. New York: Arno Press, 1972.

Cott, Nancy. *The Bonds of Womanhood: "Woman's Sphere" in New England, 1780–1835*. New Haven: Yale University Press, 1977.

Coward, Rosalind. *Patriarchal Precedent, Sexuality and Social Relations*. London: Routledge & Kegan Paul, 1983.

Curti, Merle. *The Growth of American Thought*. New York: Harper and Bros., 1943.

———. "Robert Owen in American Thought." In *Robert Owen's American Legacy*, edited by Donald Pitzer. Indianapolis: Indiana Historical Society, 1972.

Curtis, George W. *Early Letters of George William Curtis to John S. Dwight*. Edited by George Willis Cooke. New York: 1898.

Dallas, Will. "The Toon O' Maxwell." *The Canadian Magazine* 34 (1909): 323–28.

Degler, Carl. *At Odds*. New York: Oxford University Press, 1980.

Delphy, Christine. *Close to Home: A Materialist Analysis of Women's Oppression*. Amherst: University of Massachusetts Press, 1984.

Douglas, Ann. *The Feminization of American Culture*. New York: Alfred A. Knopf, 1977.

Dubin, Barbara. "A Critical Review of the Social and Educational Theories of Josiah Warren." Ph.D. diss., University of Illinois, 1973.

Dwight, Marianne. *Letters from Brook Farm*. Edited by Amy L. Reed. Poughkeepsie, 1928.

Eckhardt, Celia Morris. *Fanny Wright, Rebel in America*. Cambridge: Harvard University Press, 1984.

Eisenstein, Zillah. *The Radical Future of Liberal Feminism*. New York: Longmans, 1981.

Ekirch, Arthur, Jr. *The Idea of Progress in America, 1815–1860*. New York: Columbia University Press, 1944.

Elliott, Helen. "Development of the New Harmony Community with Special Reference to Education." Master's thesis, Indiana University, 1933.

Elliott, Josephine. "Madame Marie Fretageot: Communal Educator." *Communal Societies* 4 (1984): 167–83.

Emerson, O. B. "Frances Wright and her Nashoba Experiment." *Tennessee Historical Quarterly* 6 (1947): 291–314.

Everett, L. S. "An Exposure of the Principles of the 'Free Inquirers.' " Boston, 1831.

Fellman, Michael. *The Unbounded Frame: Freedom and Community in Nineteenth-Century America Utopias.* Westport, Conn.: Greenwood Press, 1973.

Feuer, Lewis, ed. *Marx and Engels, Basic Writings on Politics and Philosophy.* New York: Anchor Books, 1959.

Finley, Ruth E. *The Lady of Godey's: Sarah Josepha Hale.* Philadelphia, 1931.

Flower, George. *The History of the English Settlement in Edwards County Illinois.* Chicago, 1882.

Flower, Richard. *Letters From Illinois.* London, 1822.

Fogarty, Robert. *American Utopianism.* Itassa, Ill.: F. E. Peacock, 1972.

———. *Dictionary of American Communal Utopian History.* Westport, Conn.: Greenwood Press, 1980.

Fogel, Robert, and Stanley Engerman, eds. *The Reinterpretation of American Economic History.* New York: Harper and Row, 1971.

Fourier, Charles. *Oeuvres Completes.* Paris: Editions Anthropos, 1968.

Fox, Wendall P. "The Kendal Community." *Ohio Archaeological and Historical Quarterly* 20 (1911): 176–219.

French, Roderick S. "Liberation from Man and God in Boston: Abner Kneeland's Free-Thought Campaign." *American Quarterly* 32 (1980): 202–21.

Furness, Clifton, ed. *The Genteel Female: An Anthology.* New York: Alfred A. Knopf, 1931.

Galloway, William A. *The History of Glen Helen.* Columbus, Ohio: F. J. Keer Co., 1932.

Garnett, R. G. *Co-operation and the Owenite Socialist Communities in Britain, 1825–45.* Manchester: Manchester University Press, 1972.

Gasposchkin, Cecilia Payne. "The Nashoba Plan for Removing the Evil of Slavery." *Harvard Library Bulletin* 23 (1975): 221–51; 429–61.

Gilbert, Amos. *Memoir of Frances Wright.* Cincinnati, 1855.

Gilbert, Sandra M., and Susan Gubar. *The Madwoman in the Attic.* New Haven: Yale University Press, 1979.

Gray, John. *A Lecture on Human Happiness . . . to which are added the Preamble and Constitution of the Friendly Association for Mutual Interests located at Valley Forge.* 1826. New York: A. M. Kelley, 1971.

———. *A Lecture on Human Happiness. . . .* London, 1825.

Greeley, Horace. *Hints Toward Reform.* New York, 1850.

Guettel, Charnie. *Marxism and Feminism.* Toronto: Canadian Women's Educational Press, 1974.

Hall, William. "From England to Illinois in 1821." *Journal of the Illinois Historical Society* 39 (1946): 21–66; 208–54.

Haraszti, Zoltan. *The Idyll of Brook Farm.* Boston, 1937.

Haroutunian, Joseph. *Piety and Moralism.* New York: Henry Holt and Co., 1932.

Harrison, J. F. C. *Quest for the New Moral World: Robert Owen and the Owenites in Britain and America.* New York: Charles Scribner's Sons, 1969.

———, ed. *Utopianism and Education: Robert Owen and the Owenites.* New York: Teacher's College Press, 1968.

Harvey, Rowland Hill. *Robert Owen, Social Idealist.* Berkeley: University of California Press, 1949.

Haworth, A. "Planning and Philosophy: The Case of Owenism and the Owenite Communities." *Urban Studies* 13 (1976): 147–53.

Hawthorne, Nathaniel. *The American Notebooks.* Vol. II. Boston, 1868.

Hebert, William. "A Sketch for the Formation of a Society of Mutual Cooperation and Community of Property." In *Cooperative Communities.* New York: Arno Press, 1972.

Heineman, Helen. *Restless Angels: The Friendship of Six Victorian Women.* Athens, Ohio: Ohio University Press, 1983.

Heiny, Patricia Goodwin. "The Family in New Harmony, Indiana during the Owenite Experiment." Master's thesis. Indiana University, 1971.

Hendrickson, Walter B. "An Owenite Society in Illinois." *Indiana Magazine of History* 45 (1949): 175–82.

Hermann, Janet. *Pursuit of a Dream.* Oxford: Oxford University Press, 1981.

Hinds, William A. *American Communities.* Chicago, 1908.

Hine, Robert V. *California's Utopian Colonies.* San Marino: The Huntington Library, 1953.

History of Greene County. New York: J. B. Beers and Co., 1884.

Hogeland, Ronald. "The Female Appendage: Feminine Lifestyles in America, 1820–1860." *Civil War History* 17 (1971): 101–14.

Holloway, Mark. *Heavens on Earth: Utopian Communities in America, 1680–1880.* New York: Dover Publications, 1966.

Houghton, Walter. *The Victorian Frame of Mind.* New Haven: Yale University Press, 1957.

Houriet, Robert. *Getting Back Together.* New York: Avon Books, 1971.

Hugins, Walter, ed. *The Reform Impulse, 1825–1850.* Columbia, S.C.: University of South Carolina Press, 1972.

Hunt, Thomas. *Report to a Meeting of Intending Emigrants, Comprehending a Practical Plan for Funding Co-Operative Colonies of United Interests in the North-Western Territories of the United States.* London, 1843.

James, Janet. "Changing Ideas about Women in the United States, 1776–1825." Ph.D. diss., Radcliffe, 1954.

Jeffery, Kirk. "Marriage, Career, and Feminine Ideology in Nineteenth-Century America: Reconstructing the Marital Experience of Lydia Maria Child, 1828–1874." *Feminist Studies* 2 (1975): 64–113.

Johnson, Christopher. *Utopian Communism in France: Cabet and the Icarians, 1839–1851.* Ithaca: Cornell University Press, 1974.

Jones, Lloyd. *The Life, Times and Labours of Robert Owen.* 1890. New York: AMS Press, 1971.

Jones, Peter. *The Life and Journals of Kah-ke-wa-quo-na-by.* Toronto, 1860.

Kanter, Rosabeth. *Commitment and Community.* Cambridge: Harvard University Press, 1972.

Keating, J. M. *History of the City of Memphis.* Syracuse, 1888.

Kellogg, Minor K. "Recollections of New Harmony." Reprinted in Lorna Lutes Sylvester, ed., *Indiana Magazine of History* 44 (1968): 39–64.

Kelly-Gadol, Jean. "The Social Relations of the Sexes: Methodological Implications of Women's History." *Signs* 1 (1976): 809–25.

Kennedy, David. *Birth Control in America.* New Haven: Yale University Press, 1970.

Kern, Louis J. *An Ordered Love: Sex Roles and Sexuality in Victorian Utopias—The Shakers, the Mormons, and the Oneida Community.* Chapel Hill: The University of North Carolina Press, 1981.

Kirby, Georgiana Bruce. *Years of Experience.* New York: AMS Press, 1971.

Kneeland, Abner. "An Appeal to Common Sense." Boston, 1834.

———. "A Review of the Evidence of Christianity." New York, 1829.

Kolmerten, Carol. "Egalitarian Promises and Inegalitarian Practices: Women's Roles in the American Owenite Communities, 1824–1828." *Journal of General Education* 33 (1981): 31–44.

————. "Unconscious Sexual Stereotyping in Utopia: A Sample from the *New Harmony Gazette.*" In *Utopias: The American Experience,* edited by Gairdner B. Moment and Otto F. Kraushaar. Metuchen, N.J.: Scarecrow Press, 1980.

————. "Women and Work." *Georgia Review* 32 (1978): 905–11.

Lane, Margaret. *Frances Wright and the Great Experiment.* Totowa, N.J.: Manchester University Press, 1972.

Lauer, Jeanette C., and Robert H. Lauer. "Sex Roles in Nineteenth-Century American Communal Societies." *Communal Societies* 3 (1983): 16–28.

Leopold, Richard William. *Robert Dale Owen, A Biography.* Cambridge: Harvard University Press, 1940.

Lerner, Gerda. *The Creation of Patriarchy.* New York: Oxford University Press, 1986.

————. "The Lady and the Mill Girl: Changes in the Status of Women in the Age of Jackson." *Mid-Continent American Studies Journal,* 10 (1969): 5–15.

Leslie, Edmund. *Skaneateles.* New York, 1902.

Levy, Leonard W., ed. *Blasphemy in Massachusetts: Freedom of Conscience and the Abner Kneeland Case.* New York: DaCapo Press, 1973.

Lockridge, Ross. *The Old Fauntleroy Home.* New York: New Harmony Memorial Commission, 1939.

Lockwood, George. *The New Harmony Movement.* 1905. New York: Dover Publications, 1971.

McCalla, Rev. W. L. "An Examination of Miss Wright's System of Knowledge." Philadelphia, 1829.

Macdonald, Donald. "The Diaries of Donald Macdonald." Edited with an introduction by Caroline Dale Snedeker. Indianapolis: Indiana Historical Society, 1942.

McIntosh, Montgomery Eduard. "Co-operative Communities in Wisconsin." *Proceedings of the State Historical Society of Wisconsin* (1904): 99–115.

McKeen, Catherine. "Mental Education of Women." *American Journal of Education* (1856): 567–78.

M'Knight, James. "A Discourse Exposing Robert Owen's System as Practiced by the Franklin Community at Haverstraw." New York, 1826.

Maclure, William. *Opinions on Various Subjects.* 3 vols. New Harmony, Ind.: New Harmony Press, 1931.

Mannheim, Karl. *Ideology and Utopia: An Introduction to the Sociology of Knowledge.* New York: Harcourt, Brace and World, 1936.

Manuel, Frank. *The Prophets of Paris.* Cambridge: Harvard University Press, 1962.

Manuel, Frank E. and Fritzie P. *Utopian Thought in the Western World.* Cambridge: Harvard University Press, 1979.

Mariampolski, Hyman. "The Dilemmas of Utopian Communities: A Study of the Owenite Community at New Harmony, Indiana." Ph.D. diss., Purdue University, 1977.

Marshall, Peter. *William Godwin.* New Haven: Yale University Press, 1984.

Mathews, Donald G. "The Second Great Awakening as an Organizing Process, 1780–1830." *American Quarterly* 21 (1969): 23–44.

Melder, Keith. "The Beginnings of the Women's Rights Movement in the United States, 1800–1840." Ph.D. diss., Yale University 1963.

————. "Ladies Bountiful: Organized Women's Benevolence in Early Nineteenth-Century America." *New York History* 68 (1967): 231–54.

Meltzer, Milton. *Tongue of Flame: The Life of Lydia Maria Child.* New York: T. Y. Crowell, 1965.

Melville, Keith. *Communes in the Counter Culture.* New York: William Morrow & Co., 1972.

Meyers, Marvin. *The Jacksonian Persuasion: Politics and Belief.* Stanford: Stanford University Press, 1957.

Miller, Mrs. I. G. "The Icarian Community." *Transactions of the Illinois State Historical Society* 11 (1906): 103–107.

Miller, Perry. *The Life of the Mind in America: From the Revolution to the Civil War.* New York: Harcourt, Brace and World, 1965.

Minningerode, Meade. *The Fabulous Forties.* New York, 1924.

Morrison, the Rev. John. "The Toon O'Maxwell—An Owenite Settlement in Lambton County, Ont." *Ontario Historical Society Papers and Records* 12 (1914): 5–13.

Morton, Samuel George. *A Memoir of William Maclure.* Philadelphia: Merrihew and Thompson, 1844.

Motherwell and Orbiston. New York: Arno Press, 1972.

Muncy, Raymond Lee. *Sex and Marriage in Utopian Communities.* Bloomington: Indiana University Press, 1973.

Murray, Orson S. *The Struggle of the Hour: A Discourse delivered at the Paine Celebration in Cincinnati on January 29, 1861.* Warren County, Ohio, 1861.

Myerson, Joel. "Two Unpublished Reminiscences of Brook Farm." *New England Quarterly* 48 (1975): 253–60.

Newhall, Beaumont and Nancy. *Masters of Photography.* New York: Bonanza Books, 1958.

Nicholson, Linda J. *Gender and History.* New York: Columbia University Press, 1986.

Nordhoff, Charles. *The Communistic Societies of the United States.* New York: Dover Publications, 1966.

Noyes, John Humphrey. *Strange Cults and Utopias of Nineteenth-Century America* [formerly titled *History of American Socialisms*, 1870]. With an introduction by Mark Holloway. New York: Dover Publications, 1966.

Okin, Susan. *Women in Western Political Thought.* Princeton: Princeton University Press, 1979.

Owen, Robert. *The Book of the New Moral World.* 3 vols. London, 1842–52.

———. *Lectures on the Marriages of the Priesthood of the Old Immoral World.* Leeds: 1840.

———. *The Life of Robert Owen, by Himself.* New York: Alfred A. Knopf, 1920.

———. *A New View of Society.* London, 1813.

Owen, Robert Dale. *Divorce: Being a Correspondence between Horace Greeley and Robert Dale Owen.* New York, 1860.

———. "An Earnest Sowing of Wild Oats." *Atlantic Monthly* 34 (1874): 67–78.

———. *To Holland and to New Harmony: Robert Dale Owen's Travel Journal, 1825–1826.* Edited by Josephine M. Elliot. Indiana Historical Society, 1969.

———. "An Outline of the System of Education at New Lanark." 1824. Reprinted in *Robert Owen at New Lanark.* New York: Arno Press, 1972.

———. *Robert Dale Owen's Travel Journal, 1827.* Edited by Josephine M. Elliott. *Indiana Historical Society Publications* 23 (1969): 178–288.

———. "Situations." N.p., 1839.

———. *Threading My Way.* New York, 1874.

Owen, William. "Diary of William Owen from November 10, 1824–April 20, 1825." Edited by Joel W. Hiatt. *Indiana Historical Society Publications* 4 (1906): 7–134.

Owenism and the Working Class. New York: Arno Press, 1972.

Pancoast, Elinor, and Anne E. Lincoln. *The Incorrigible Idealist, Robert Dale Owen in America.* Chicago: Principia Press, 1940.

Pankhurst, Richarde K. P. "Anna Wheeler: A Pioneer Socialist and Feminist." *Political Quarterly* 25 (1954): 132–43.

———. *William Thompson.* London: Watts and Co., 1954.

Parks, Edd Winfield. "Dreamer's Vision, Frances Wright at Nashoba." *Tennessee Historical Magazine* 2 (1932): 75–86.

Pears, Thomas, ed. *New Harmony, An Adventure in Happiness: The Papers of Thomas and Sarah Pears.* Indianapolis: Indiana Historical Society, 1933.

Pease, William H., and Jane H. Pease. *Black Utopia.* Madison: State Historical Society of Wisconsin, 1963.

Pelham, William. "The Letters of William Pelham." 1916. In *New Harmony as Seen by Participants and Travelers.* Philadelphia: Porcupine Press, 1975.

Perkins, A. J. G. and Teresa Wolfson. *Frances Wright, Free Enquirer.* 1939. Philadelphia: Porcupine Press, 1972.

Perrin, William Henry, ed. *The History of Stark County.* Chicago, 1881.

Pierson, Stanley. *British Socialists.* Cambridge: Harvard University Press, 1979.

Piotrowski, Sylvester. "Étienne Cabet and the *Voyage en Icarie.*" Ph.D. diss., Catholic University, 1935.

Pitzer, Donald, ed. *Robert Owen's American Legacy.* Indianapolis: Indiana Historical Society, 1972.

Podmore, Frank. *Robert Owen, A Biography.* New York: D. Appleton and Co., 1924.

Powers, Rev. H. P. "Female Education." Newark, 1826.

Prudhommeaux, Jules. *Étienne Cabet et les Origines du Communisme Icarien.* Nîmes, 1907.

———. *Histoire de la Communauté Icarienne.* Nîmes, 1906.

Puffin, Peter. "Heaven on Earth." Philadelphia, 1825.

Reed, Evelyn. "In Defense of Engels on the Matriarchy." In *Feminism and Socialism.* New York: Pathfinder Press, 1972.

Reed, John F. "Vision at Valley Forge." *Bulletin of the Historical Society of Montgomery County* 15 (1966): 27–38.

Riasanovsky, Nicholas V. *The Teaching of Charles Fourier.* Berkeley: University of California Press, 1969.

Rich, Adrienne. *Of Woman Born: Motherhood as Experience and Institution.* New York: W. W. Norton, 1976.

Riley, Glenda Gates. "From Chattel to Challenger: The Changing Image of the American Woman, 1828–1848." Ph.D. diss., Ohio State University, 1967.

Robert Owen at New Lanark, by a Former Teacher at New Lanark. Manchester, 1839.

Rohrlich, Ruby, and Elaine Hoffman Baruch, eds. *Women in Search of Utopia.* New York: Schocken Books, 1984.

Roll, Eric. *A History of Economic Thought.* Homewood, Ill.: Richard Irwin, 1973.

Rosenberg, Charles E. "Sexuality, Class and Role in Nineteenth-Century America." *American Quarterly* 25 (1973): 131–53.

Royle, Edward. "The Owenite Legacy to Social Reform, 1845–1900." *Studies in History and Politics* 1 (1980): 56–74.

Rozwenc, Edwin C. *Ideology and Power in the Age of Jackson.* New York: New York University Press, 1964.

Russell, Amelia. "Home Life of the Brook Farm Association." *Atlantic Monthly* 42 (1878): 458–66; 556–63.

Rutherford, Virginia. "A Study of the Speaking Career of Frances Wright in America." Ph.D. diss., Northwestern University, 1960.

Ryan, Mary P. *Womanhood in America.* New York: New Viewpoints, 1975.

Sams, Henry W., ed. *Autobiography of Brook Farm.* Gloucester, Mass.: Peter Smith, 1974.

Sargant, William. *Robert Owen and his Social Philosophy.* 1860. New York: AMS Press, 1971.

Sargent, Lyman Tower. "The Icarians in Iowa." *Annals of Iowa* 41 (1972): 957–68.

———. "The Relationship between Political Philosophy and Political Ideology." Ph.D. diss., University of Minnesota, 1965.

Schott, Hilda. *Does Socialism Liberate Women?* Boston: Beacon Press, 1974.

Schuster, Eunice. "Native American Anarchism." *Smith College Studies in History* 17 (1931–32): 87–117.

Sears, John Van Der Zee. *My Friends at Brook Farm.* New York, 1912.

Sedgwick, Catharine. *Means and Ends.* Boston, 1839.

Shaw, Albert. *Icaria, A Chapter in the History of Communism.* New York: G. P. Putnam's Sons, 1884.

Shelley, Mary Wollstonecraft. *The Letters of Mary Wollstonecraft Shelley.* Edited by Betty T. Bennett. Baltimore: Johns Hopkins University Press, 1983.

Shepperson, W. S. *British Emigration to North America.* Minneapolis: University of Minnesota Press, 1957.

Sigourney, Lydia. *Letters to Mothers.* New York: 1838.

Simons, Richard. "A Utopian Failure." *Indiana History Bulletin* 18 (1941): 98–114.

Sklar, Kathryn Kish. *Catharine Beecher: A Study in American Domesticity.* New York: W. W. Norton, 1976.

Smith, Timothy L. *Revivalism and Reform: American Protestantism on the Eve of the Civil War.* New York: Abingdon Press, 1970.

Smith-Rosenberg, Carroll. "Beauty, the Beast and the Militant Woman: A Case Study of Sex Roles and Social Stress in Jacksonian America." *American Quarterly* 23 (1971): 562–84.

———. "The Hysterical Woman: Sex Roles and Role Conflict in Nineteenth-Century America." *Social Research* 39 (1972): 652–78.

———. "Puberty to Menopause: The Cycle of Femininity in Nineteenth-Century America." In *Clio's Consciousness Raised.* Edited by Mary Hartman and Lois W. Banner. New York: Harper Torchbooks, 1974.

Smith-Rosenberg, Carroll, and Charles Rosenberg. "The Female Animal: Medical and Biological Views of Women in Nineteenth-Century America." *Journal of American History* 60 (1973): 332–56.

The Social Pioneer and Herald of Progress. The New England Social Reform Society, 1844.

Spann, Edward K. *Brotherly Tomorrows: Movements for a Cooperative Society in America, 1820–1920.* New York: Columbia University Press, 1989.

Spurlock, John C. *Free Love: Marriage and Middle-Class Radicalism in America, 1825–1860.* New York: New York University Press, 1988.

Sumner, Arthur. "A Boy's Recollections of Brook Farm." *New England Magazine* 16 (1894): 309–13.

Taylor, Anne. *Visions of Harmony.* Oxford: Clarendon Press, 1987.

Taylor, Barbara. *Eve and the New Jerusalem: Socialism and Feminism in the Nineteenth Century.* New York: Pantheon Books, 1983.

Taylor, William, and Christopher Lasch. "Two Kindred Spirits: Sorority and Family in New England, 1839–1846." *New England Quarterly* 36 (1963): 23–41.

Teselle, Sallie, ed. *The Family, Communes and Utopian Societies.* New York: Harper and Row, 1972.

Thomas, John. "Romantic Reform in America." *American Quarterly* 17 (1965): 656–82.

Thompson, E. P. *The Making of the English Working Class.* New York: Vintage Books, 1963.

Thompson, William. *Appeal of One Half of the Human Race, Women, Against the Pretensions of the Other Half, Men. . . .* London, 1825.

———. *An Inquiry into the Principles of the Distribution of Wealth.* 1824. New York: Burt Franklin, 1968.

———. *Practical Directions for the Speedy and Economical Establishment of Communities on the Principles of Mutual Co-operation, United Possessions, and Equality of Exertions and of the Means of Enjoyments.* London, 1830.

Tocqueville, Alexis de. *Democracy in America.* 2 vols. New York: Harper and Row, 1966.

Trollope, Frances. *Domestic Manners of the Americans.* New York, 1894.

Tyler, Alice Felt. *Freedom's Ferment: Phases of American Social History from the Colonial Period to the Outbreak of the Civil War.* Minneapolis: University of Minnesota Press, 1944.

Underhill, Samuel. "An Address." Shalersville, Ohio, 1837.

———. *The Annals of Magnetism.* Cleveland, 1838.

———. "Lectures on Mysterious Religious Emotions." Bethlehem, Ohio, 1829.

———. "Oration." Brecksville, Ohio, 1836.

Vallet, Emile. *An Icarian Communist in Nauvoo: Commentary by Emile Vallet.* Introduction and notes by H. Roger Grant. Springfield, Ill.: Illinois State Historical Society, 1971.

Wagner, Jon. "Sexuality and Gender Roles in Utopian Communities: A Critical Survey of Scholarly Work." *Communal Societies* 6 (1986): 172–88.

Waterman, William R. *Frances Wright.* New York: Columbia University Studies in History, Economics, and Public Law, 1924.

Weiss, Harry B., and Grace M. Ziegler. *Thomas Say.* Springfield: Charles C. Thomas, 1931.

Welter, Barbara. "Anti-Intellectualism and the American Woman." *Mid-America* 48 (1967): 258–70.

———. "The Cult of True Womanhood, 1820–1860." *American Quarterly* 18 (1966): 151–74.

———. "Female Complaints: Medical Views of American Women." In *Dimity Convictions: American Women in the Nineteenth Century.* Athens, Ohio: Ohio University Press, 1976.

Wildes, Harry E. *Valley Forge.* New York, 1938.

Wilson, Edmund. *To the Finland Station.* New York: Doubleday, 1953.

Wood, Ann Douglas. " 'The Fashionable Diseases': Women's Complaints and their Treatment in Nineteenth-Century America." In *Clio's Consciousness Raised.* Edited by Mary Hartman and Lois Banner. New York: Harper and Row, 1974.

———. "Mrs. Sigourney and the Sensibility of Inner Space." *New England Quarterly* 45 (1972): 163–81.

———. "The Scribbling Women and Fanny Fern: Why Women Wrote." *American Quarterly* 23 (1971): 3–24.

Wright, Frances. "An Address to the Industrious Classes." New York, 1830.

———. *Biography.* In *Life, Letters, and Lectures.* New York: Arno Press, 1972.

———. *A Course of Popular Lectures,* including "On the Nature of Knowledge," "Of Free Inquiry," and "On Existing Evils." In *Life, Letters, and Lectures.* New York: Arno Press, 1972.

———. *View of Society and Manners in America.* 1822. Cambridge: Harvard University Press, 1963.

Index

Albion, 33–35
Associationists, 150. *See also* Fourier, Charles
Atwood, Margaret, 170

Bakewell, Benjamin, 40, 62
Bassett, T. D. Seymour, 149
Bentham, Jeremy, 114
Bernhard, Duke of Saxe-Weimer-Eisenach, 76, 184*n*
Bestor, Arthur, 52, 125–26, 143, 179*n*, 183*n*
Birkbeck, Morris, 33–34, 61, 189*n*
Blatchly, Cornelius, 31, 38
Blue Spring Community: begins, 63; constitution, 63, 66, 80; tensions of inequality, 75; disbands, 72; limit on women's political rights, 83; married women's unhappiness, 98–99
Bradford, George, 173
Brisbane, Charles, 149
Brook Farm, 172–75
Brown, Paul, 32, 45, 46–47, 65, 70, 75, 142, 152

Cabet, Etienne, 161–65
Cabot, Fred, 173
Campbell, Frances, 112
Caroline (a *New Harmony Gazette* correspondent), 89
Cheltenham Community, 165
Child, Lydia Maria, 7
Claeys, Gregory, 180*n*
Clinton, DeWitt, 38, 117
Coal Creek Community, 31–32
Cole, G. D. H., 180*n*
Collins, John, 159–60
Combe, Abram, 20, 21–22, 24–25, 28
Communitist, 192*n*
Community of Equality: established at New Harmony, 8; Constitution, 53–55
Cooper, James Fenimore, 189*n*
Countercultural communities of the 1960s, 1
Craig, Thomas, 147
Cult of True Womanhood, 5–8, 79–80, 88–89, 131. *See also* True Woman; Welter, Barbara
Cultural practices, 12, 171
Curtis, George William, 173

Dana, Charles, 174
D'Arusmont, Madame. *See* Wright, Frances
D'Arusmont, Phiquepal, 51, 52, 57, 135, 136–39
D'Arusmont, Sylva, 137–39, 141
Davis, Joseph, 60–61
Davis Bend, 61

Degler, Carl, 4
Dorsey, James, 32
Duncan, Judge H. D., 187*n*
Dupalais, Virginia, 76
Dwight, Marianna, 174–75

Eastman, Sophia, 172
Edinburgh Practical Society, 21–22
Education: at New Harmony, 57–58, 81–83; at the Friendly Association for Mutual Interest at Valley Forge, 65; at Blue Spring, 66; at Franklin, 66; at Yellow Springs, 67; at Kendal, 81; at Nashoba, 119–20; importance to Frances Wright, 132–33; at the Icarian Communities, 164
Engels, Friedrich, 10
Equality: importance to Robert Owen and the Owenites, 13, 19–20, 28–29, 37–38, 43, 44, 48, 56, 58, 67; importance in the Owenite communities, 12, 37, 53–54, 65–67
Equality Community, 154–58

Fisher, Mrs. (at New Harmony), 187*n*
Flower, Eliza, 123–25
Flower, George: establishes Albion, 33; marries Eliza Andrews, 34; devotes himself to Frances Wright's plan to free America's slaves, 35, 115–18, 123–24; leaves Nashoba, 124–25, 189*n*
Flower, Richard, 28, 34
Forestville Community at Coxsackie, 64, 72
Fourier, Charles, 37, 52, 149–50, 182*n*
Franklin Community at Haverstraw: established, 62, 64; Abner Kneeland encourages membership, 64; constitution, 66; Robert Jennings, president, 66; disbands, 72; class problems, 77–79; unhappiness of married women, 96, 98
Free Enquirers, 125–26, 130–35. *See also* Wright, Frances; Owen, Robert Dale
Free thought, 10, 74
Fretageot, Marie: meets Owen, 40; as Owen devotee, 50; joins Maclure and travels to New Harmony on the "Boatload of Knowledge," 52; as worker at New Harmony, 92; visits Wright in Paris, 138; continues the Owenite tradition in New Harmony, 143–44
Friendly Association for Mutual Interests at Kendal. *See* Kendal Community
Friendly Association for Mutual Interests at Valley Forge, 51, 63, 65, 72, 75, 80–81

206

Carol A. Kolmerten is Associate Professor of English at
Hood College in Frederick, Maryland.